IMAGES
of America

CITRUS HEIGHTS

On the Cover: Pictured in 1903, the Sylvan School was originally constructed in 1862. It had green clapboard shutters on its eight windows around the one classroom. Heating was provided by a potbellied stove. For more information on this historical school and others, see chapter five. (Courtesy Jim Van Maren.)

IMAGES
of America

CITRUS HEIGHTS

Jim Van Maren

ARCADIA
PUBLISHING

ISBN 978-0-7385-7459-2

Published by Arcadia Publishing
Charleston, South Carolina

Printed in the United States of America

Library of Congress Control Number: 2010938333

For all general information, please contact Arcadia Publishing:
Telephone 843-853-2070
Fax 843-853-0044
E-mail sales@arcadiapublishing.com
For customer service and orders:
Toll-Free 1-888-313-2665

Visit us on the Internet at www.arcadiapublishing.com

Dedicated to the men and women whose vision over the years created Citrus Heights

Contents

Acknowledgments 6

Introduction 7

1. Native Americans 9
2. Trek to the Gold Fields 15
3. Land and Early Settlers 25
4. Early Government 41
5. Education and Worship 49
6. Growth of the Community 67
7. War Years 89
8. Compassion 97
9. The Spirited People 105
10. The New City 119

ACKNOWLEDGMENTS

Special associates: Wilma Camilleri, Stephanie Cotter, and Teena Stern

Laren Metzer, California State Archives
Melinda Peak, Peak & Associates
Kristie Stevens, City of Roseville, California
City of Citrus Heights: Rhonda Sherman
Katherine Weedman-Cox, Cox B&W Lab, Inc.
April Orsi
Manon Marketing
Richard Kniesel
Carrick family (Ernestine Botts Smith)
Evelyn Coldani
Leineke family
Beverly Sales (Hollingsworth family)
Roeley Giusti
Mary Purvis
Bruce Ellithorpe
Chuck and Joy Engvall
Andrew Felsenstein
Margrethe and Steven Law
Sacramento Metropolitan Fire Department (Randy Wooton)
June Kreisch
Sacramento Bee
Christ the King Retreat Center (Margaret Hinshaw and Brother Kirk)
Mitzi Valerio, Holy Family Catholic Church
Phil Kampel Photography, *The Messenger*, 2nd edition, September 2010
Dana Sauerland
Center for Sacramento History
California State Library
Carol Spiker (Women's Club)
Emily Neeland (Women's Club)
Citrus Heights Historical Society
Ted Mitchell
Leonard M. Davis
Jean Duncan
Jack Duncan
Kiwanis Club (Bill Hooper)
Soroptimist Club (Bonnie Hunt)
Lions Club (Rebekkah McCurry)
Guy Coates (Fireman's Fund)
Fair Oaks Historical Society
San Juan High School Alumni Association
Hodsons
Jim Van Maren

INTRODUCTION

In a prominent area of Sacramento County, California, is a city known as Citrus Heights. It was 150 years ago that portions of Citrus Heights were part of a vast Mexican land grant known as the Rancho Del San Juan. In 1850, the area encompassed by the city was known as the Sylvan District. It was covered with stately groves of oak trees and bisected by trails made by settlers and miners. These pioneers traveled through the district on a trek that paralleled old Highway 40 to the north and east to the town of Auburn. The route was used by teamsters hauling supplies to the mining camps and roadhouses that served these adventurers who came to California over the Sierra Nevada Mountains. The roadhouses were numbered by the distances between them—12, 14, 15, 16, 17, and 18—even though they did not measure true miles. With the coming of the railroad in the 1860s, the once popular teamster trails began to close out to the faster, more economical train service, and the roadhouses closed their doors. The original land grants that constituted the area (San Juan and Norris) were later divided into large farms. The locale remained largely rural until after World War II. Since then, the population has grown from a modest 20 families in the early 1850s to the current population of over 80,000.

The early settlers were primarily of English, Irish, and German descent. They became farmers, particularly of wheat, which was in demand by grain mills. Oak trees were cleared to create farms. After the 1890s, farmers changed from grain feeds to almonds, limited supplies of citrus, olives, strawberries, turkeys, and a small amount of cattle. Crops were raised on dryland farms, and water was obtained from hand-dug wells. Public water conveyance was not available until after 1916.

The community fathers decided that an organization made up of local residents must be formed to deal with schools and other community services. The Citrus Heights Community Club met for the first time on April 24, 1924. It became the hub where farmers and local residents came together to work out problems of growth and development. The club remained in operation until the late 1980s.

In 1862, residents built the first grammar school in the eastern part of Sacramento County at Sylvan Corners. Many of the early graduating students did not go on to high school but stayed home to work on the family farm. Some attended the high schools in nearby communities, often riding a horse to get to school. By 1911, community leaders decided to pursue the effort to construct a high school in this part of the county. San Juan High School (named after the Mexican land grant) was the first fully constructed high school in the area and accepted its first students in 1915. A second high school, Mesa Verde High School, was built in 1976 to accommodate the increase in students.

In 1910, a real estate firm began to buy up large tracts of land. As a promotional ploy to attract buyers, the name Sylvan District was discarded and Citrus Heights was chosen. The firm, Trainor-Desmond Company, felt this would imply that citrus products grew easily there. The Community Club supported the new name.

With the Depression came unemployment, but with a strong spirit, families pulled together. After World War II came new job opportunities, and the community began to grow. New home development and retail sales contributed to a greater tax base. The community was in a positive position. Yet, problems with the Sacramento Board of Supervisors persisted, with property tax money from the area not being returned to the community for the repair of roads and police protection. In 1927, the Community Club passed a position "to incorporate to form a strong organization for the welfare of the community." Due to the Depression and the poor economy, no further action took place.

After several more attempts, the city of Citrus Heights was incorporated in 1997 (see chapter 10). It is a magnificent place to work and live. The schools are well structured from preschool to high school, and a high percentage of high school graduates are accepted to college. It is a diamond.

One

NATIVE AMERICANS

At the time of the California Gold Rush, the Sacramento Valley was home to the Nisenan (or Southern Maidu) peoples, who had a unique language and rich cultural traditions. They lived in permanent village sites at the edges of rich ecotones oriented to the natural resources, rivers, and landforms. The Maidu depended on seasonal activities, including the ripening of plant foods, the movements of animals, and the runs of fish. Steelhead and salmon ran up many of the streams, including Secret and Auburn Ravines. With the valley flooding in the winter and spring, a great number of animals—such as elk, antelope, and bears—moved to the natural levees along the rivers and into the lower foothills. Flocks of waterfowl visited the flooded areas between the rivers and foothills, coveys of quail gathered in the fall, and pigeons were common in both fall and spring. The hunting of these plentiful resources was part of the Nisenan lifeway. Local culture was centered on the gathering, storage, and year-round use of acorns; continual foraging of resources by everyone in the group; hunting strategies; and plant availability. Valley Maidu built their villages on low natural rises along the waterways or on gentle slopes with a southern exposure. Village size varied from 3 to 7 houses up to 40 or 50. Houses were dome shaped, 10 to 15 feet across, constructed of willow poles and covered with earth, tule, and grasses. For winter living, more substantial shelters were required. Winter quarters included a dance house and acorn granaries. Firewood availability may have been a factor in the preference for living by oak trees. Winter was the time of ceremonies, social gatherings, and marriages. Life was punctuated by contests, children were trained, and trade items, tools, baskets, and equipment were made and repaired. There was very little material for clothing, therefore, the dress for women and men was usually the same year-round. Women preferred short aprons made of wire grass tule, shredded maple, or willow bark. To keep warm, fur blankets, skin, and feather robes were utilized. Rabbit robes required about 40 skins. Disaster struck the Sacramento Valley Nisenan in 1833 when a great epidemic, believed to be malaria, decimated the native population. It is estimated that 75 percent died. There were but a few Maidu left to face the settlers and gold miners who soon followed.

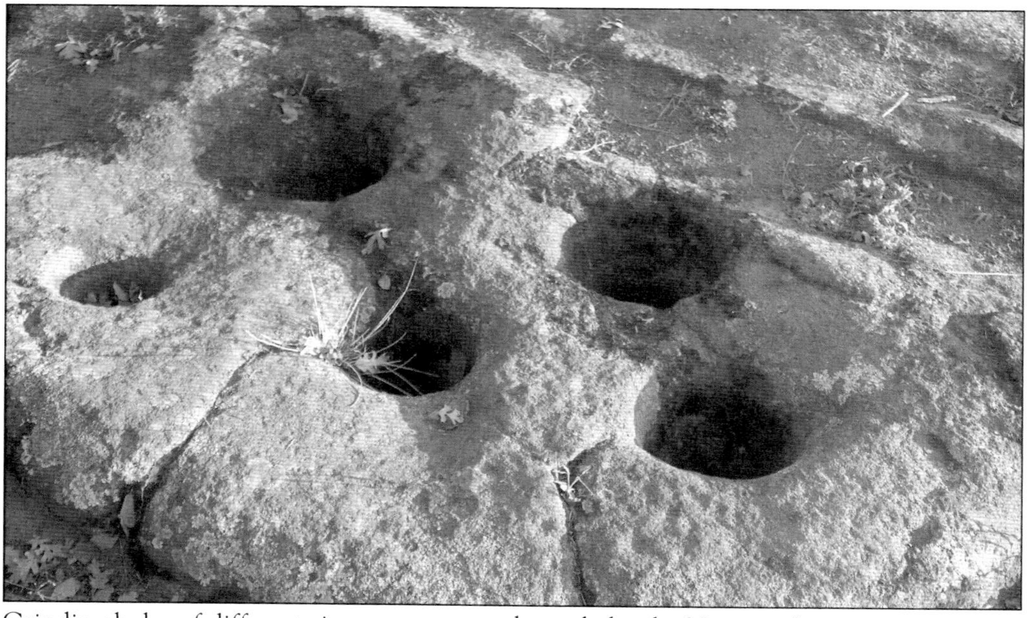

Grinding holes of different sizes were purposely made by the Nisenan for processing acorns and other items. Several such grinding sites are located near Citrus Heights. (Courtesy City of Roseville, California.)

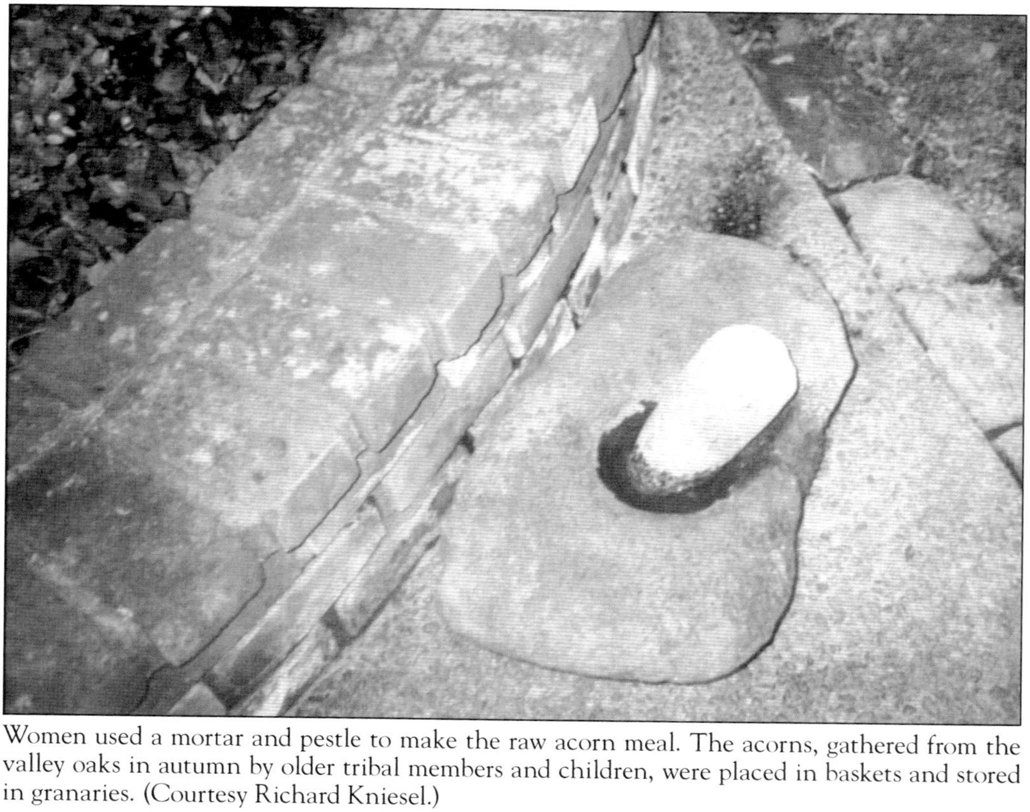

Women used a mortar and pestle to make the raw acorn meal. The acorns, gathered from the valley oaks in autumn by older tribal members and children, were placed in baskets and stored in granaries. (Courtesy Richard Kniesel.)

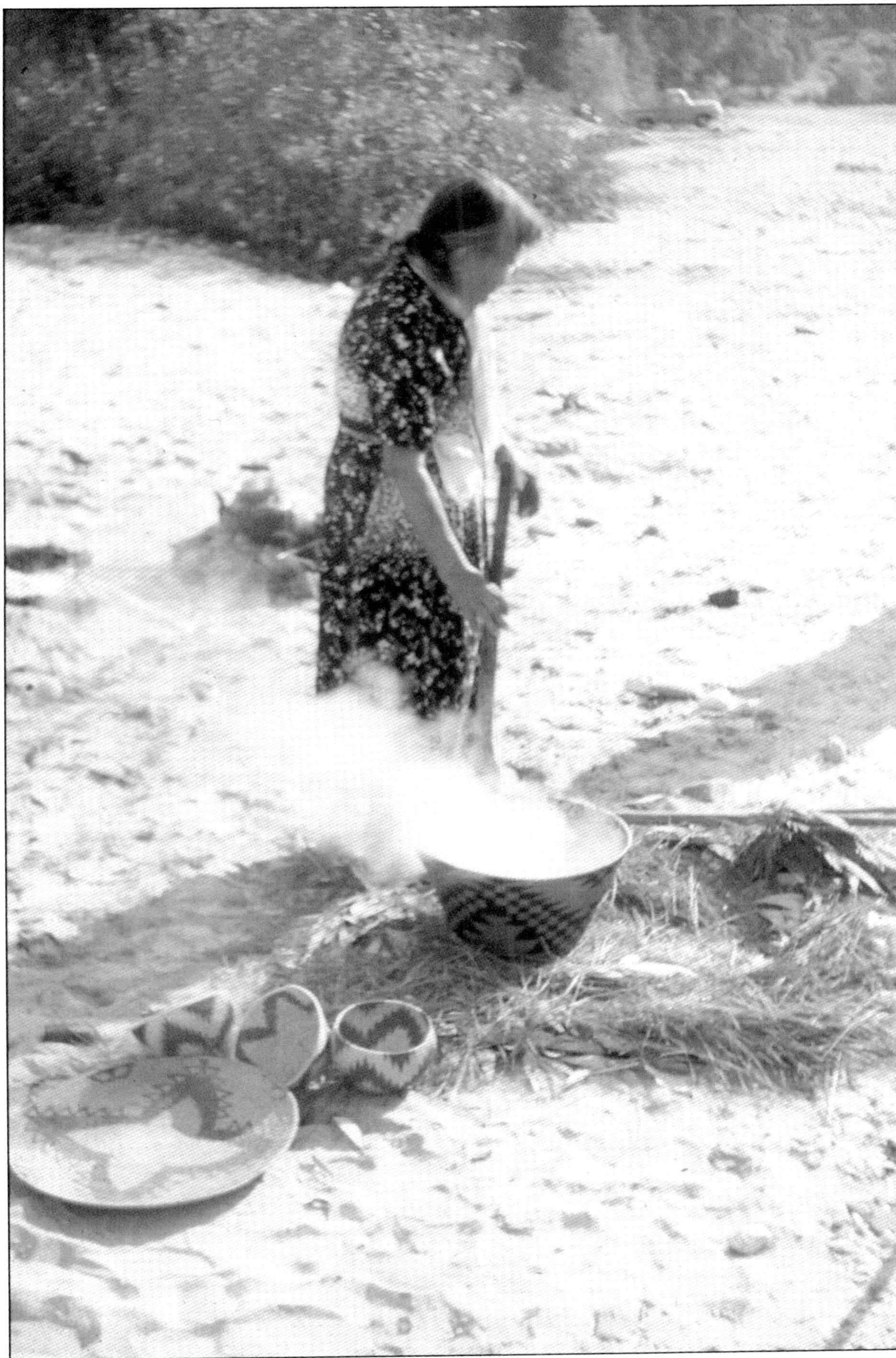

Marie Potts is cooking acorn mush with heated rocks in a basket that she made. This photograph was taken during demonstration days at Sutter's Fort in Sacramento in 1957. (Courtesy Francis A. Riddell Papers, California State Archives.)

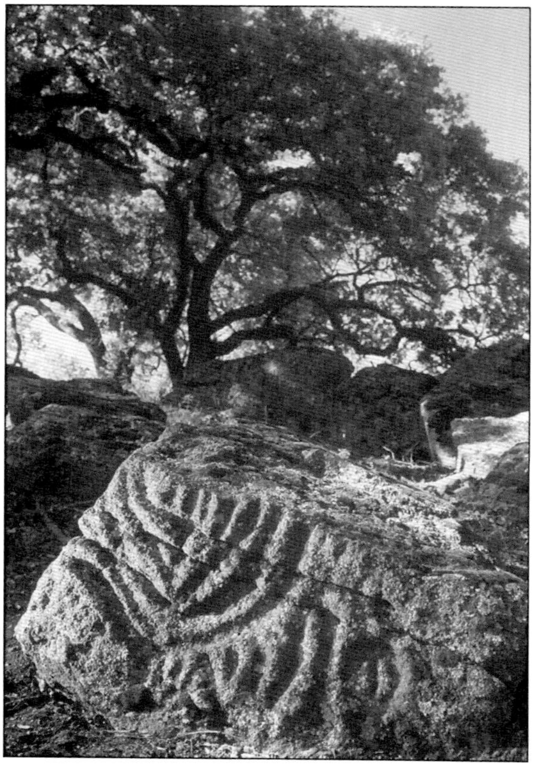

Petroglyphs (carvings on stone) are evidence of a sophisticated Nisenan culture in the Sacramento Valley. These are located at the Maidu Historic Site in Roseville; others can be found throughout the region. Note the Tree of Life carved into the stone. (Both, courtesy City of Roseville, California.)

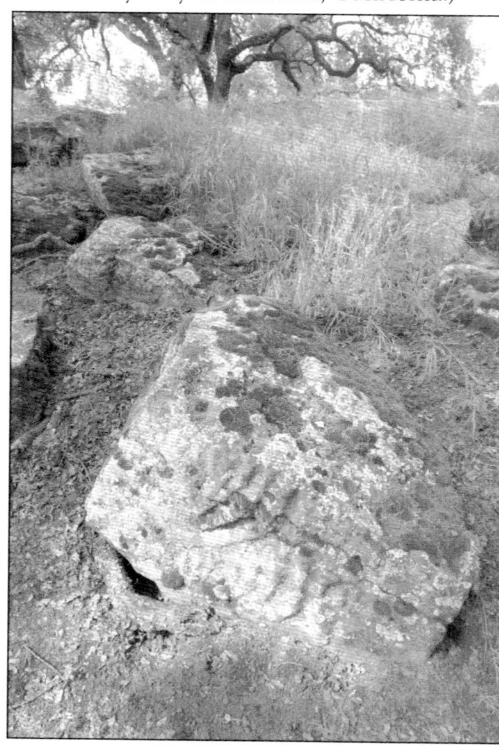

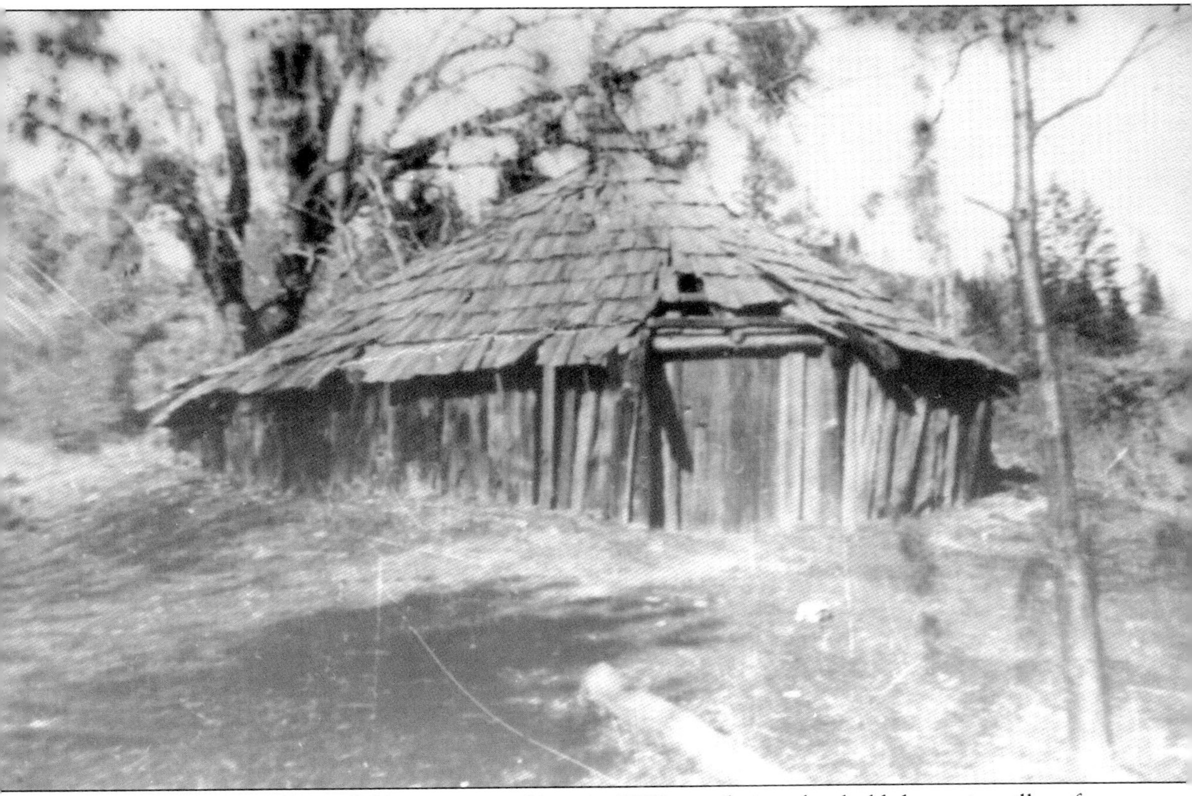

The Maidu Dance (Round) House, pictured here in 1907, was designed to hold the entire village for feasts and ceremonies. (Courtesy Francis A. Riddell Papers, California State Archives.)

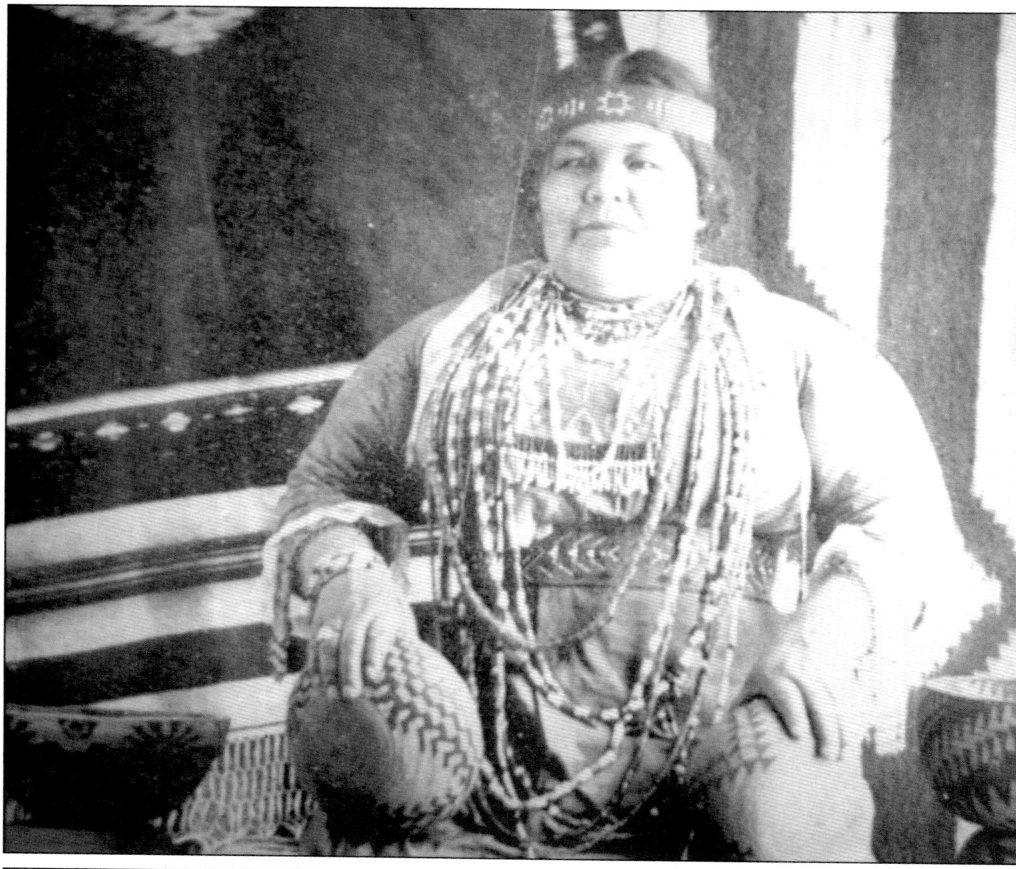

This is typical dress for the Maidu women, worn here by Lena Peconom. (Courtesy Francis A. Riddell Papers, California State Archives.)

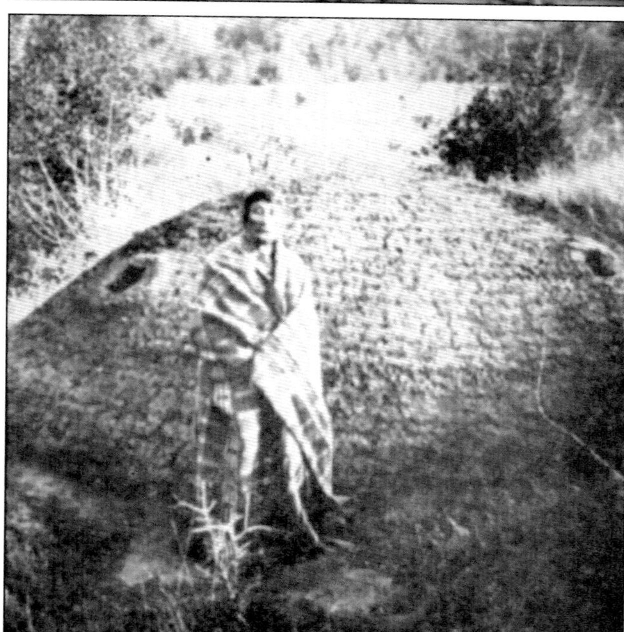

In this image from *Fair Oaks and San Juan Memories*, John Ricketts is standing in front of an Indian sweat house in 1902. It was located on the Ricketts farm in Fair Oaks, close to where Walnut Avenue joins Winding Way. (Courtesy San Juan Record Press.)

Two

TREK TO THE GOLD FIELDS

The earliest trail from Sacramento to the city of Auburn was an arduous route. History records this trail as one of the busiest of those used by miners heading to the gold fields. Where possible, the trail would follow Arcade Creek, which is located a short distance north of present-day Auburn Boulevard. Halfway on the route, it took a more direct path toward the city of Auburn. Today, that portion is known as Old Auburn Road. Prior to 1864, settlers hauled their belongings in wagons pulled by oxen or horses. The Central Pacific Railroad came through nearby Roseville that year and provided the settlers with an easier and cheaper alternative: to turn north at Sylvan Corners and meet the train at the Roseville junction. Roadhouses designed to help travelers by providing way stations were established along the trail. There were six roadhouses on Auburn and Old Auburn Roads. Each was identified by a number indicating the mileage from downtown Sacramento. The numbers, however, did not accurately measure the true distance between each of them.

The first roadhouse was 12 Mile Roadhouse located about a quarter of a mile from Auburn Boulevard on Devecchi Avenue. This roadhouse was demolished in the 1870s. Lumber salvaged from it was used to build the bar located at the entrance to Devecchi Avenue on Auburn Boulevard. The bar was given the name 12 Mile Roadhouse. The only roadhouse still existing is No. 14 at 6540 Auburn Boulevard. It was built by Joseph Gray in 1851. He and his wife, Ann, operated it until 1869. The wood used to construct it is stamped "Norwic." It is possible that this very hard wood may have come from Norway, gone through the East Coast ports of this country, and then around Cape Horn to San Francisco. The present home is built around the original roadhouse. Joseph Gray is also known to have grown the first grapes and grain in the region. The first building in the Sierra Mountain town of Truckee was also built by Gray. Today, the 14 Mile Roadhouse is a private home.

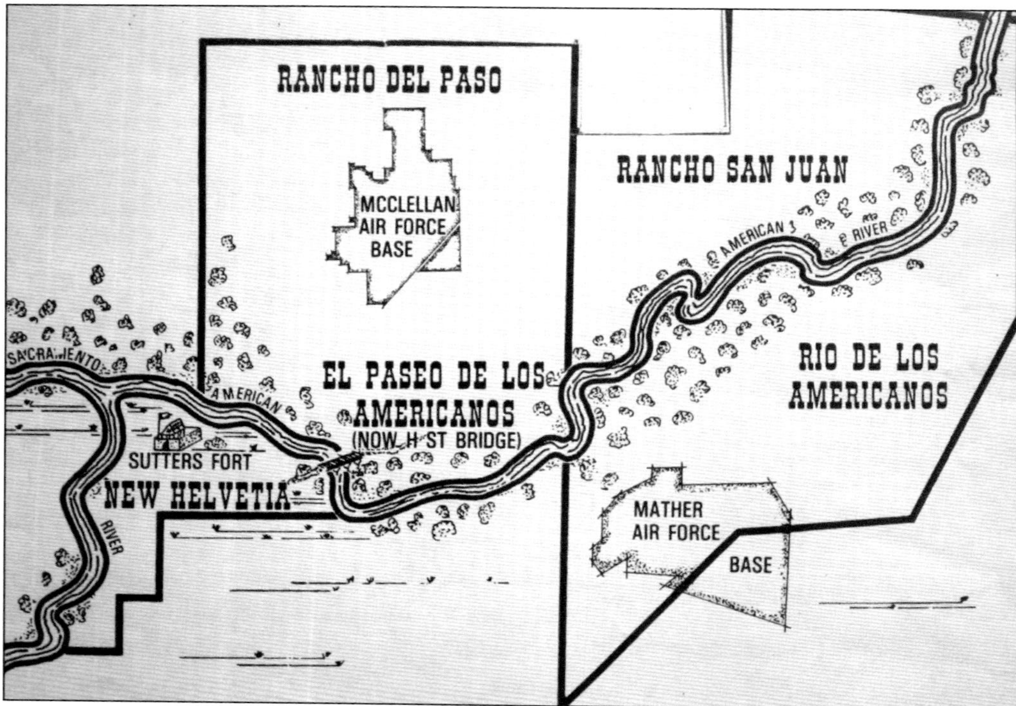

Rancho Del San Juan grant was part of the large Mexican land grant where Citrus Heights is located. Rancho Del Paso is directly east, and Rio Del Los Americanos is southeast of the Rancho Del San Juan grant. Greenback Lane is in the center of the San Juan grant line. (Courtesy Jim Van Maren.)

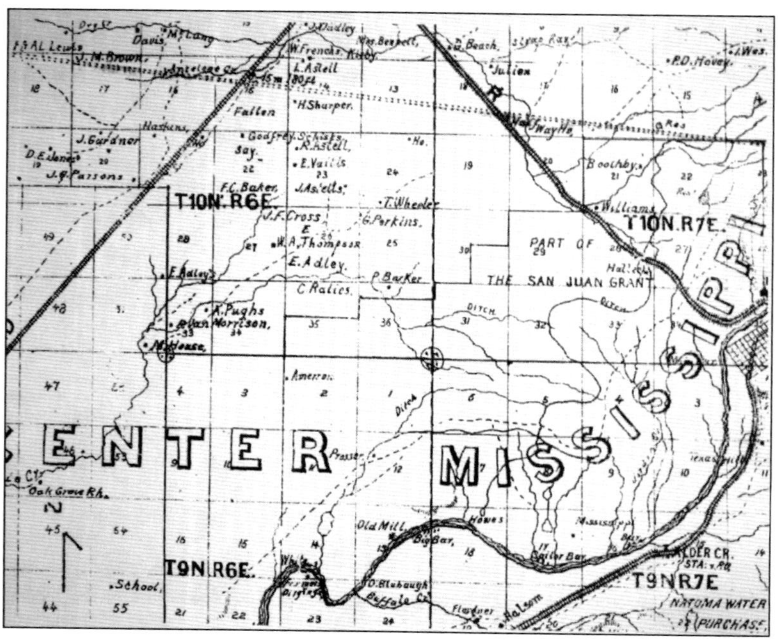

The map shows the Center Mississippi Township as it was in 1868. The Central Pacific Railroad tracks are shown in the bottom right corner. The dotted line that begins at section 22 and ends at section 27 is the original trek by miners along what is Auburn Boulevard today (Courtesy Center for Sacramento History.)

This map of Citrus Heights includes the trail used by settlers and miners traveling from Sacramento north to the city of Auburn. (Courtesy Jim Van Maren.)

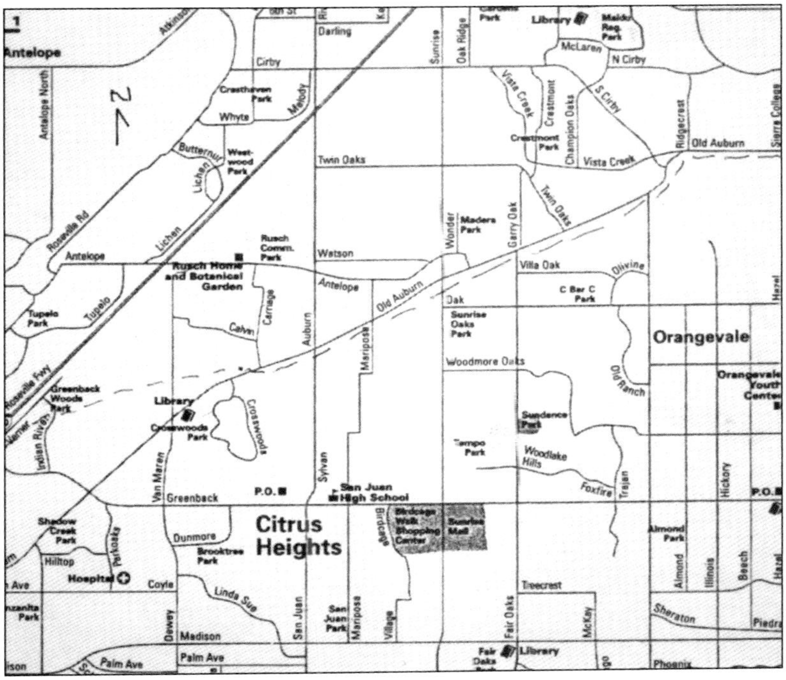

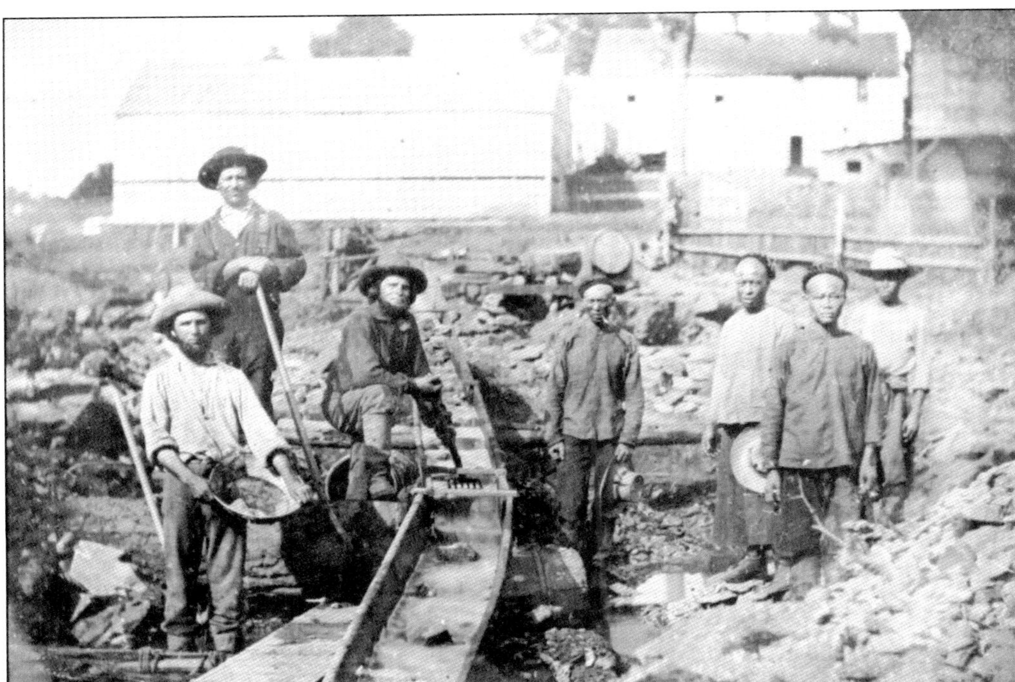

The three men on the left in this lithograph by George C. Cooper are flushing water down their sluice with gravel. The others are Chinese immigrants helping to work the mines. (Courtesy Center for Sacramento History.)

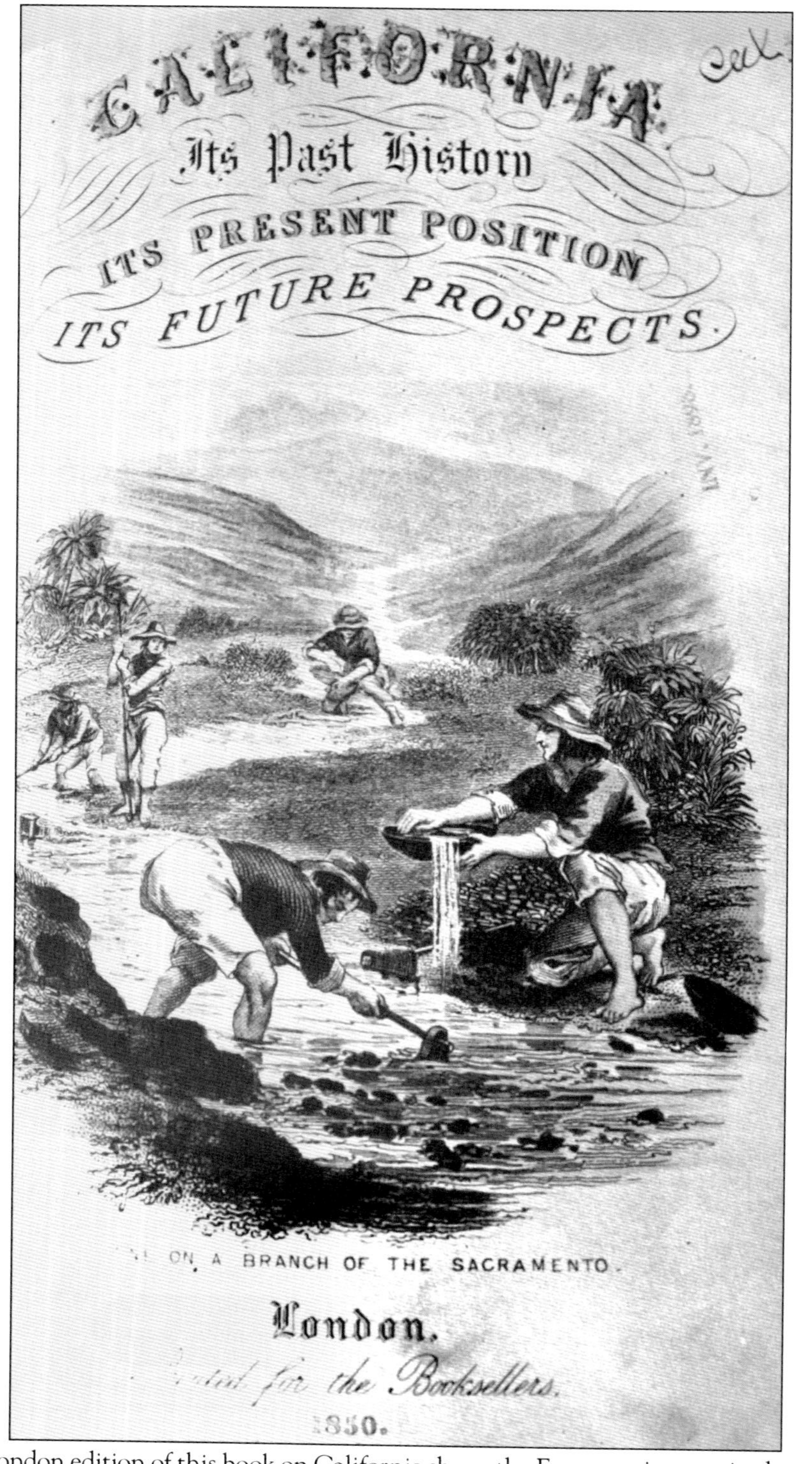

An 1859 London edition of this book on California shows the European interest in the American West and the lure of gold. (Courtesy California State Library.)

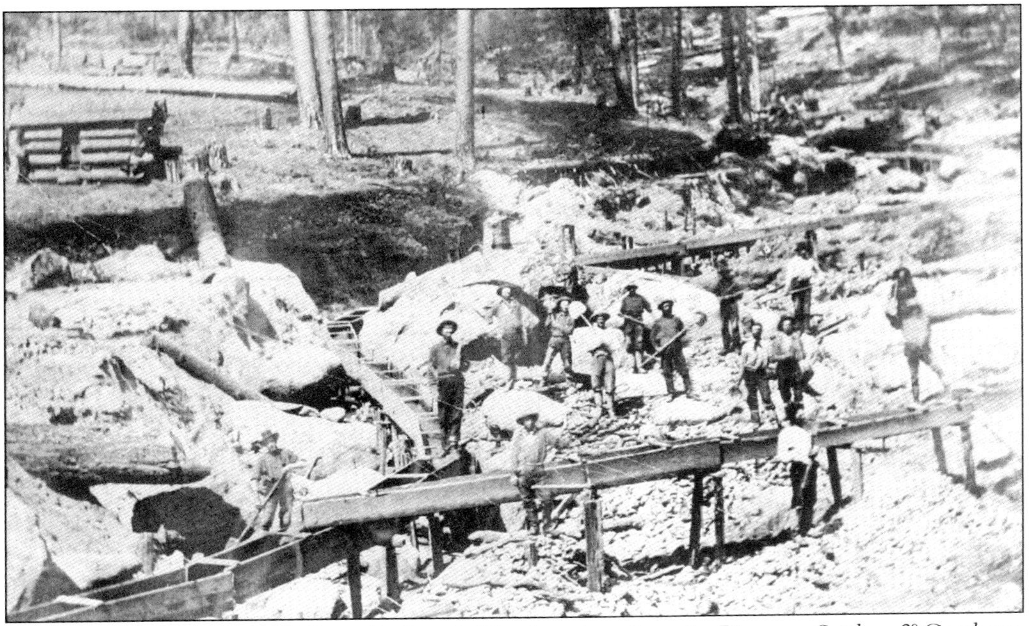

In this image depicted in William C. Davis's *The American Frontier Pioneers, Settlers & Cowboys, 1800–1899* (1992), gold miners are looking for their fortune at the head of Auburn Ravine. The trail to get to the ravine was the trek through Sylvan District. This image includes a group of miners with their troughs, or sluices, which contain gravel that washes over riffles to trap the gold. (Courtesy California State Library.)

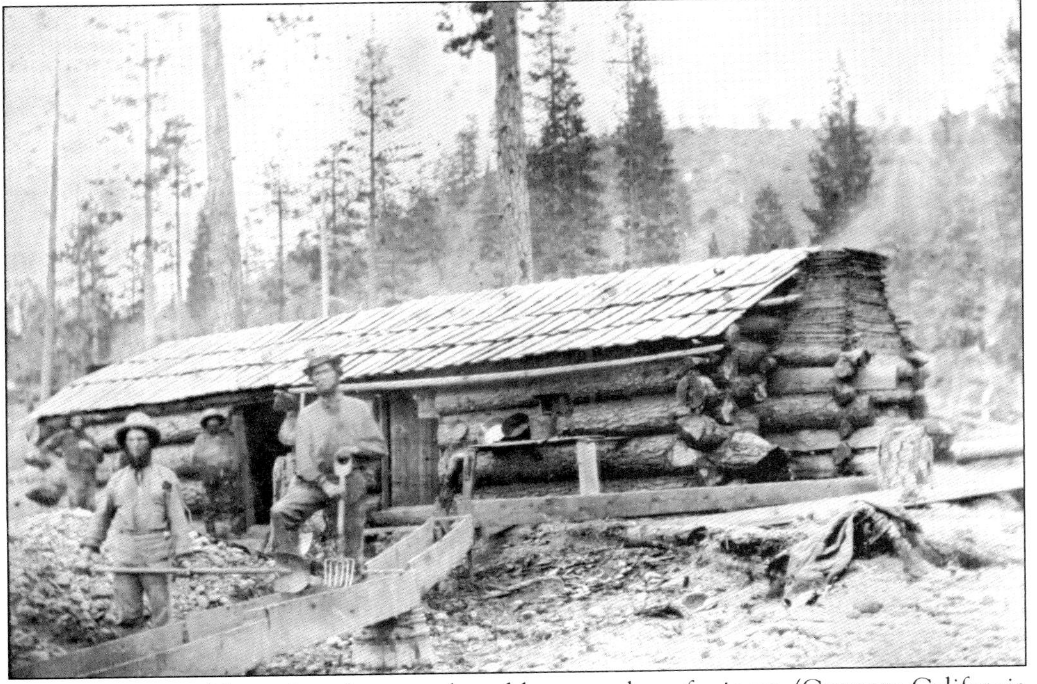

Above is a typical log cabin that was shared by a number of miners. (Courtesy California State Library.)

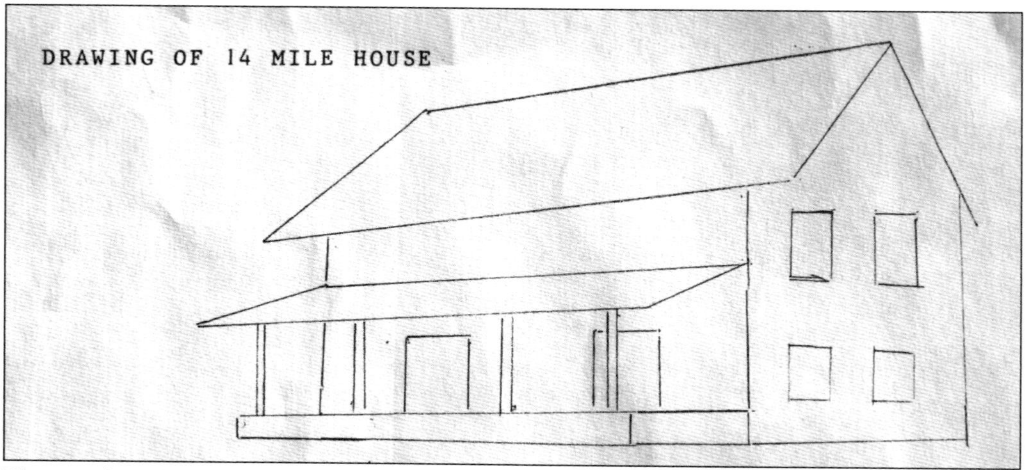

This is a line drawing of 14 Mile Roadhouse as it is today: a home at 6540 Auburn Boulevard. The original wood still remains within the walls. It is one of three wooden buildings that are the oldest such structures in Sacramento County. (Courtesy Jim Van Maren.)

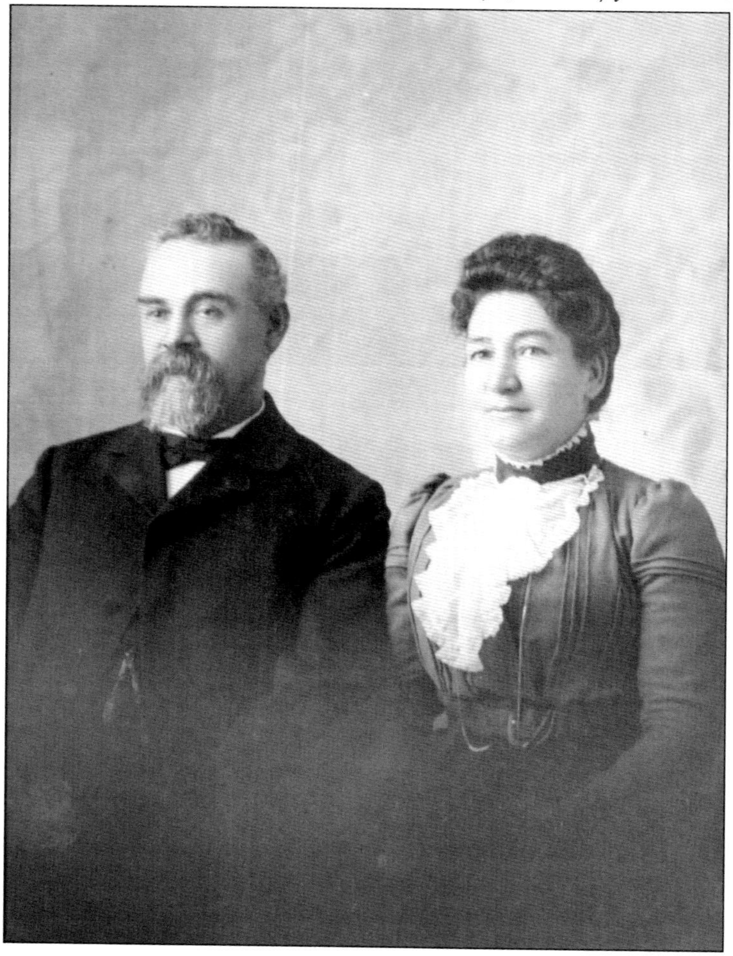

In this image are Joseph and Ann Gray. Joseph built the 14 Mile Roadhouse around 1850. Gray is also credited with constructing the first building in the town of Truckee, California. (Courtesy Guy Coates, Fireman's Fund, Truckee.)

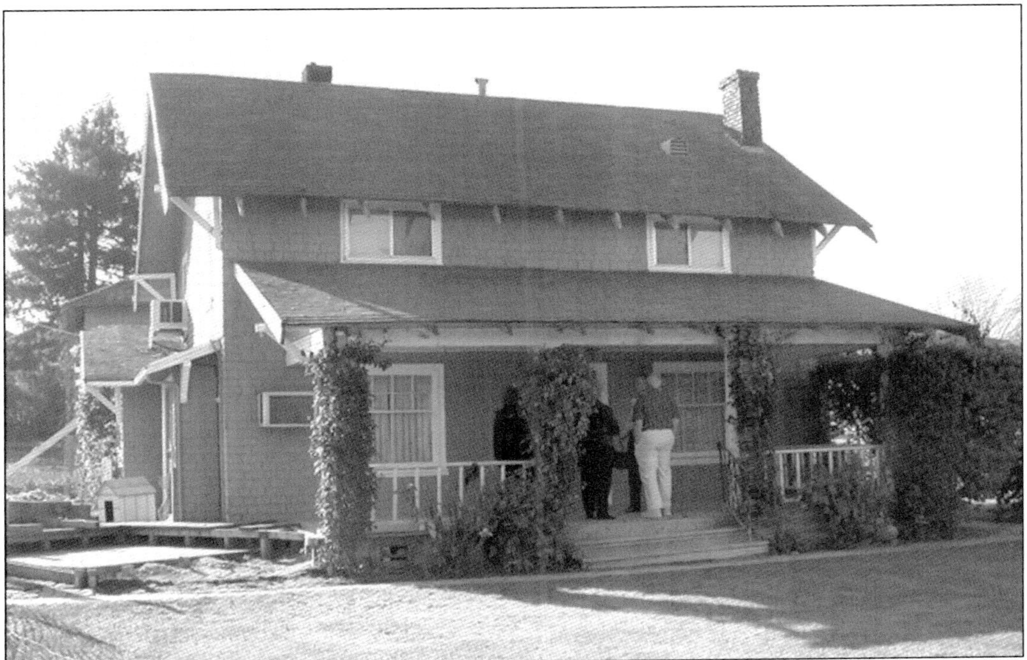

The 14 Mile Roadhouse was purchased from R. Lauppe in 1919 by Adolph Van Maren, father of Guy Van Maren, as a wedding gift. This home was built around the original roadhouse, where it has been preserved. (Courtesy Jim Van Maren.)

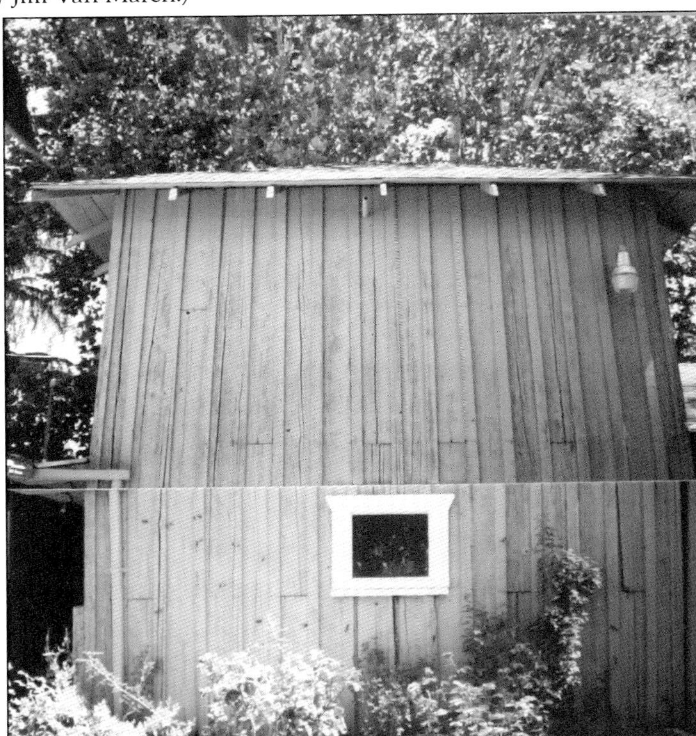

At the rear of 14 Mile Roadhouse is a tank house that was built in 1919. Inside the tank house is a 1,000-gallon water tank raised up about 10 feet from the floor. It provided water for the home, outbuildings, and lawns. Under the water tank is a cellar to keep perishables cool. The 14 Mile Roadhouse had only a windmill for its water supply, which was brought up from a hand-dug well. (Courtesy Jim Van Maren.)

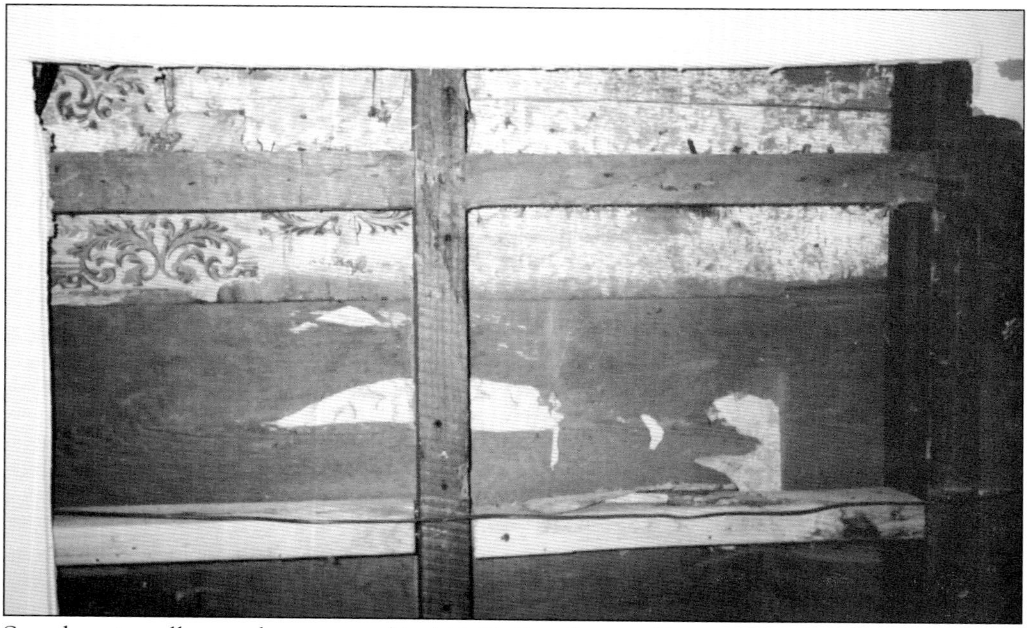

Seen here is wallpaper that was used in 14 Mile Roadhouse. (Courtesy Jim Van Maren.)

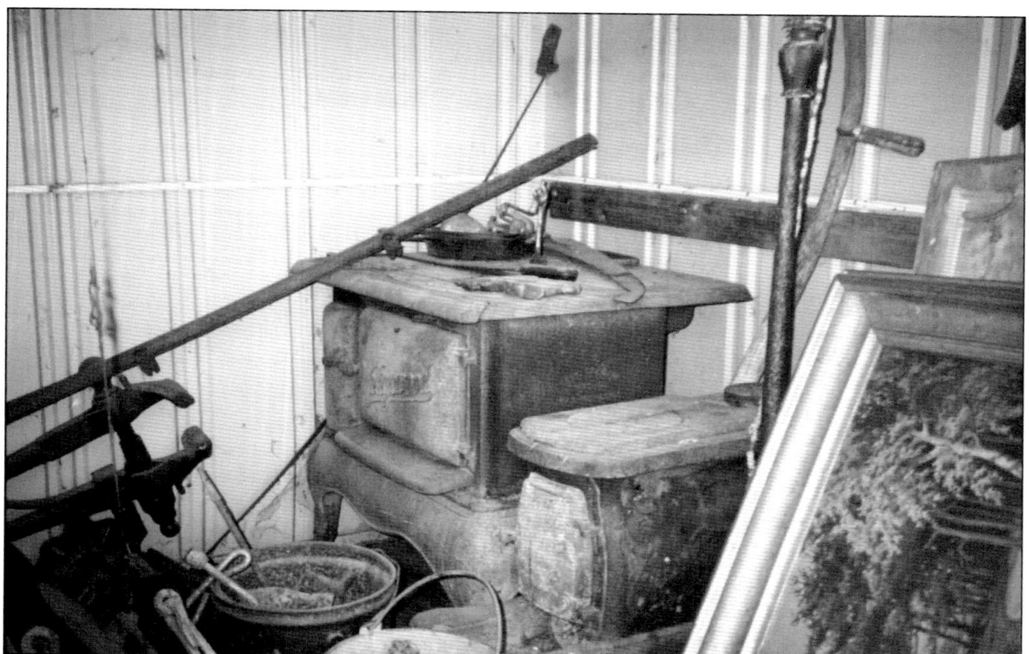

The large woodstove was used from 1919 until 1939 for cooking and heating at 6540 Auburn Boulevard. Attached to the stove was a 15-gallon water tank that piped hot water at the end of the stove. The smaller woodstove provided heat in the sleeping quarters of the hired help. (Courtesy Jim Van Maren.)

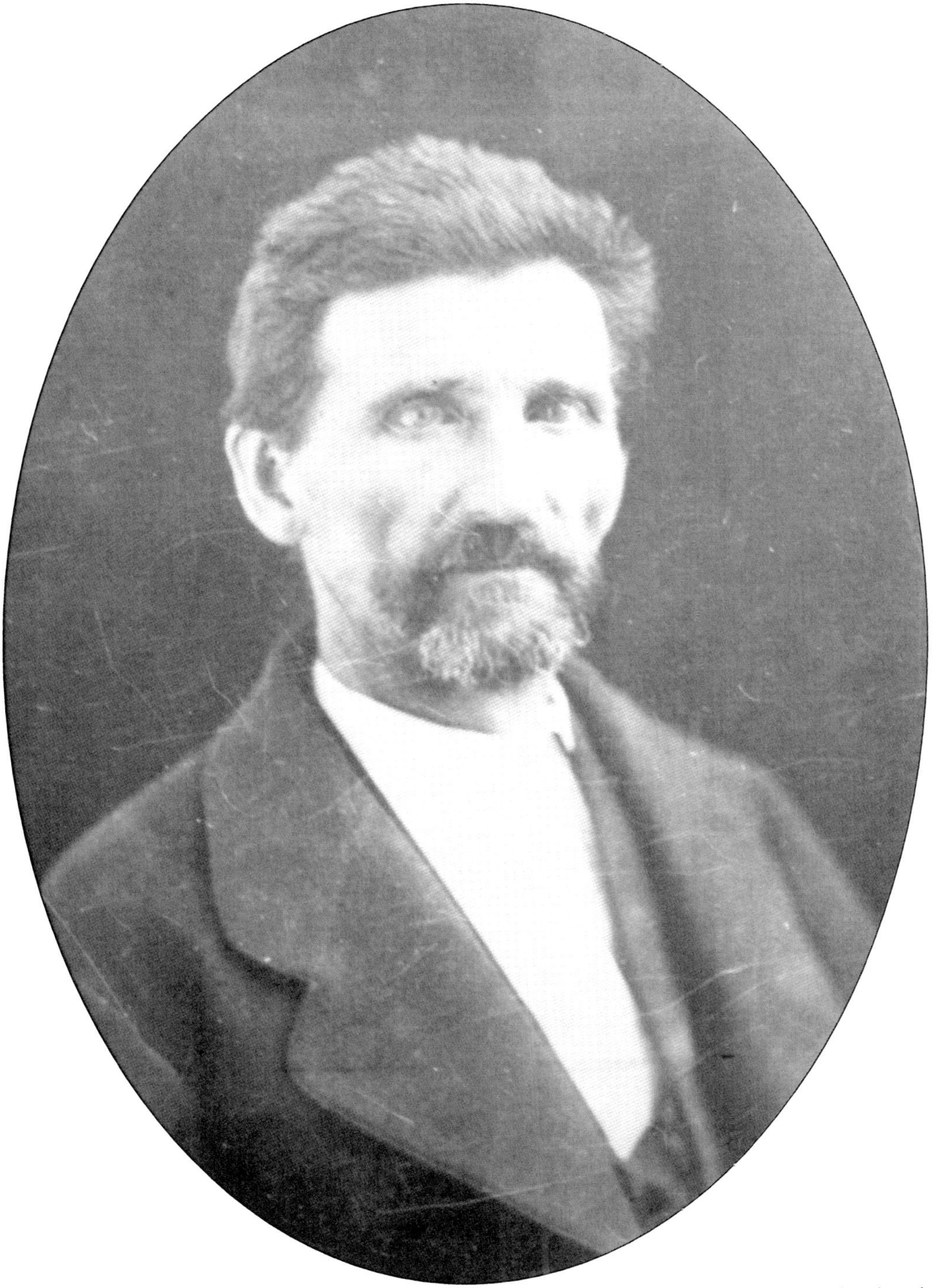

W.A. Thomas owned and operated 15 Mile Roadhouse (since demolished) and is credited with conferring the name Sylvan upon the community. In 1919, a real estate company changed the name to Citrus Heights. (Courtesy Leonard M. Davis.)

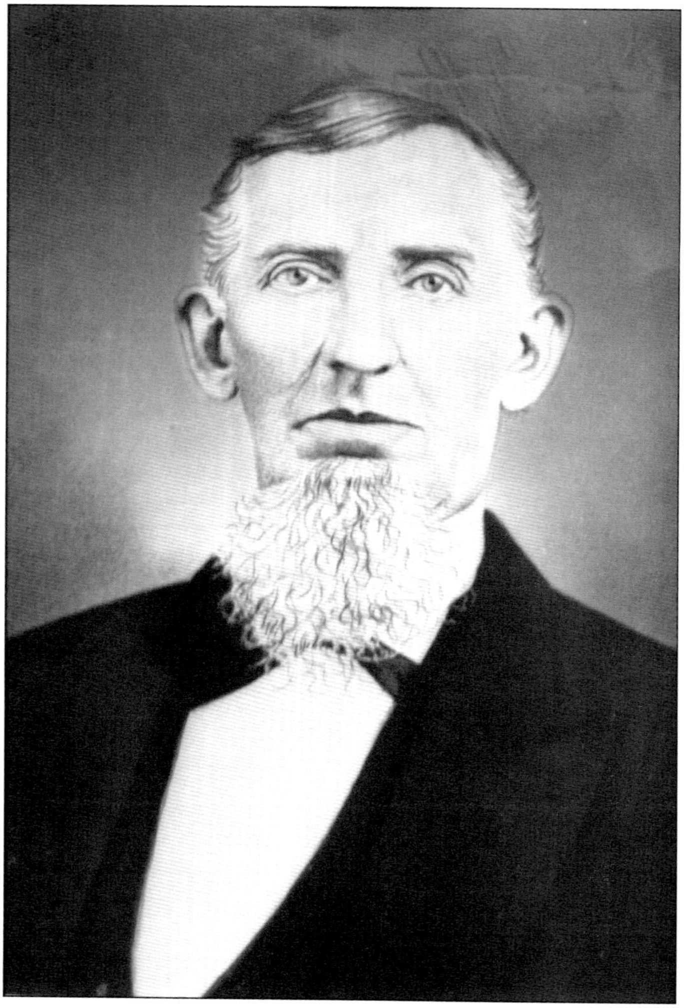

D.S. Neff was the proprietor of 17 Mile Roadhouse, once a popular teamster stop. (Both, courtesy Center for Sacramento History.)

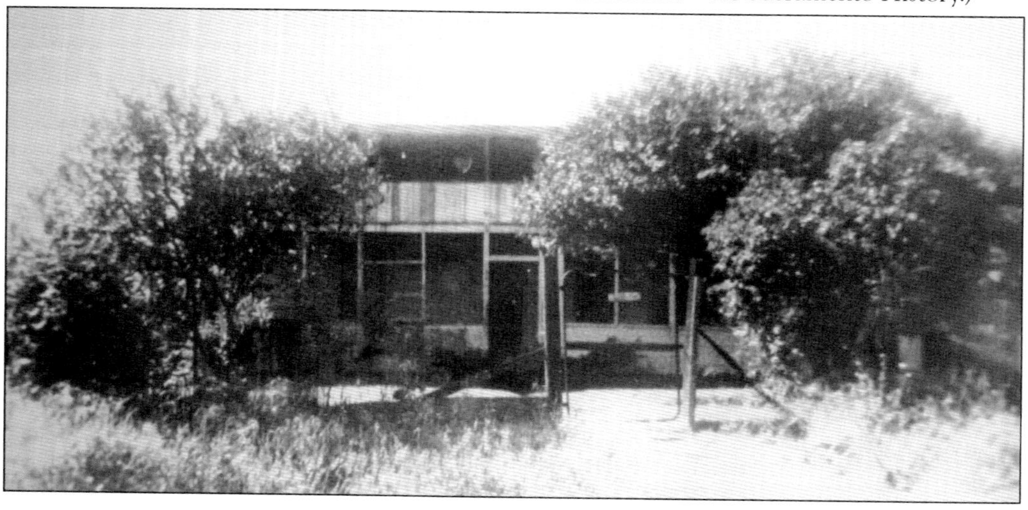

Three

Land and Early Settlers

The first groups of venturous explorers to penetrate the Nisenan territories were inspired by the fertile lands and the possibility of gold. With the rivers full of water for irrigation and domestic use, there were great opportunities for agricultural growth, and word spread across the country. Immigrants and easterners came to California over the Sierra Nevada Mountains and by ship around Cape Horn. With the availability of government lands, the preemption program was a unique means to secure property, but it was soon replaced by the Homestead Act of 1862. It permitted adult males to obtain, without cost, 160 acres under special conditions that included farming and creating a dwelling. Citrus Heights had a great beginning in the 1850s, started by those who took advantage of these land grant programs. Some farm acreage was given in the form of a patent by the US president.

Of the settlers, one of the first couples was Joseph Gray and his wife, Ann, pioneers of 1849. They settled along Auburn Road, where they owned and operated 14 Mile Roadhouse. In 1854, Peter Van Maren farmed 40 acres and lived at 12 Mile Roadhouse. Later, his holdings expanded to 800 acres. Others who came to the area are as follows: John Cross arrived in 1861 and owned 320 acres; John Aiston came in 1857 and owned 440 acres; Frederick Volle arrived in 1858 and had 480 acres (the historical Rusch House is on a portion of the Volle property); Georgiana Jane Pitcher settled in 1868 with 650 acres (named Sunrise Ranch and Sunrise Road); Rudolph Lauppe's 1869 land extended 320 acres; Cornelius O'Donahue came in 1863, receiving 160 acres, which grew to 1,000 acres; and William Carrick, a resident since 1873, received 320 acres from governmental programs. Today, William Carrick's ranch is the location of C-Bar-C Park on Oak Avenue. This is just a small sampling of those who built in the area.

Until the 1950s, Citrus Heights was considered an agricultural community. It began to grow and diversify when Aerojet General arrived in 1942. Intel Corporation came to the Folsom area in 1984, specializing in the use of technology in science, industry, engineering, farming, and medicine. Both companies contributed to mid-20th-century growth of entrepreneurship and population, which helped to create to the vibrant Citrus Heights of today.

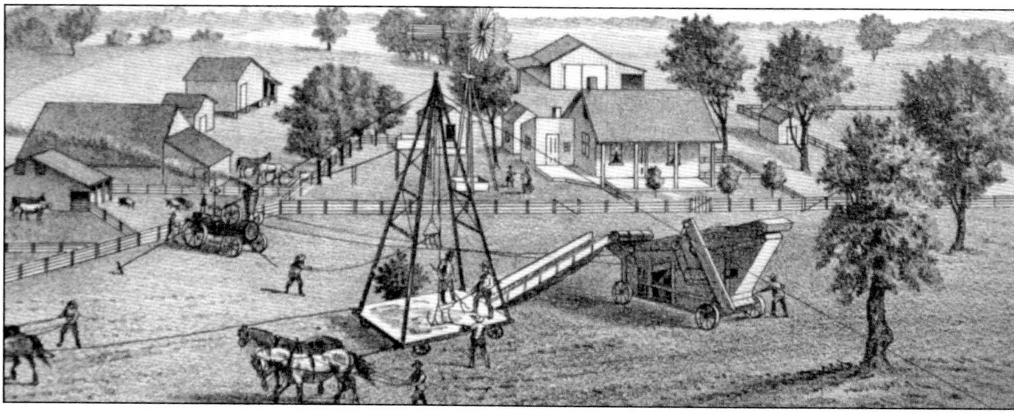

Pictured above is the ranch of John Aiston Sr., while the one below belonged to his son J.A. Aiston Jr. These drawings originally appeared in *History of Sacramento County, California*, published in 1880. (Both, courtesy Thompson and West; reproduced by Howell-North.)

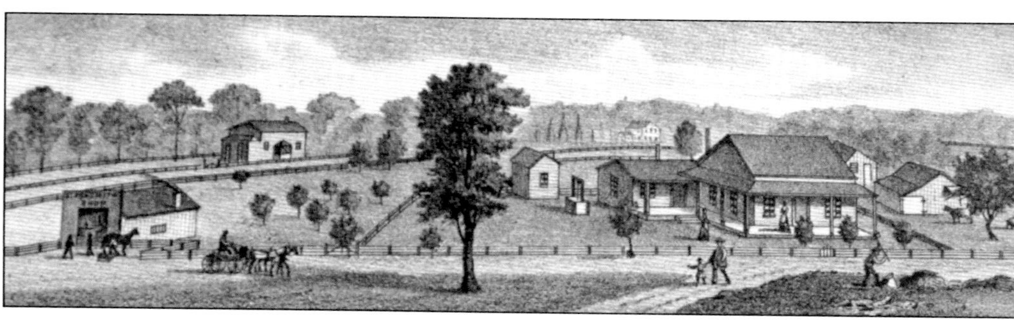

John and Mary Aiston lived at the northeast point of Sylvan Corners and assisted in the construction of the Sylvan School in 1862. Their ranch was located in the Antelope area connecting to the Sylvan District. (Courtesy Leonard M. Davis.)

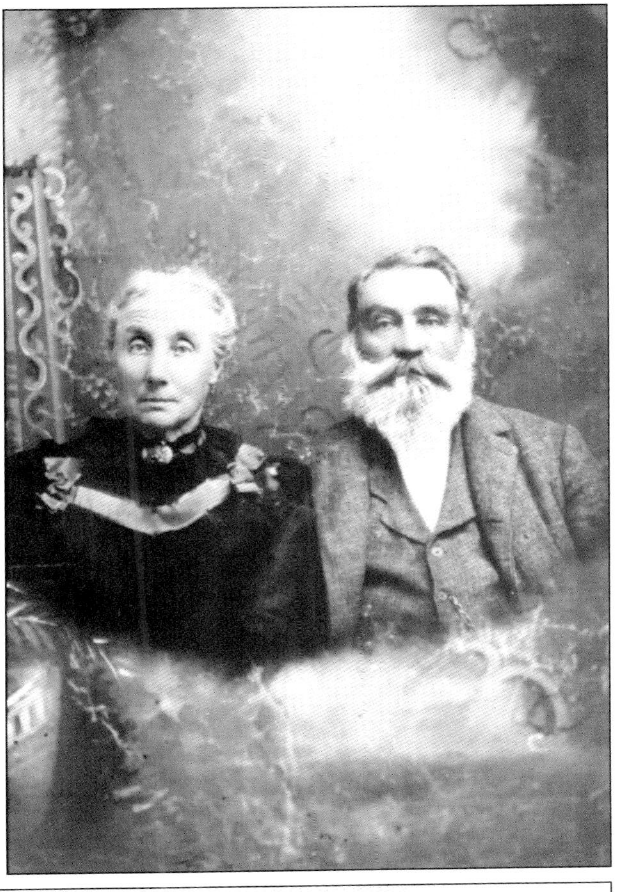

The Sylvan District ranch of pioneers John and Mary Aiston was sold to Trainor-Desmond Company for residential development early in the 20th century. San Juan High School is situated on what was Aiston property. (Courtesy Leonard M. Davis.)

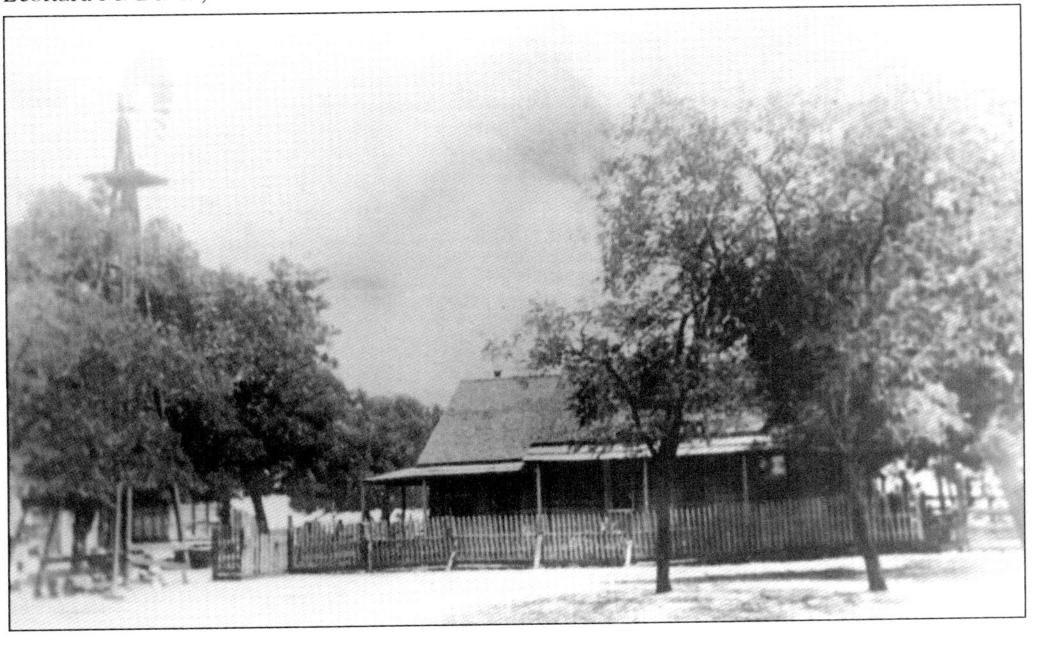

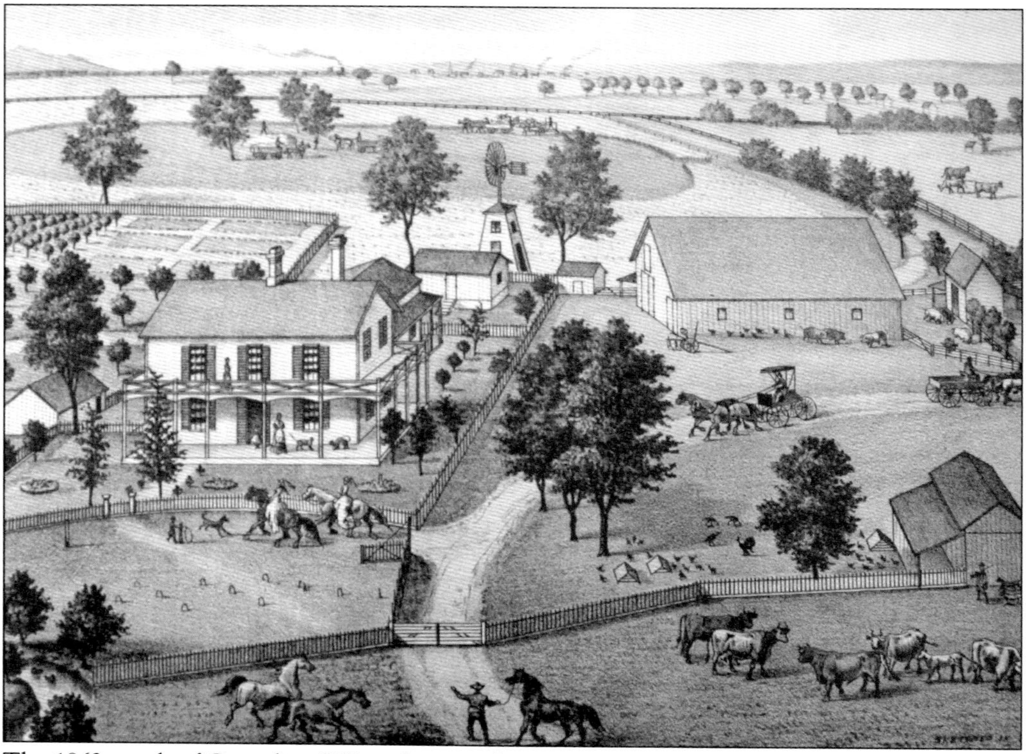

The 1862 ranch of Cornelius O'Donahue was located on what was to become Van Maren Lane. O'Donahue purchased additional properties that are now occupied by Sunrise Mall, Birdcage Walk, and Fair Oaks Presbyterian Church. This drawing originally appeared in *History of Sacramento County, California*, published in 1880. (Courtesy Thompson and West; reproduced by Howell-North, Berkeley, California, 1960.)

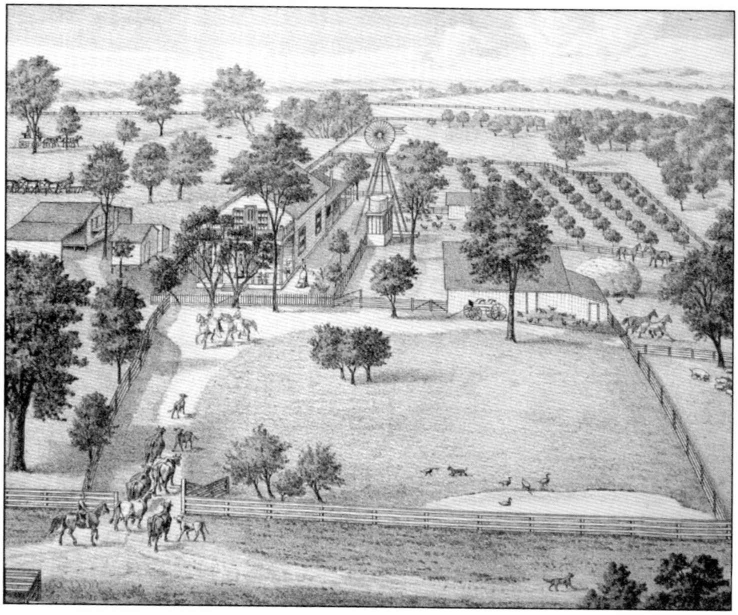

The Grand Oaks Shopping Plaza is located on the former farm of Fred and Julia Volle. Part of the original Volle land is today's Rusch Park, which includes the Rusch home built in 1914. The Volle family settled in the area in 1858. This drawing originally appeared in *History of Sacramento County, California*, published in 1880. (Courtesy Thompson and West; reproduced by Howell-North, Berkeley, California, 1960.)

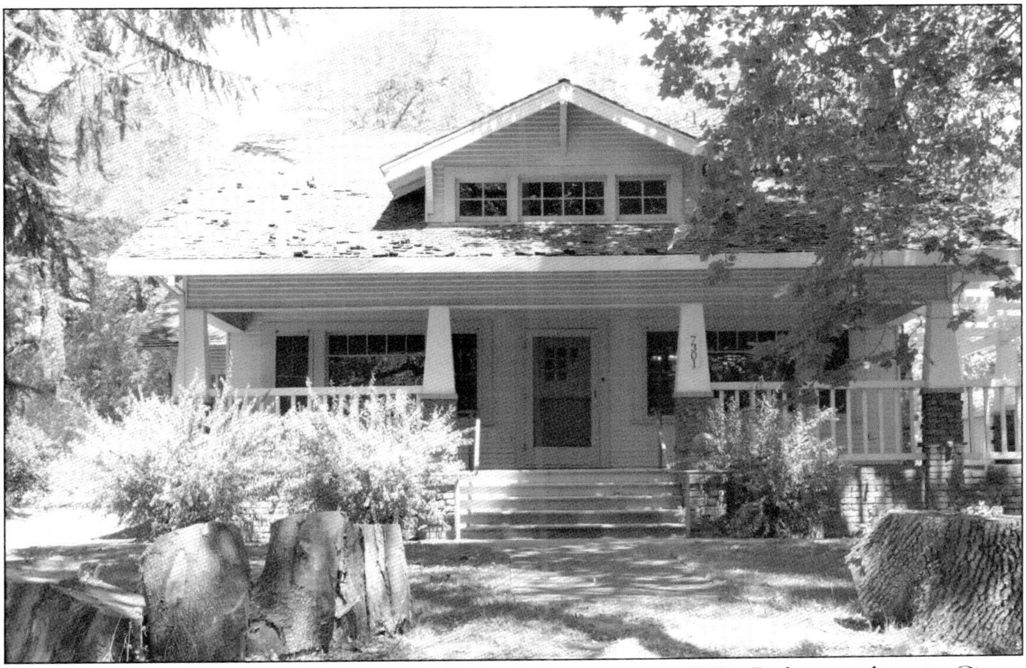

Fred and Julia Volle crossed the plains by covered wagon in 1853. Before settling in Citrus Heights, they owned a small place on L Street in Sacramento that later became part of the State Capitol grounds. Of their 11 children, 10 were raised at this site. Their daughter Louisa died shortly after giving birth to Fred Rusch in 1881. Following the death of their mother, Fred and Julia Rusch were raised by their grandparents and inherited the ranch in 1916. (Courtesy City of Citrus Heights.)

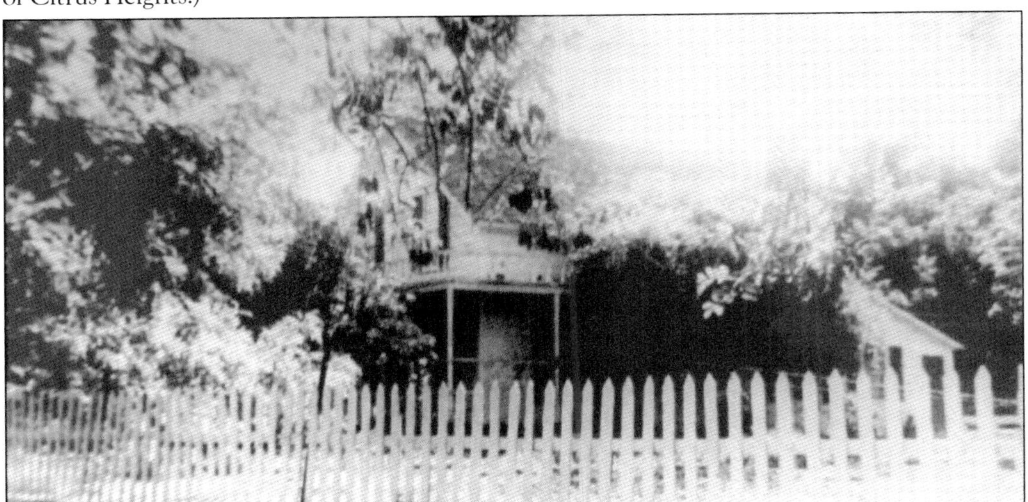

The home of carpenter John F. Cross was built about a quarter of a mile east of 14 Mile Roadhouse along Auburn Boulevard. Cross first built a one-room house for his family and later remodeled it into a two-story structure. It was razed in the 1970s. (Courtesy Leonard M. Davis.)

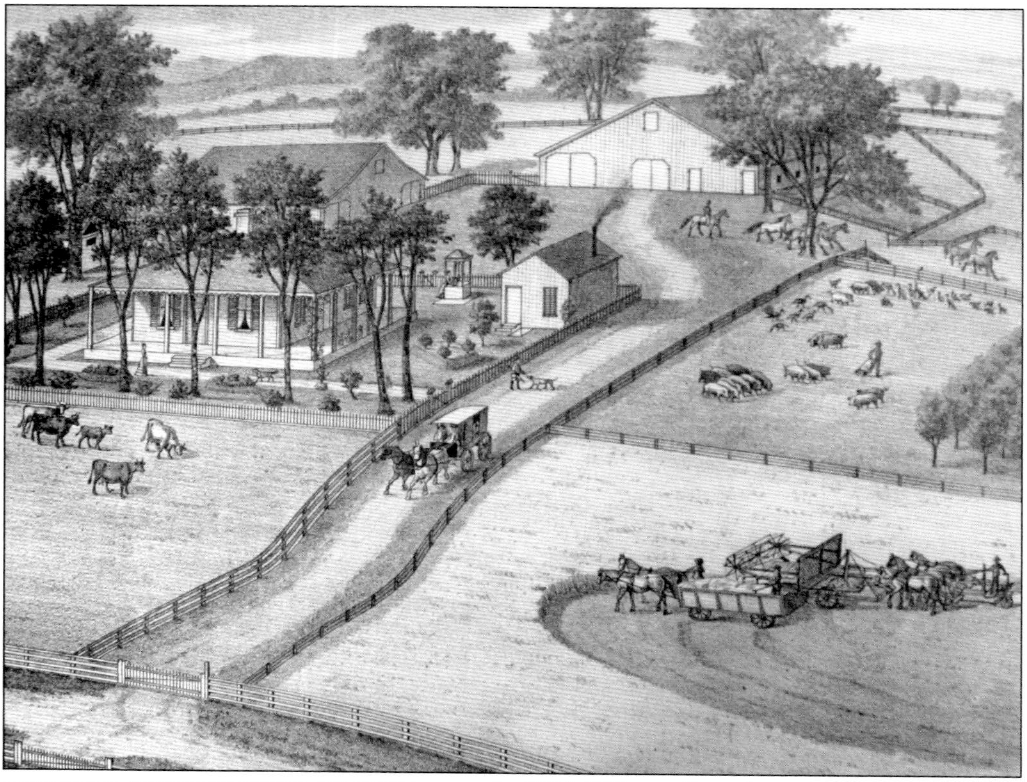

In 1873, William Carrick, a native of Ireland, moved to California, where he acquired his ranch in the Sylvan District. It was located off Oak Avenue. William's nephew Lester Carrick and wife Pansy operated the ranch and a popular hay and barbecue business at the C-Bar-C Park on Oak Avenue. This drawing originally appeared in *History of Sacramento County, California*, published in 1880. (Courtesy Thompson and West; reproduced by Howell-North, Berkeley, California, 1960.)

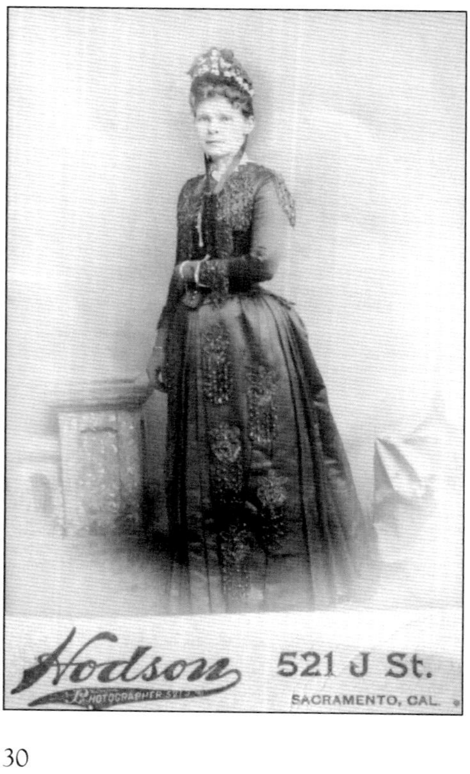

Eliza Carrick Pond models a black dress worn in 1880 at the inaugural ball of Gov. George Perkins. (Courtesy Ernestine Botts Smith.)

Lester Carrick is seated on threshing equipment used to smooth fields after plowing. (Courtesy Ernestine Botts Smith.)

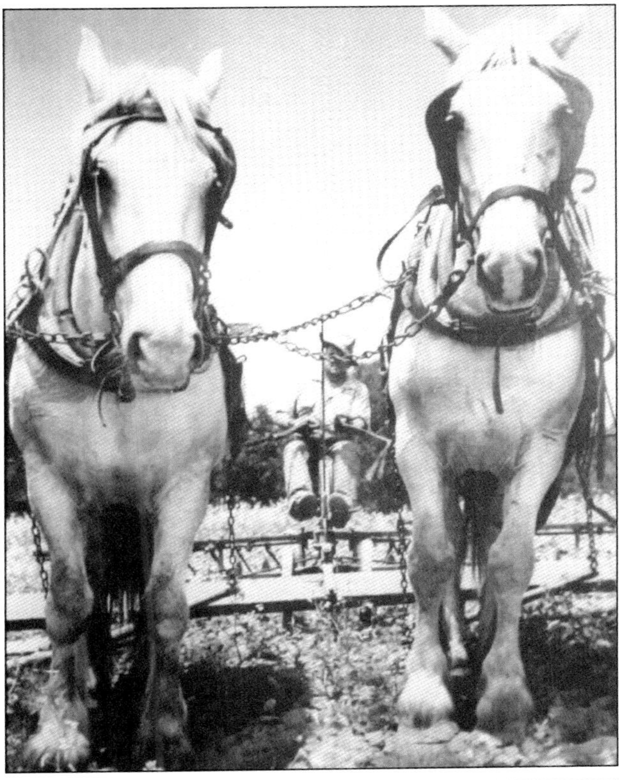

Lester Carrick's horses are preparing to pull a wagon full of hay. A pitchfork was used to gather the hay, which was a very labor-intensive feat. (Courtesy Ernestine Botts Smith.)

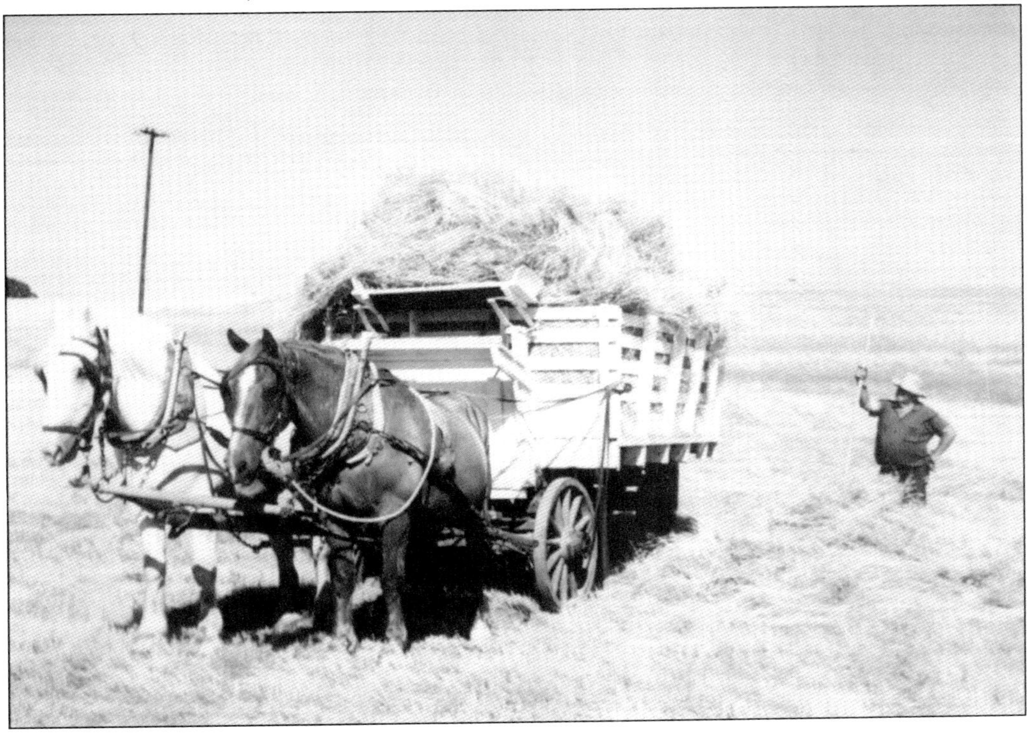

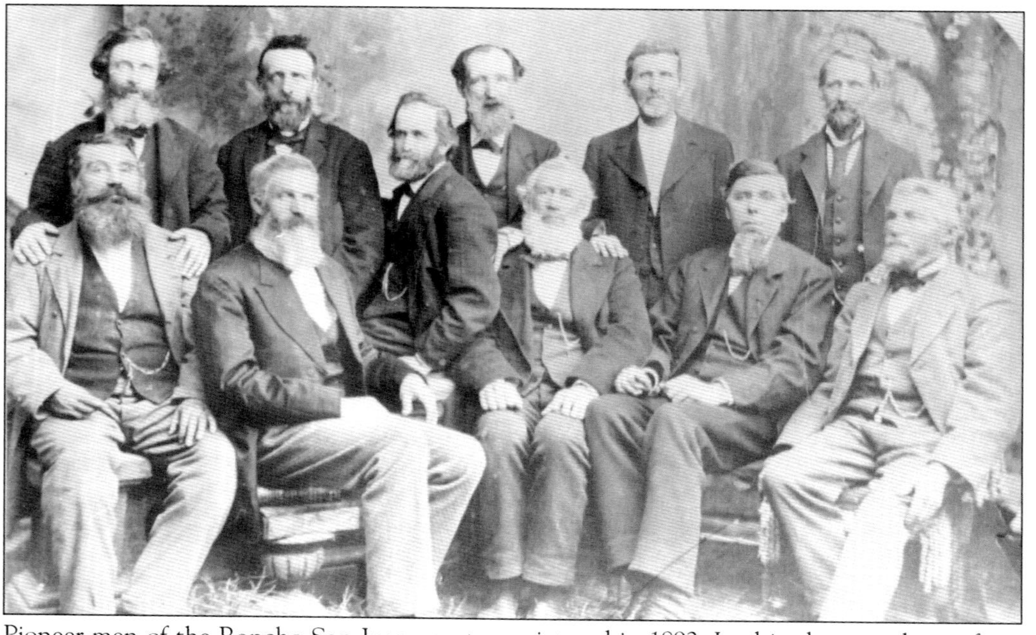

Pioneer men of the Rancho San Juan grant are pictured in 1892. In this photograph are, from left to right, (first row) Mr. Aiston (age 58), Mr. Cross (age 54), Mr. Gardner (age 55), Mr. Brown (age unknown), Mr. Cavitt (age 50), and Mr. Mertel (age 57); (second row) Mr. Daly (age 56), Mr. Johnson (age 51), Mr. McClory (age 64), Mr. Thomas (age 62), and Mr. Leonard (age 55). (Courtesy Leonard M. Davis.)

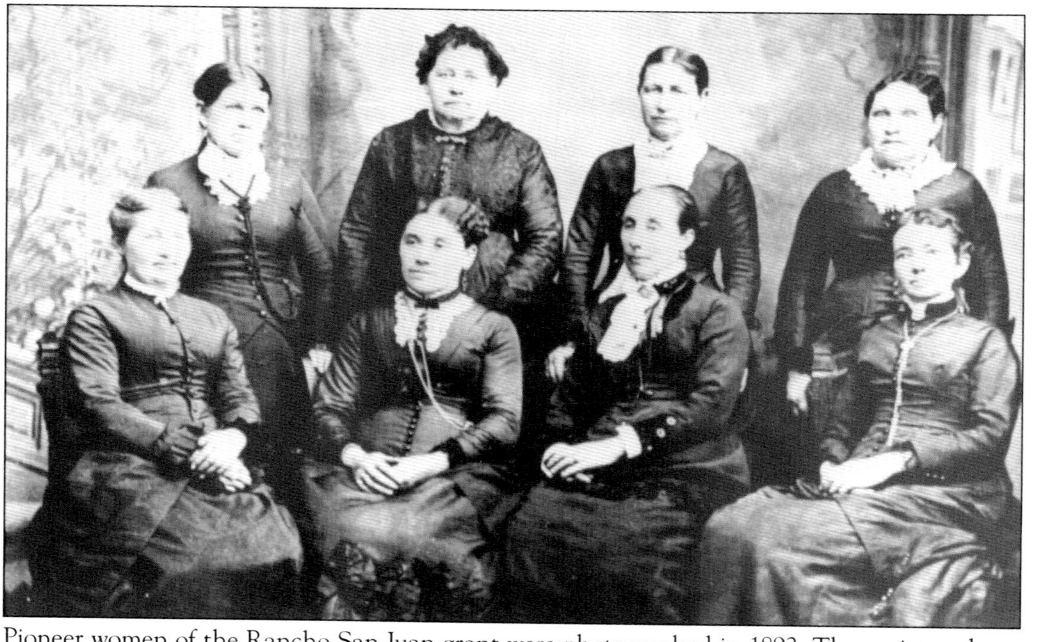

Pioneer women of the Rancho San Juan grant were photographed in 1892. Those pictured are, from left to right, (first row) Ms. Johnson (age 42), Ms. Mertes (age 52), Ms. Aiston (age 59), and Ms. Cross (age 48); (second row) Ms. Daly (age 52), Ms. Thomas (age 60), Ms. Cavitt (age 51), and Ms. Gardner (age 50). (Courtesy Leonard M. Davis.)

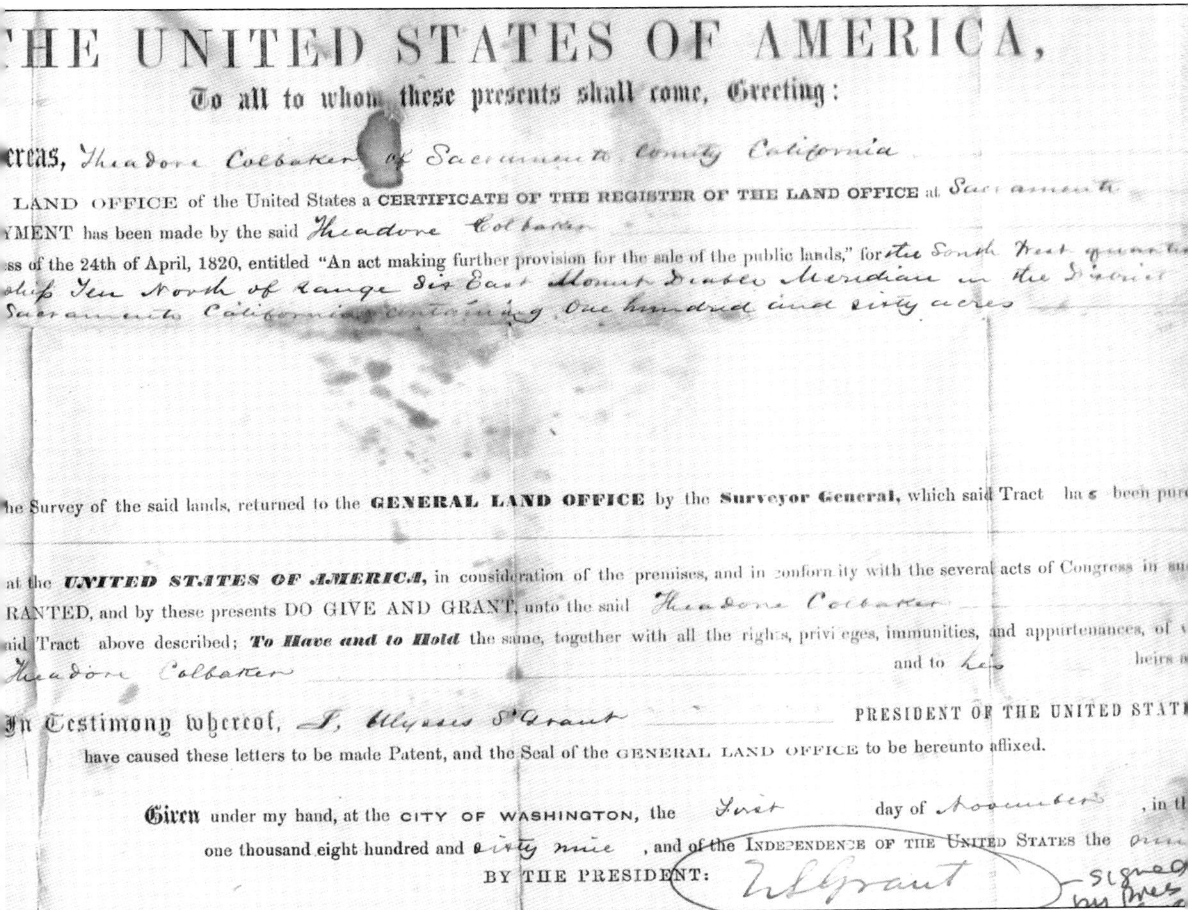

HE UNITED STATES OF AMERICA,

To all to whom these presents shall come, Greeting:

ereas, Theadore Colbaker of Sacramento County California

LAND OFFICE of the United States a CERTIFICATE OF THE REGISTER OF THE LAND OFFICE at Sacramento

YMENT has been made by the said Theadore Colbaker

ss of the 24th of April, 1820, entitled "An act making further provision for the sale of the public lands," for the South West quarter

ship Ten North of Range Six East Mount Diablo Meridian in the District

Sacramento California containing One hundred and sixty acres

he Survey of the said lands, returned to the GENERAL LAND OFFICE by the Surveyor General, which said Tract has been pur

at the UNITED STATES OF AMERICA, in consideration of the premises, and in conformity with the several acts of Congress in su

RANTED, and by these presents DO GIVE AND GRANT, unto the said Theadore Colbaker

aid Tract above described; To Have and to Hold the same, together with all the rights, privileges, immunities, and appurtenances, of

Theadore Colbaker and to his heirs a

In Testimony whereof, I, Ulysses S Grant PRESIDENT OF THE UNITED STAT

have caused these letters to be made Patent, and the Seal of the GENERAL LAND OFFICE to be hereunto affixed.

Given under my hand, at the CITY OF WASHINGTON, the First day of November , in th

one thousand eight hundred and sixty nine , and of the INDEPENDENCE OF THE UNITED STATES the

BY THE PRESIDENT: U S Grant — signed by Pres.

When given as a patent, land came with all rights, privileges, and immunities, and no payment was required. This patent was signed by Pres. Ulysses Grant on November 1, 1866. The original land parcel was located near the intersection of Van Maren Lane and Antelope Road. It was given to Theodore Colbaker, the great-grandfather of Ted Mitchell. (Courtesy Ted Mitchell.)

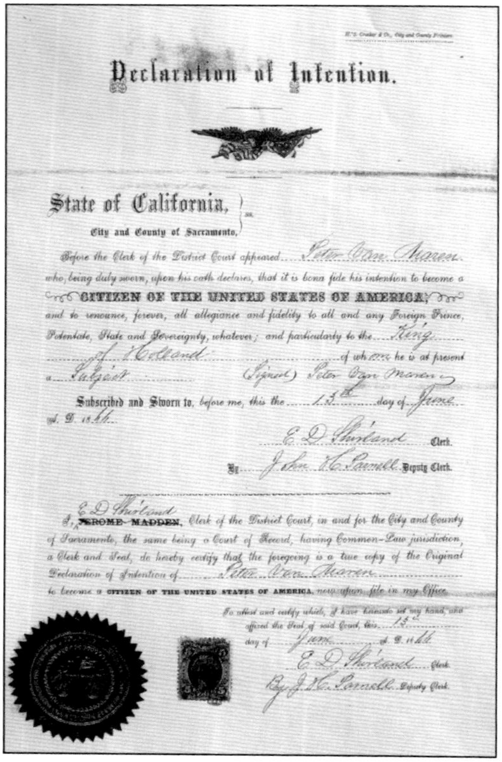

Declaration of Intention.

State of California, } ss.
City and County of Sacramento.

Before the Clerk of the District Court appeared Peter Van Maren who, being duly sworn, upon his oath declares, that it is bona fide his intention to become a CITIZEN OF THE UNITED STATES OF AMERICA; and to renounce, forever, all allegiance and fidelity to all and any Foreign Prince, Potentate, State and Sovereignty, whatever; and particularly to the King of Holland of whom he is at present a Subject (Signed) Peter Van Maren

Subscribed and Sworn to, before me, this the 13th day of June A.D. 1866.

E. D. Shirland Clerk.
By John H. Powell Deputy Clerk.

I, E. D. Shirland ~~JEROME MADDEN~~, Clerk of the District Court, in and for the City and County of Sacramento, the same being a Court of Record, having Common-Law jurisdiction, a Clerk and Seal, do hereby certify that the foregoing is a true copy of the Original Declaration of Intention of Peter Van Maren to become a CITIZEN OF THE UNITED STATES OF AMERICA, now upon file in my Office.

To attest and certify which, I have hereunto set my hand, and affixed the Seal of said Court, this 13th day of June A.D. 1866

E. D. Shirland Clerk.
By J. H. Powell Deputy Clerk.

This declaration of intention from 1866 is a sworn document to the fact that Peter Van Maren intended to become a citizen of the United States. In addition, he would renounce allegiance and fidelity to all and any foreign prince, potentate, state, and sovereignty, and particularly to the King of Holland. (Courtesy Jim Van Maren.)

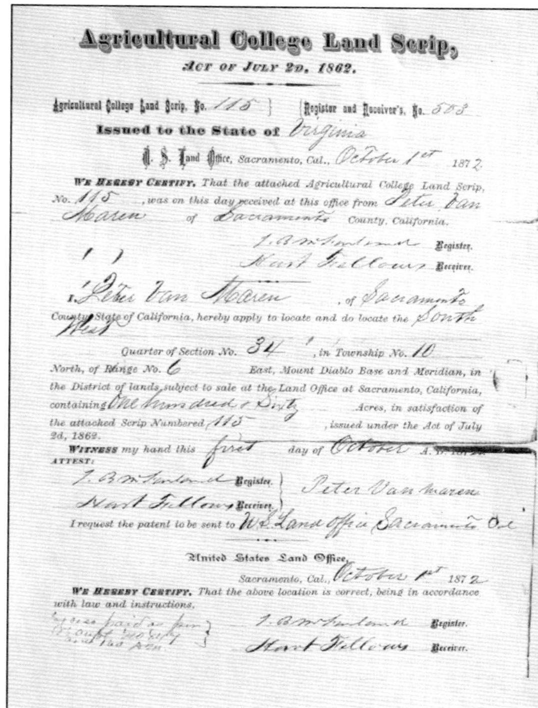

Agricultural College Land Scrip,

Act of July 2d, 1862.

Agricultural College Land Scrip, No. 115 } Register and Receiver's, No. 505

Issued to the State of Virginia

U. S. Land Office, Sacramento, Cal., October 1st 1872.

We Hereby Certify, That the attached Agricultural College Land Scrip, No. 115, was on this day received at this office from Peter Van Maren of Sacramento County, California.

T. B. McFarland Register.
Hart Fellows Receiver.

I, Peter Van Maren, of Sacramento County, State of California, hereby apply to locate and do locate the South West Quarter of Section No. 34, in Township No. 10 North, of Range No. 6 East, Mount Diablo Base and Meridian, in the District of lands subject to sale at the Land Office at Sacramento, California, containing One hundred & Sixty Acres, in satisfaction of the attached Scrip Numbered 115, issued under the Act of July 2d, 1862.

Witness my hand this first day of October A.D. 1872.

Attest:
T. B. McFarland Register. } Peter Van Maren
Hart Fellows Receiver. }

I request the patent to be sent to U.S. Land Office Sacramento Cal

United States Land Office,
Sacramento, Cal., October 1st 1872

We Hereby Certify, That the above location is correct, being in accordance with law and instructions.

T. B. McFarland Register.
Hart Fellows Receiver.

Under the Agricultural College Land Scrip Act of July 20, 1862, Peter Van Maren paid $2.50 per acre to the US government for the 160 acres he settled. The monies from this program went to the development of agricultural land grant colleges, such as the University of California. (Courtesy Jim Van Maren.)

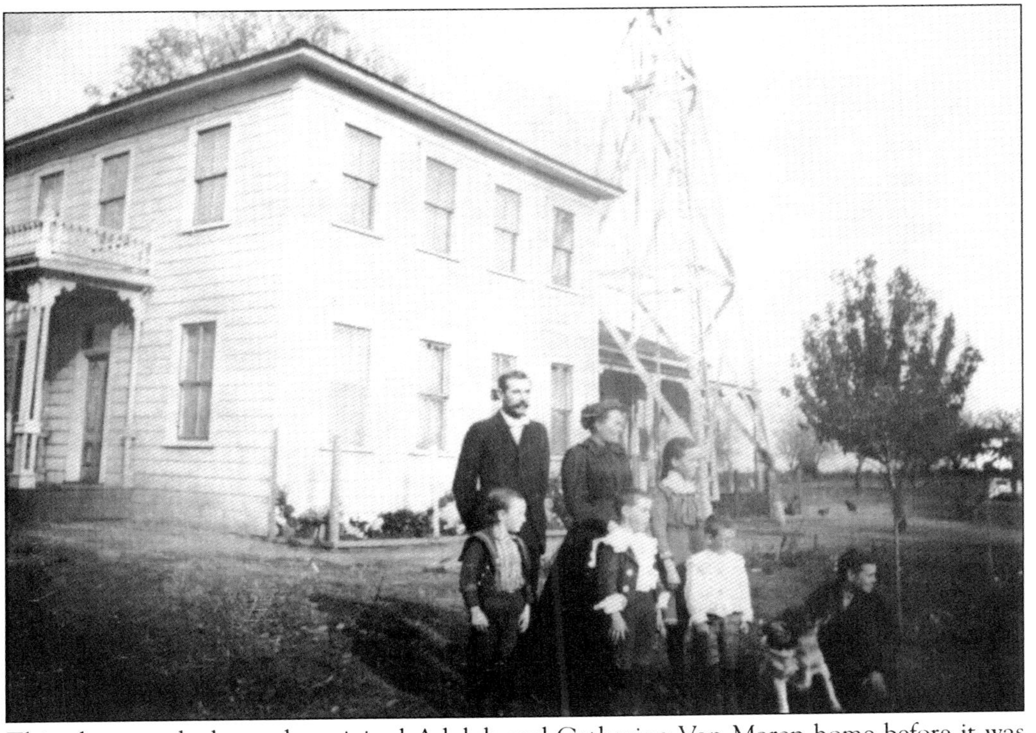

This photograph shows the original Adolph and Catherine Van Maren home before it was remodeled in 1900. Today, it would be located at the north end of Van Maren Park. Posed in front of the home are, from left to right, (first row) Adolph Jr., Cornelius, Guy Van Maren, and Daniel Lehan; (second row) Adolph and Catherine Van Maren and May (Stock) Corlett. (Courtesy Jim Van Maren.)

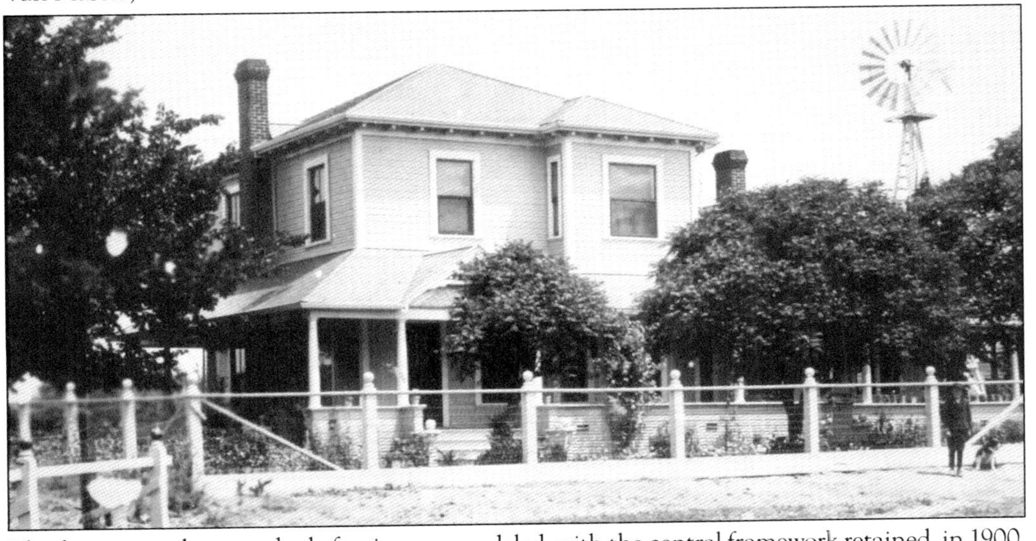

This home was photographed after it was remodeled, with the central framework retained, in 1900. The home had an exterior porch, and inside was a parlor, living room, four bedrooms, a bath with piped water, and a large kitchen and pantry. Shown is Guy Van Maren. The home burned beyond repair on March 23, 1969. (Courtesy Jim Van Maren.)

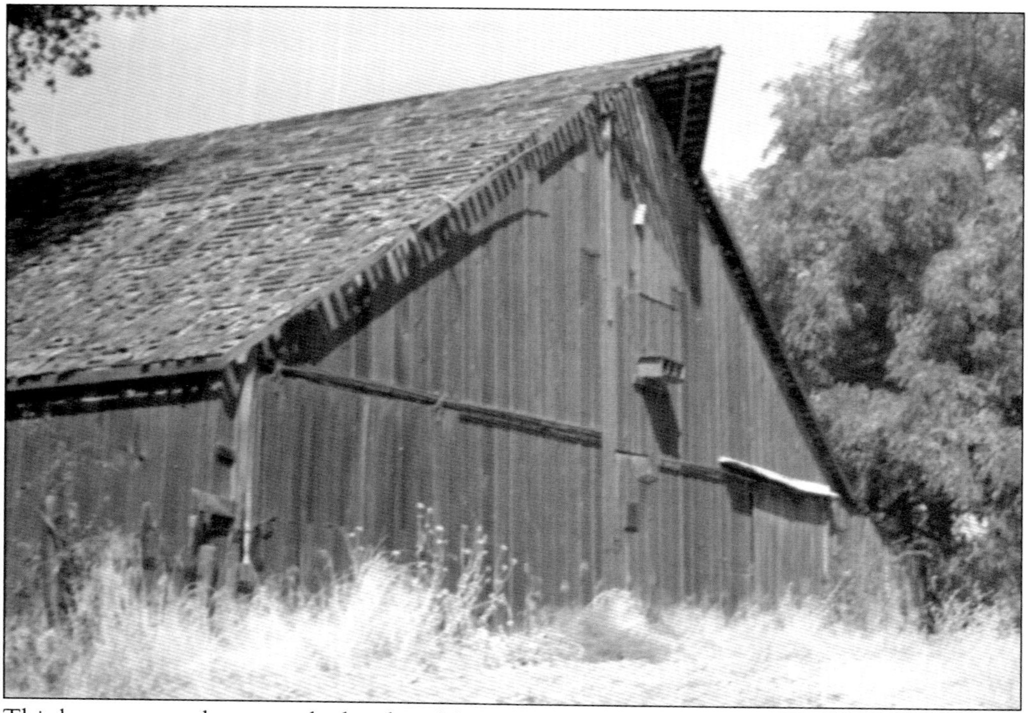

This barn was used to store the header of the harvester during winter. In the center of the barn, loose hay was stored to feed the horses, which was done on the other side of the structure. The barn was demolished to make way for residential development. It was located on the Cornelius Van Maren homesite on Van Maren Ranch. (Courtesy Jim Van Maren.)

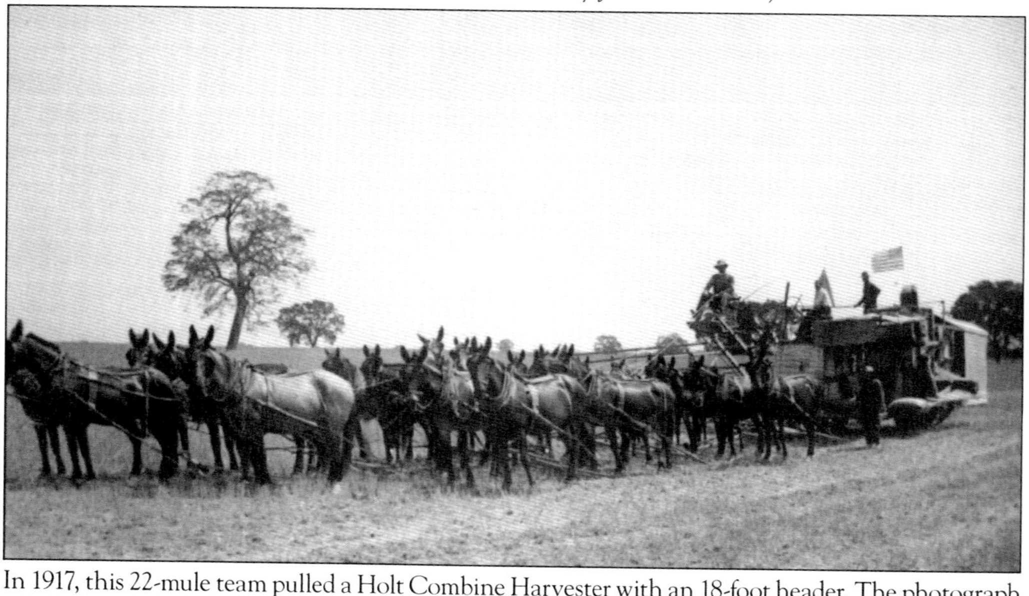

In 1917, this 22-mule team pulled a Holt Combine Harvester with an 18-foot header. The photograph was taken east of Van Maren Lane on July 4. Shown from left to right are Adolph, Connie, and Guy Van Maren and Ralph Sandstad (on the ground). In later years, the harvester was pulled by a 75-horsepower Holt tractor. (Courtesy Jim Van Maren.)

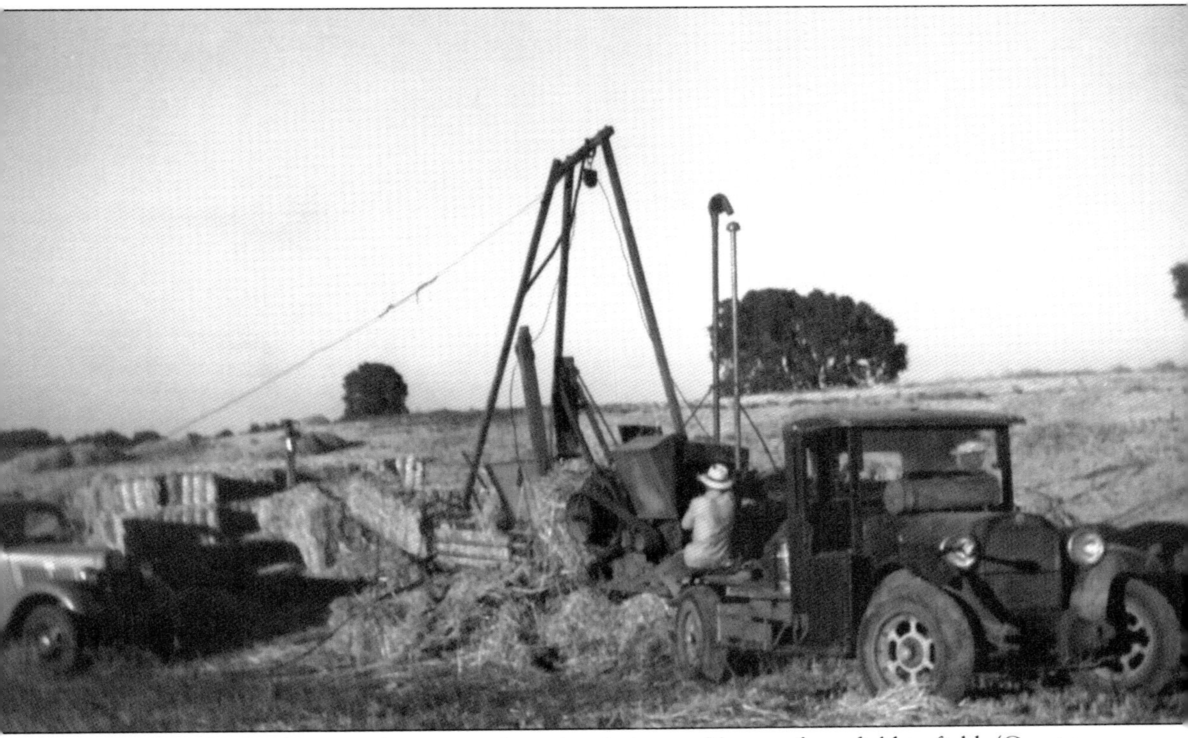

A 1947 Dodge Graham truck converted to a hay baler could move from field to field. (Courtesy Jim Van Maren.)

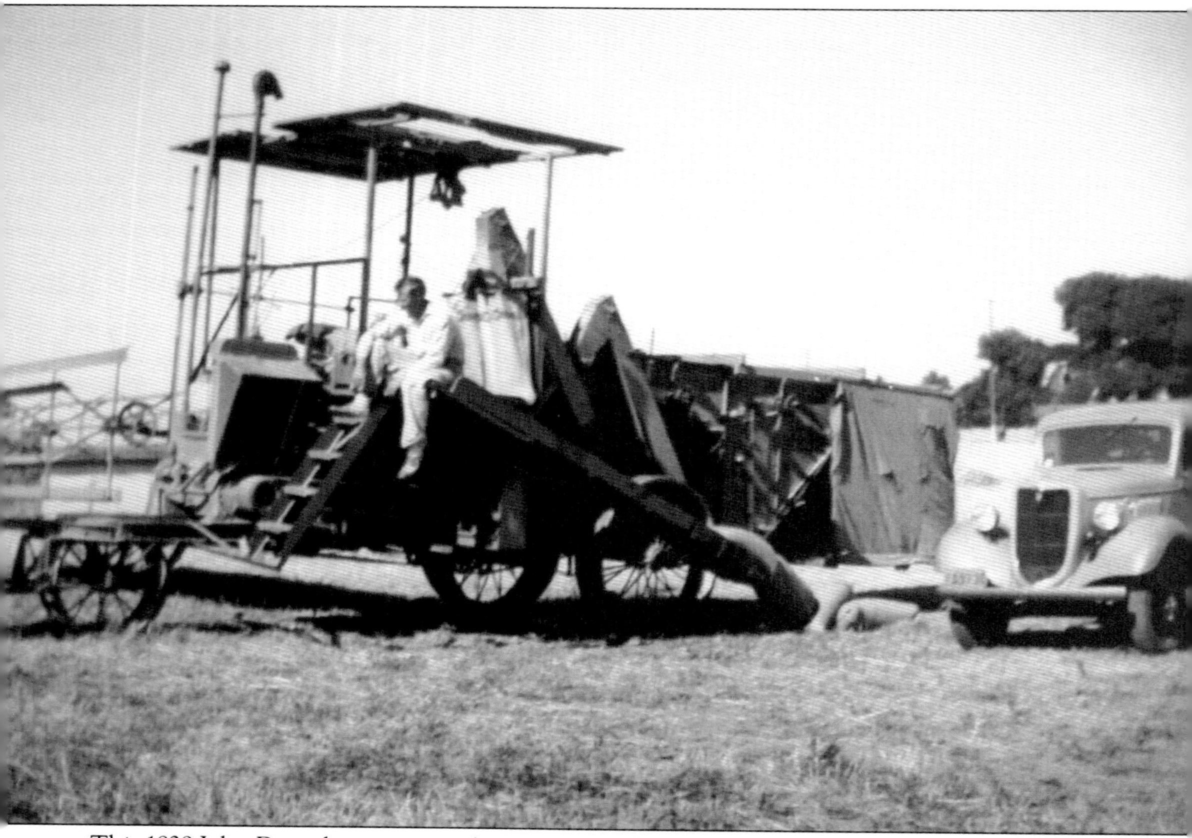

This 1939 John Deere harvester combine is seen with sacks of wheat sliding down the shoot to the ground to be picked up. The harvester had a 14-foot header and was pulled by an International 14 tracklayer. Shown is John Stock waiting to go to work. (Courtesy Jim Van Maren.)

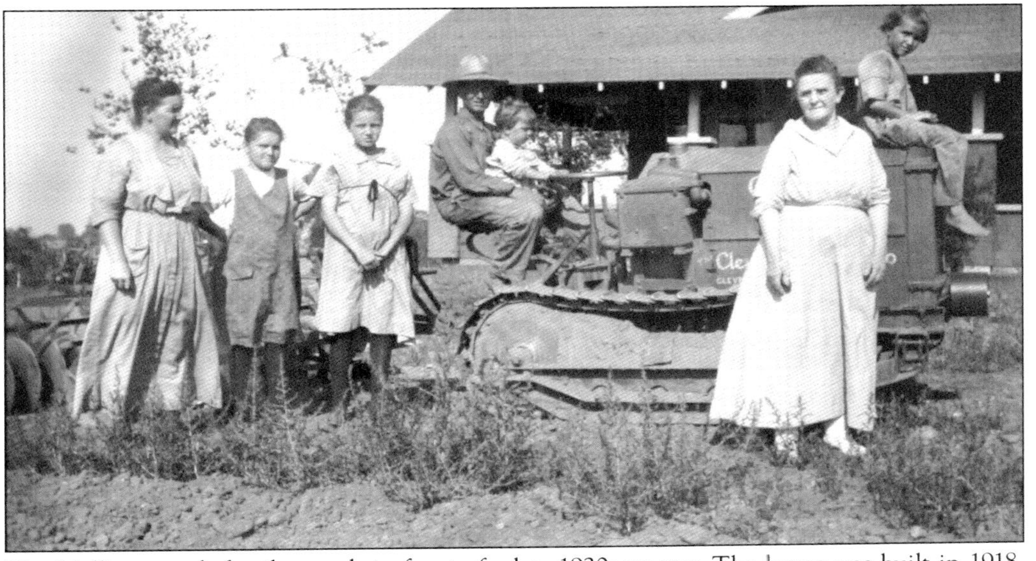

The Hollingsworth family stands in front of a late-1920s tractor. The home was built in 1918. Lois Hollingsworth is sitting on the tractor. (Courtesy Beverly Sales.)

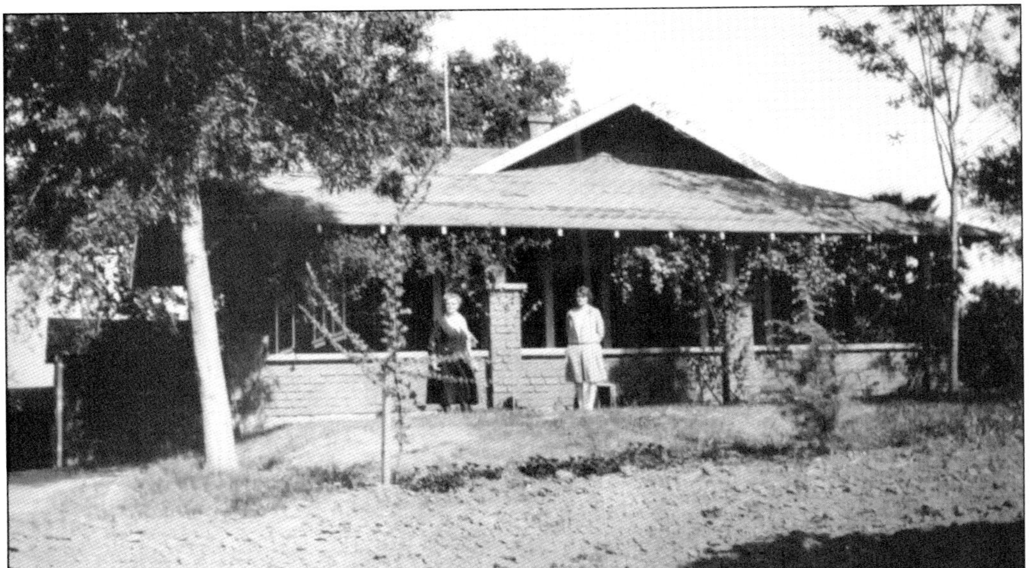

In this image from the 1920s is the Hollingsworth home located north of Sylvan Corners along Auburn Boulevard on a 10-acre fruit ranch. (Courtesy Hollingsworth family.)

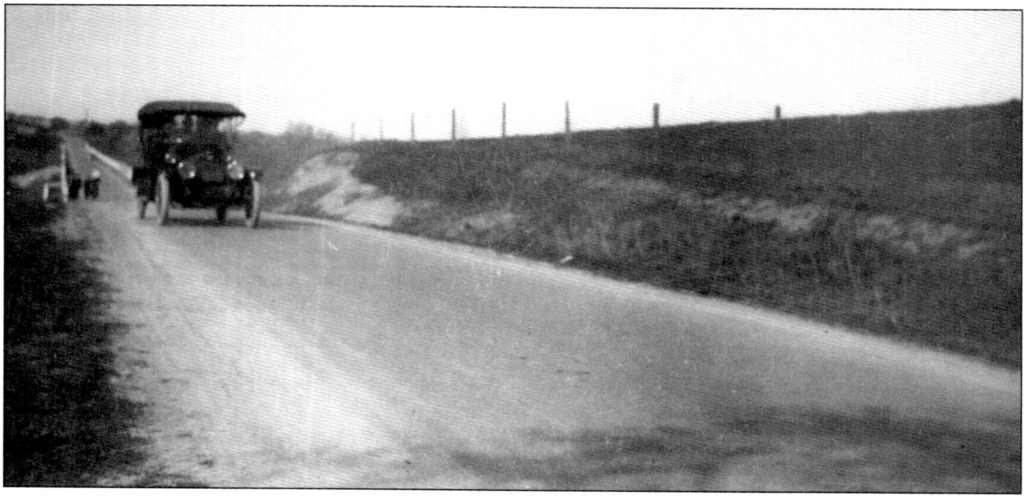

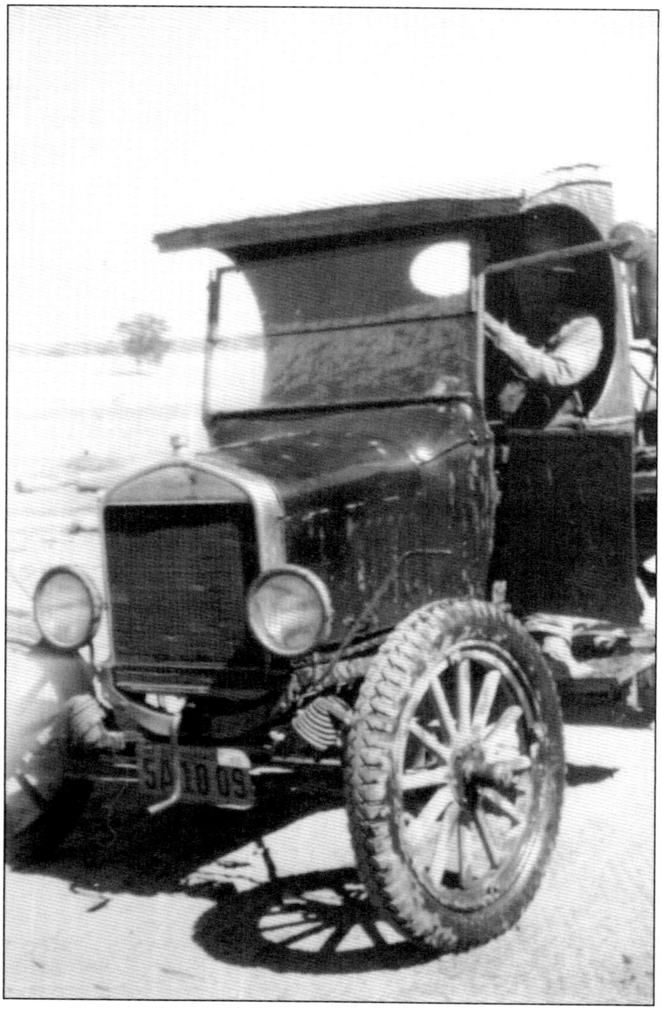

Old Highway 40 later became Auburn Boulevard. This 1912 Ford touring car is traveling south toward Citrus Heights after crossing the Dry Creek bridge. (Courtesy Leonard M. Davis.)

This 1926 Ford Model T truck is driven by Lester Pilcher, who farmed near Oak Avenue and Sunrise Boulevard in the 1930s. (Courtesy Ernestine Botts Smith.)

Four

EARLY GOVERNMENT

Irrigation water, the vital life of farmsteads, came to the area in 1911 and transformed grain fields to the present active community of residences, businesses, and retail of today. In the late 19th century, water was supplied from the American Canyon & Water Company. The Citrus Heights Water Takers Association was created when the population began to grow. The name was changed to Citrus Heights Water District on October 25, 1920. In 1951, the Citrus Heights Water District, the Fair Oaks Water District, and the Orangevale Water District combined to form the San Juan Water District Association, which ultimately led to the 1954 creation of the San Juan Suburban Water District. This was the first community services district in California. The Citrus Heights Water District remains, with residents receiving their water from Folsom Lake. In 1923, the Citrus Heights Community Club, a volunteer group composed of regional leaders, decided that an organization should be formed to deal with mutual service problems. Joining the club in its earliest years were members from the communities of Orangevale, Roberts, Fair Oaks, Carmichael, and Citrus Heights. Citrus Heights soon separated from the other regional members so that it could deal with its own special public service needs.

In 1928, the Community Club appointed a fire committee, which was headed by Adolph Van Maren. Four years later, Eugene Desimone was appointed the first fire chief. In 1934, an all-volunteer fire department was formed. The following year, it became the Citrus Heights Fire District, Inc., covering a vast area that included Citrus Heights, Orangevale, Antelope, and Del Paso. This fire district was the forerunner to today's Sacramento Metropolitan Fire District. During World War II, the Ladies Auxiliary (1942 through 1947) replaced the men who left for military service. When it was apparent that the fire district needed assistance in emergencies, the Ladies in White (1951 through 1986) formed. These volunteers, who received specialized emergency training, created a rescue squad to deal with automobile accidents and emergency medical issues. The Ladies in White was the first group of its kind in the country, and they received national and international recognition.

In November 1975, the Citrus Heights and Foothill Farms branch libraries merged to form the Sylvan Oaks Community Library. Since 1993, it has been located at the corner of Auburn Boulevard and Van Maren Lane.

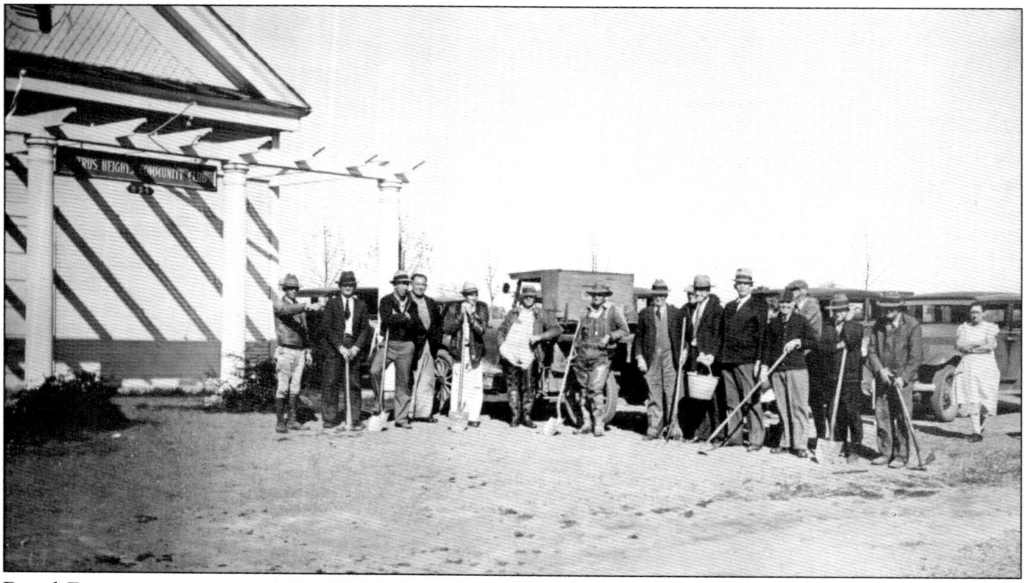

Road Days was sponsored by the Community Club. Members would voluntarily come together to clean the ditches and fill in chuckholes in the roads. While the men were engaged in road repair, the women would prepare a potluck lunch. Local farmers supplied tools and their trucks to support the program. (Courtesy Jim Van Maren.)

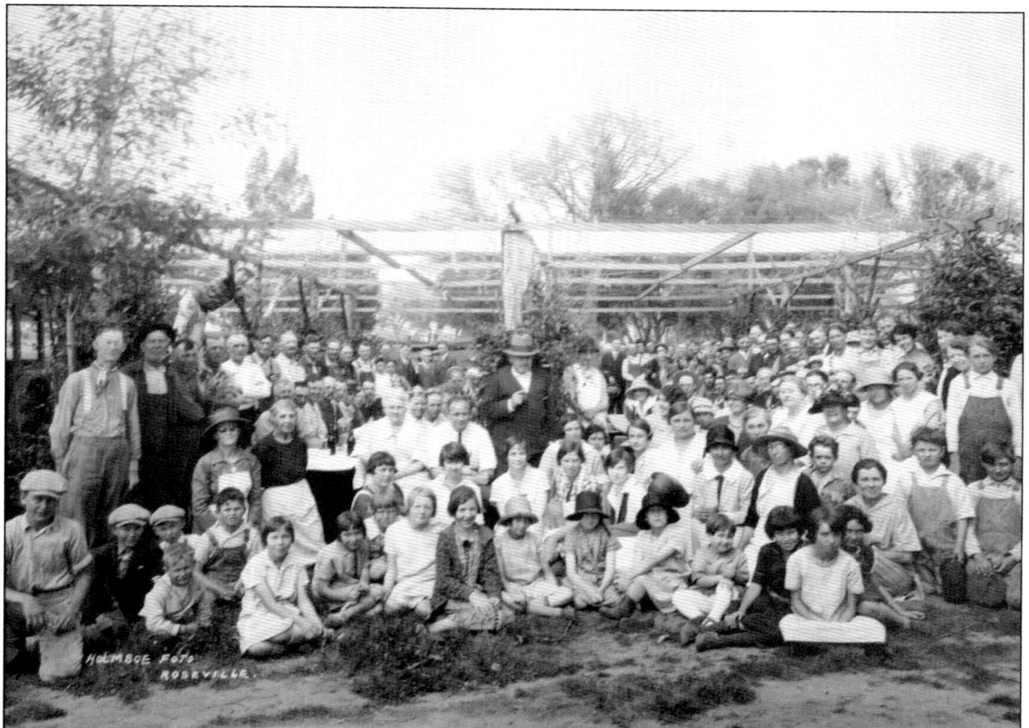

In 1926, Road Day volunteers gathered at Sylvan Corners. (Courtesy Jim Van Maren, Holmboe Foto.)

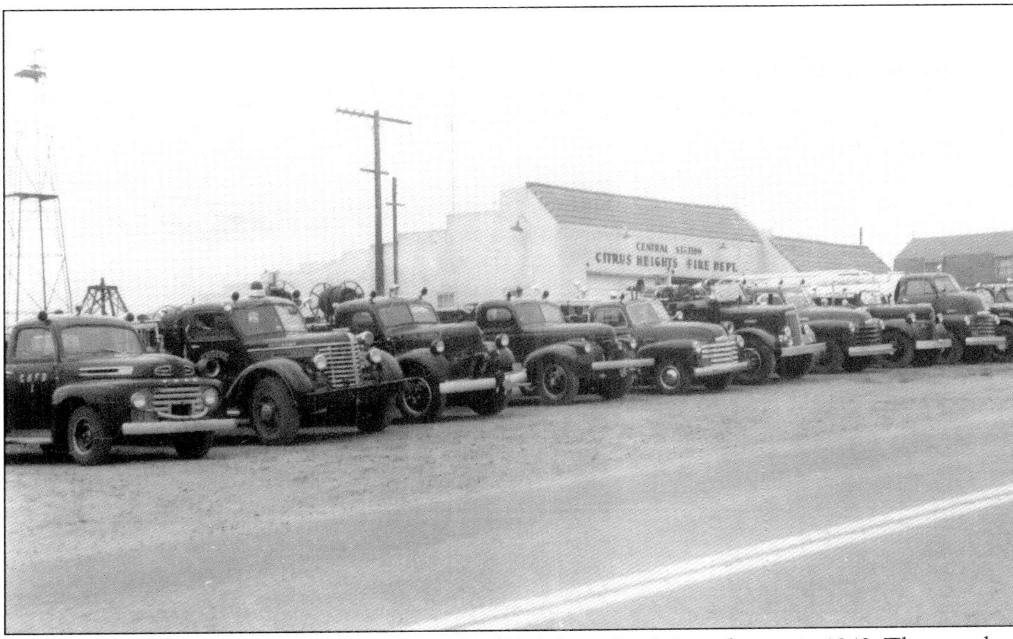

Construction on the Central Station located at 7641 Greenback Lane began in 1942. The attached home was purchased from San Juan High School, and volunteers built the rest. (Courtesy Warren Desimone collection, City of Citrus Heights.)

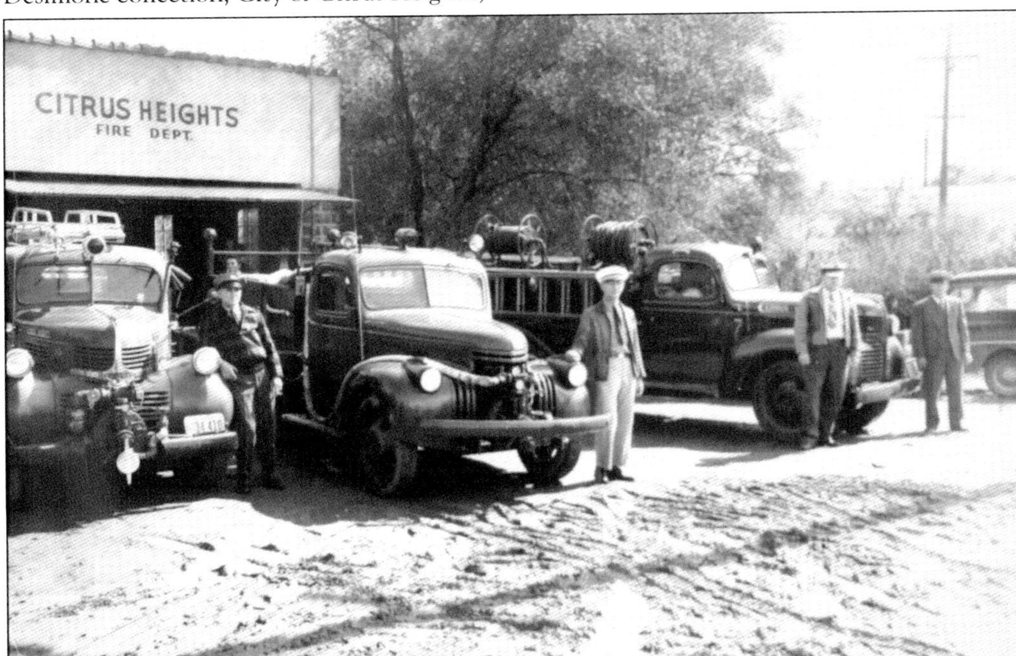

Formed in 1935, the Citrus Heights Fire District was an all-volunteer department. This association was a forerunner to the Sacramento Metropolitan Fire District. The first fire station in the area was located on Mariposa Street, just north of Greenback Lane. (Courtesy Roseville Historical Society photograph collection, City of Citrus Heights.)

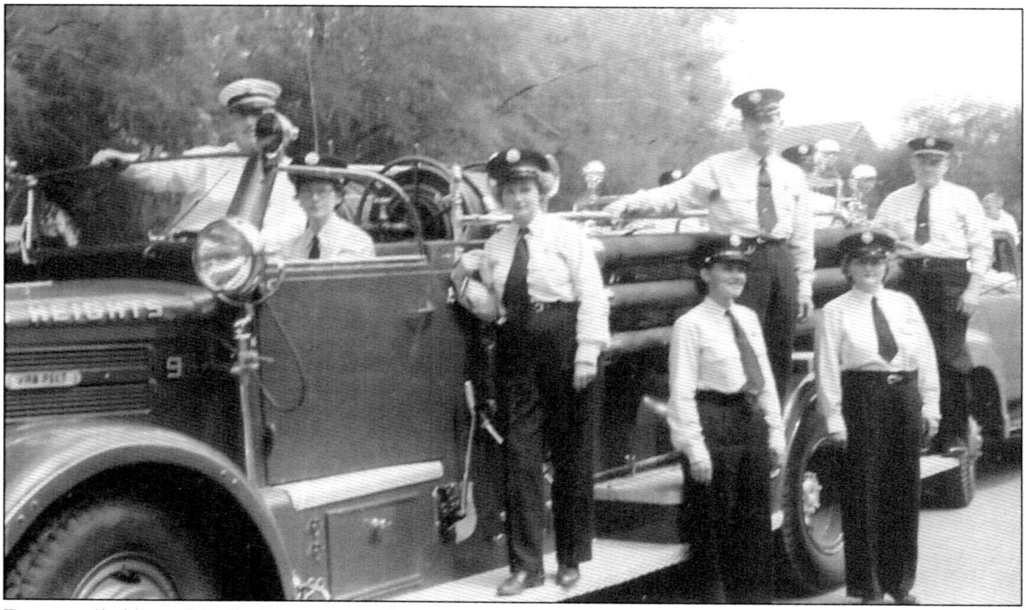

Eugene (left) and Zella Desimone drive truck No. 9. (Courtesy Warren Desimone collection, City of Citrus Heights.)

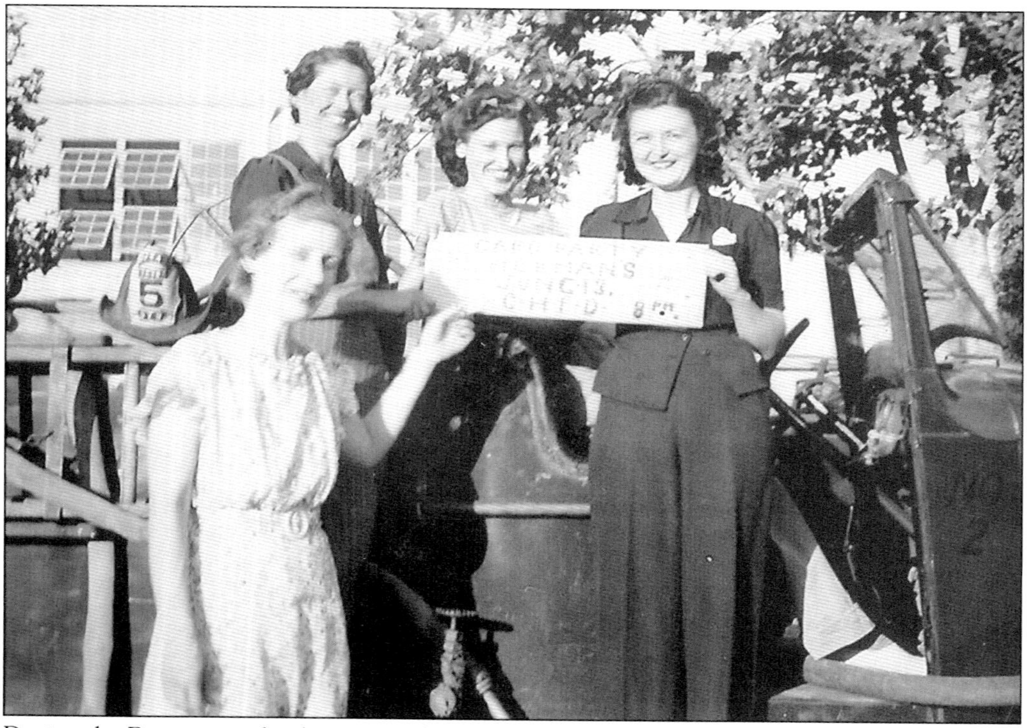

During the Depression, funds were needed to buy equipment and vehicles for the Citrus Heights Fire District. These four women raised $19.99 at a card party to purchase some necessary tools, including a shovel and crowbar. Estaline Mulch is in front, with Zella Desimone behind her. (Courtesy Warren Desimone collection, City of Citrus Heights.)

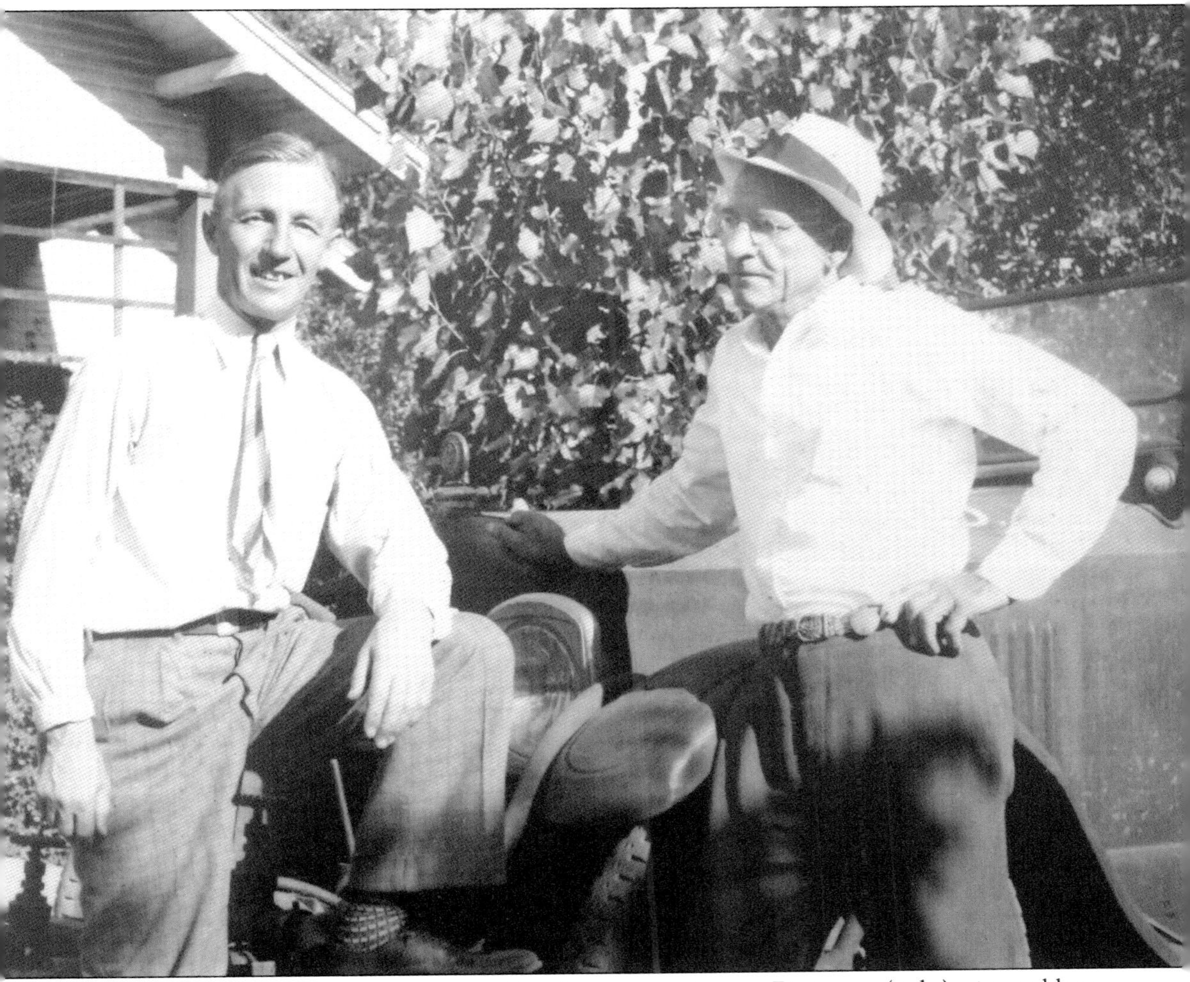

The first fire chief of the Citrus Heights Fire District was Eugene Desimone (right), pictured here with Ed Voltz, who later became a fire chief. (Courtesy Warren Desimone collection, City of Citrus Heights.)

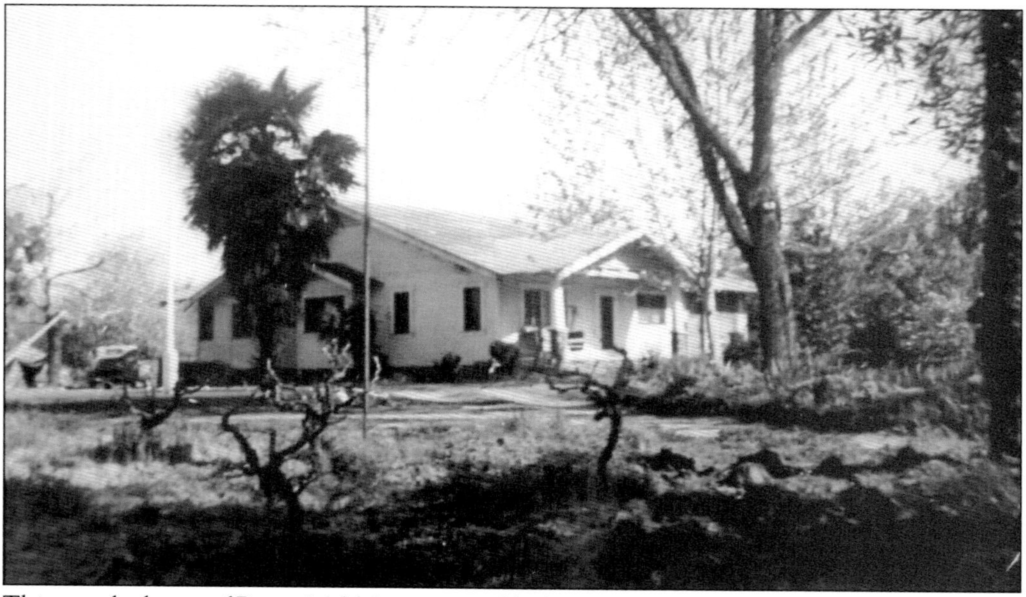

This was the home of Byron Myklebost, constable from 1926 to 1950. The home was demolished to make room for a group of retail stores at the southeast corner of Sylvan and Auburn Boulevards. (Courtesy Margrethe Law.)

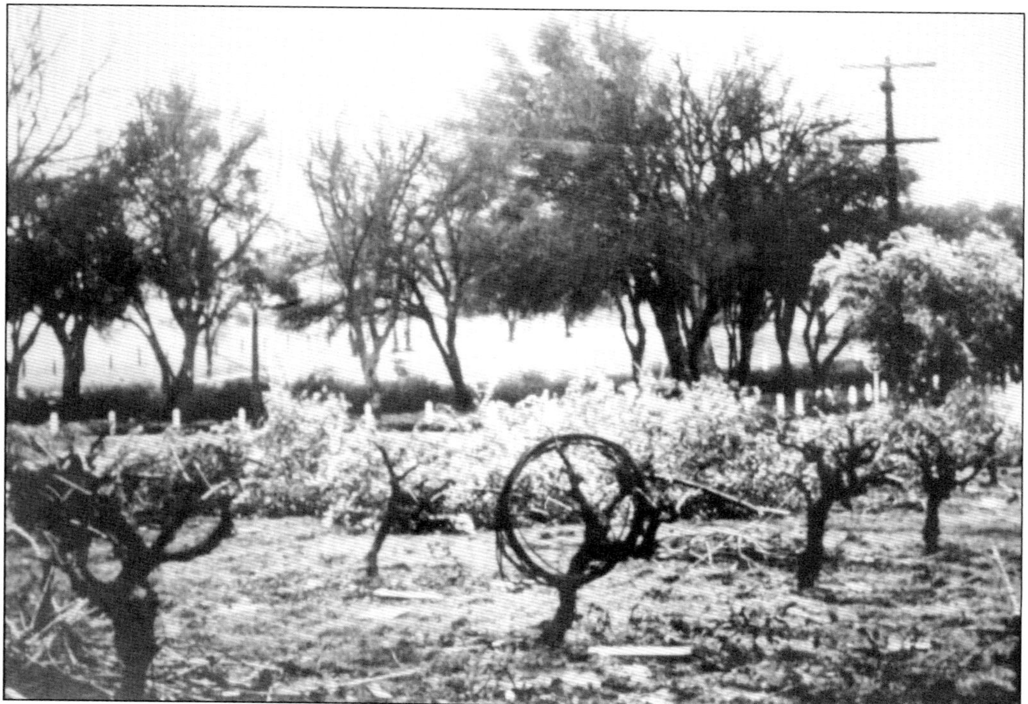

This image was shot looking at Sylvan Corners from a southeast vantage point. Constable Byron Myklebost had a vineyard here. In the distance is the yard at today's Sylvan Middle School. Note the oak trees that still stand today near a 2010 monument to Citrus Heights. (Courtesy Margrethe Law.)

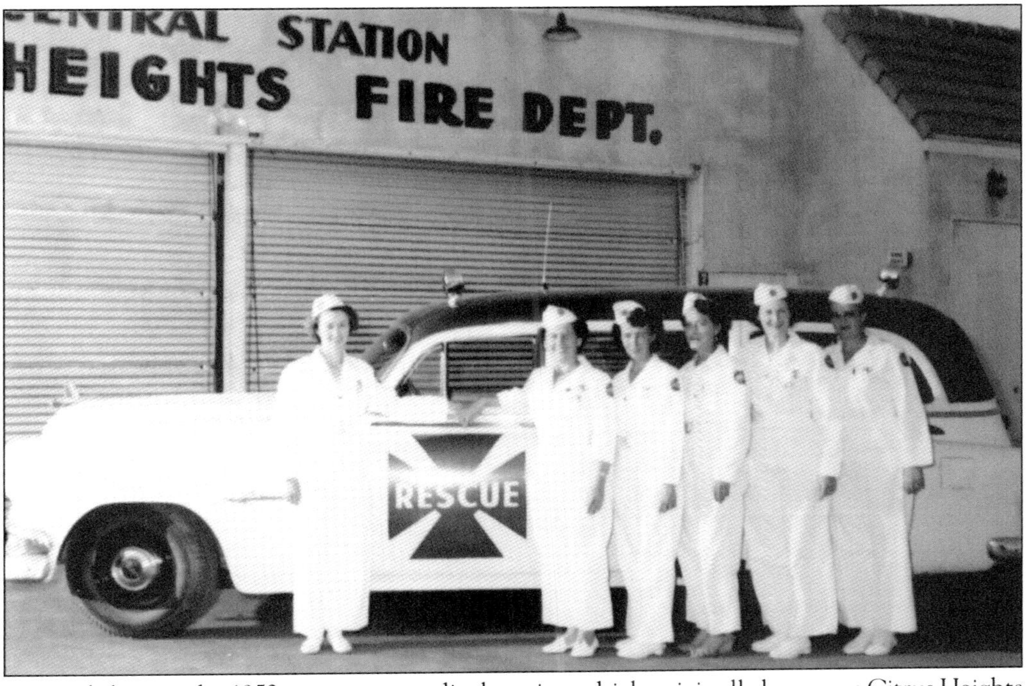

Pictured above is the 1953 emergency medical service vehicle originally known as Citrus Heights Fire District Rescue One. The ambulance was purchased by the Sacramento County Board of Supervisors for $2,119. In 1953, it was donated to the Citrus Heights Fire District. "Ol' Rescue" served as the only ambulance in the northeast portion of Sacramento County. It was operated by the Ladies in White Rescue Squad, known as "angels of mercy in white overalls." As noted by the *Sacramento Bee* in 2004, they pioneered the concept of first aid units working in conjunction with firefighters. Many other communities have replicated the concept of the Ladies in White Rescue Squad. (Both, courtesy Sacramento Metropolitan Fire District.)

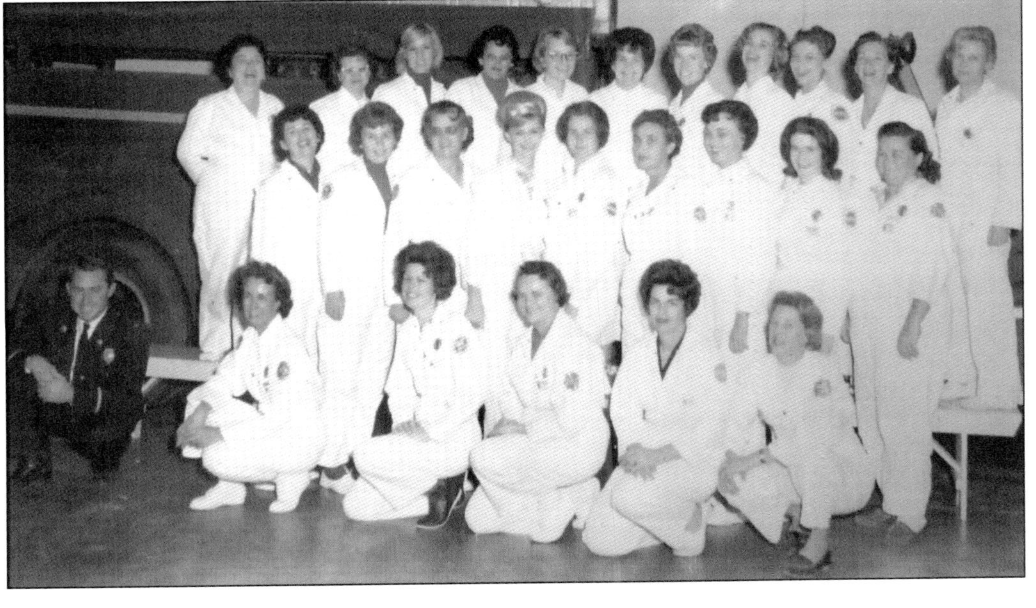

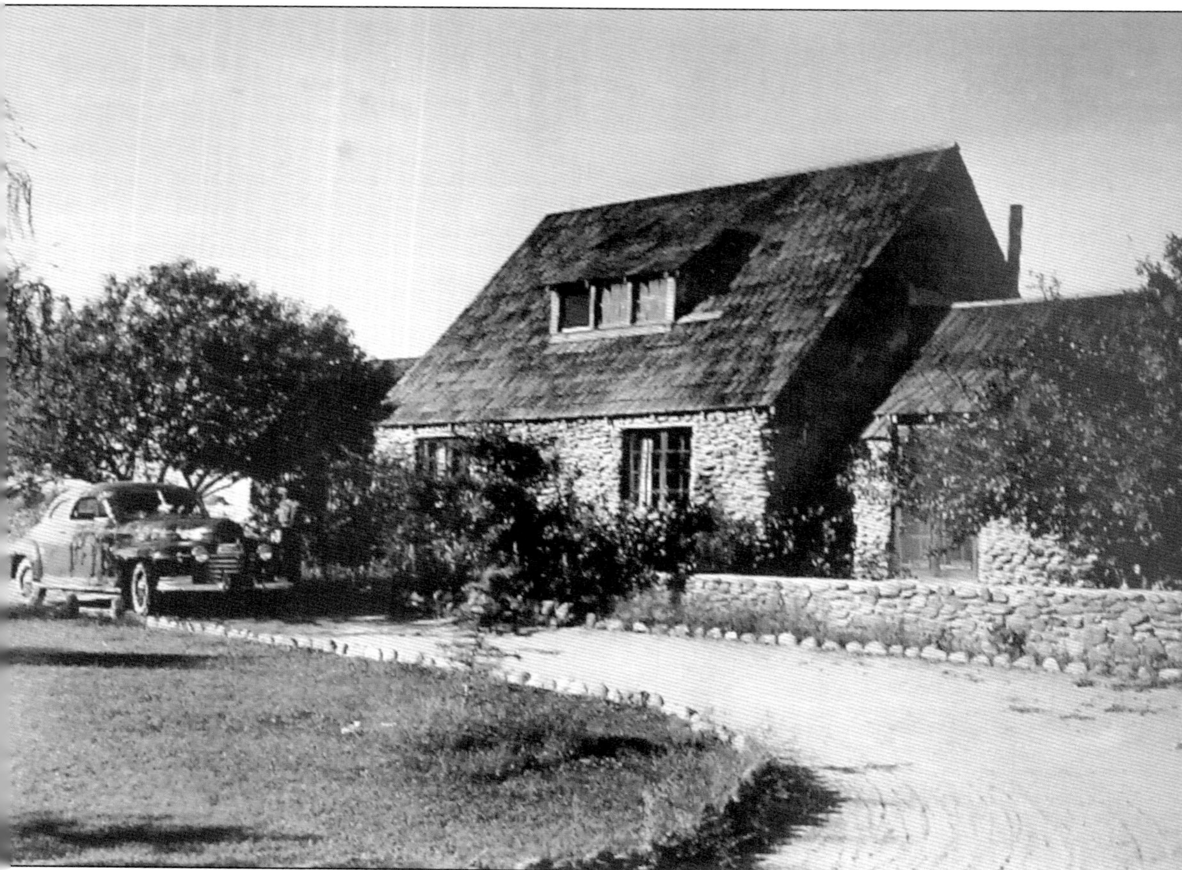

This rock house is one of five that the Desimone family had built in the area, probably because these structures were fairly safe from fire. In 2006, Warren Desimone recalled that the rocks were gathered in Folsom near the American River. (Courtesy Warren Desimone collection, City of Citrus Heights.)

Five

Education and Worship

Originally, grammar school was held in an old home on Plum Ranch, located one and a half miles north of the Cross home on Auburn Boulevard. Classes were later moved to a shed on the property of Sarah Cross, remaining there for almost two years. Recognizing the need for a stable building dedicated to education, residents built the first grammar school in 1862. William Thomas donated the school site at Sylvan Corners. He was also responsible for naming the district Sylvan. John Cross led the school's construction with the assistance of John Aiston and Peter Van Maren. A community high school held its first classes in a Carmichael grammar school located about two blocks south from the intersection of Dewey Drive and Winding Way. Due to the building's high occupancy level, the students from Sylvan District had to move to Fair Oaks Grammar School, where they remained until a permanent facility was built.

In 1911, a committee representing Orangevale, Fair Oaks, Roberts, Carmichael, and Citrus Heights came together to consider the construction of a high school, and in 1913, San Juan High School was built on land donated by real estate promoter Trainor-Desmond Company. From 1911 through 1914, students attended Christian Brothers, Sacramento High School, or Roseville High School, which was located in an old hotel building. On November 20, 1959, one superintendent replaced six school principals to create the new San Juan Unified School District, though each principal remained in charge of their respective school under the superintendent. The district included five elementary schools and San Juan High School. Currently, San Juan High School is undergoing renovation, and as a result, it will celebrate its centennial as one of the most modern and updated schools in the area. A second high school, Mesa Verde, was created in 1976.

Religious services were held temporarily in the Sylvan School by Rev. Harry Hollingsworth of the Society of Friends faith. In 1921, Walter Leonard, Martin Taylor, and L. Bert Morgan led the construction of the first Society of Friends church in the community, located at 7600 Old Auburn Road. Rev. Everett Scotten was the first pastor. The church is now the site of the Pioneer Baptist Church. The first Catholic church, Holy Family Catholic Church, was dedicated in June 1949, with Fr. Vita Mistretta presiding. Father Mistretta was instrumental in building the current edifice located at 7817 Old Auburn Road.

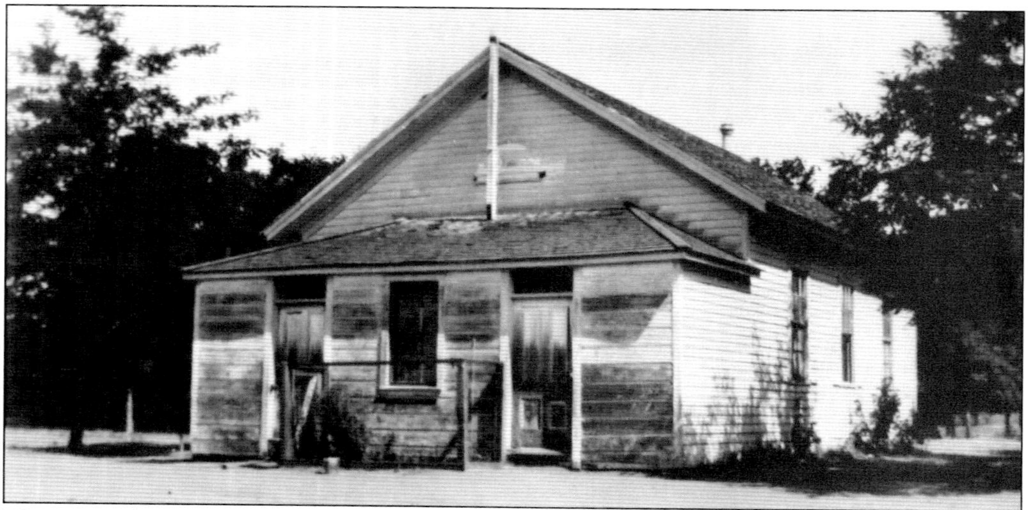

The original Sylvan School was constructed in 1862. The white building had green clapboard shutters covering eight windows. The interior consisted of a single classroom and two broom or hat closets. Girls sat on one side and boys on the other. Next to the teacher's desk was a potbellied stove. The first teacher was Alfred Spooner, who was paid $50 per month to teach about 40 students. (Courtesy Jim Van Maren.)

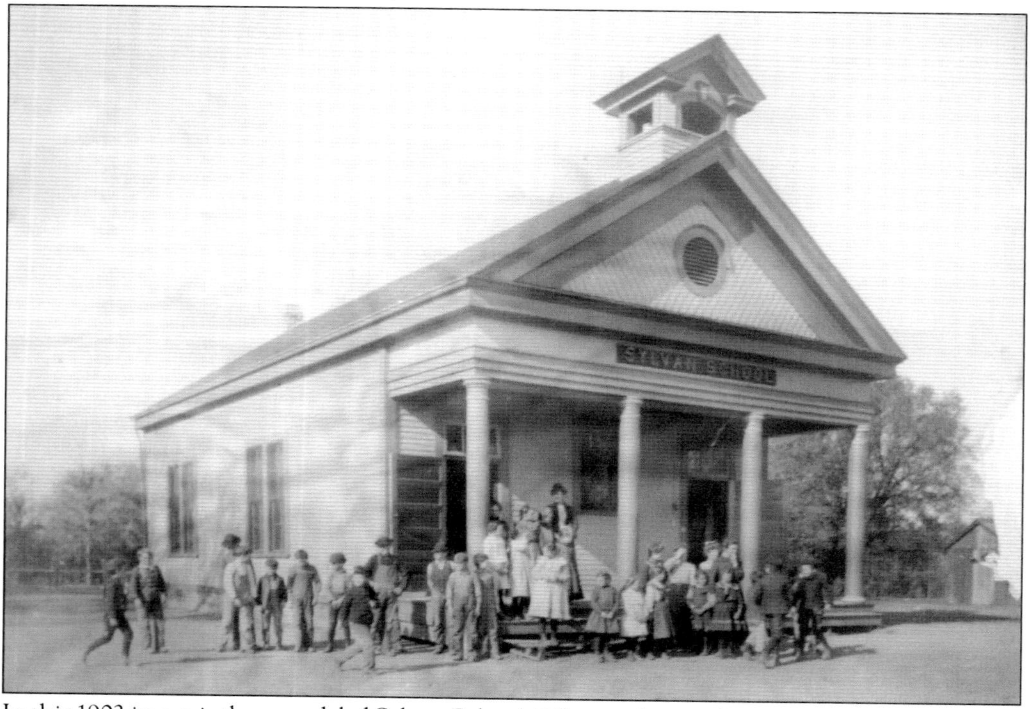

In this 1903 image is the remodeled Sylvan School. Pillars and a cupola were added. In the absence of electricity, the windows were enlarged to provide better lighting. There was an outhouse for the students and teacher. The school was remodeled again in 1927 when it was moved from Sylvan Corners to the present site on Sylvan Road, on land donated by Adolph Van Maren. The cupola was removed at that time. (Courtesy Jim Van Maren.)

Vote FOR the School Bonds

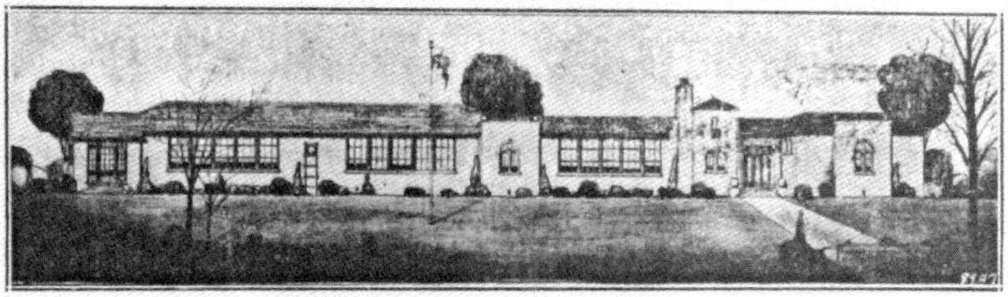

HOW THE SYLVAN GRAMMAR SCHOOL WILL LOOK WHEN THE ALTERATIONS AND ADDITIONS ARE COMPLETED.

COFFMAN-SAHLBERG-STAFFORD ARCHITECTS AND ENGINEERS SACRAMENTO, CALIF.

Our present buildings are overcrowded and we require additional class rooms, and if we make the much needed alterations and additions our School will become an immense asset to our district and a lasting blessing to our children so,

VOTE FOR THE BONDS ON SATURDAY, MAY 21st, 1927

The $15,000 called for in the Bond Election is intended to cover the cost of three additional class rooms, a new heating plant to take care of all the rooms, and alterations to our present building to bring our school up to date in all respects.

The plans are so drawn that additional rooms may be added from time to time without tearing out anything or destroying the original plan.

It isn't economy to employ first-class teachers and expect them to produce results under present conditions.

Let's Put SYLVAN on the Map by Voting These Bonds.

Election Saturday, May 21, 1927

POLLS OPEN: 8:00 a. m. to 8:00 p. m.

POLLING PLACE: Sylvan School Building

VOTE FOR THE BONDS

In 1927, Citrus Heights residents voted for $15,000 in bonds for the Sylvan School. Guy Van Maren, clerk of the Sylvan Board of Trustees, noted that the bonds carried 148 to 49. Three rooms were added to the schoolhouse. (Courtesy Jim Van Maren.)

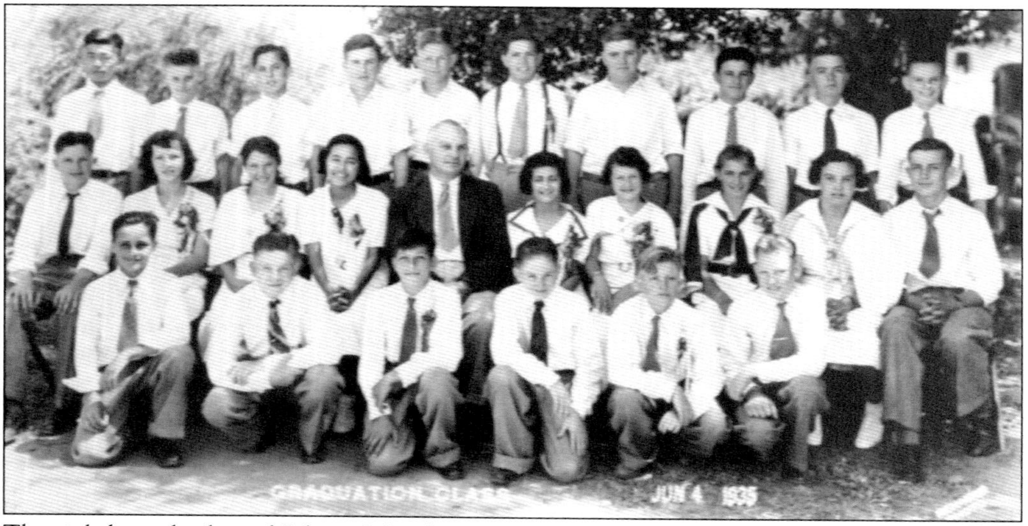

The eighth-grade class of Sylvan School is pictured in 1935. (Courtesy Roeley Giusti.)

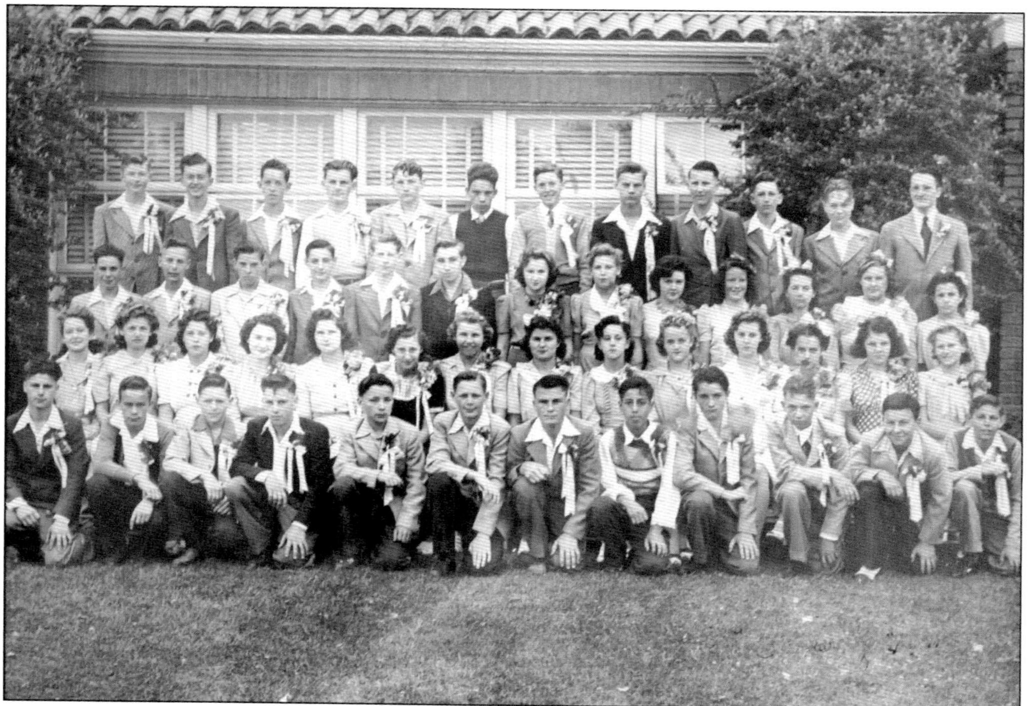

Sylvan School's 1942 eighth-grade class gathered for this photograph. (Courtesy Jim Van Maren.)

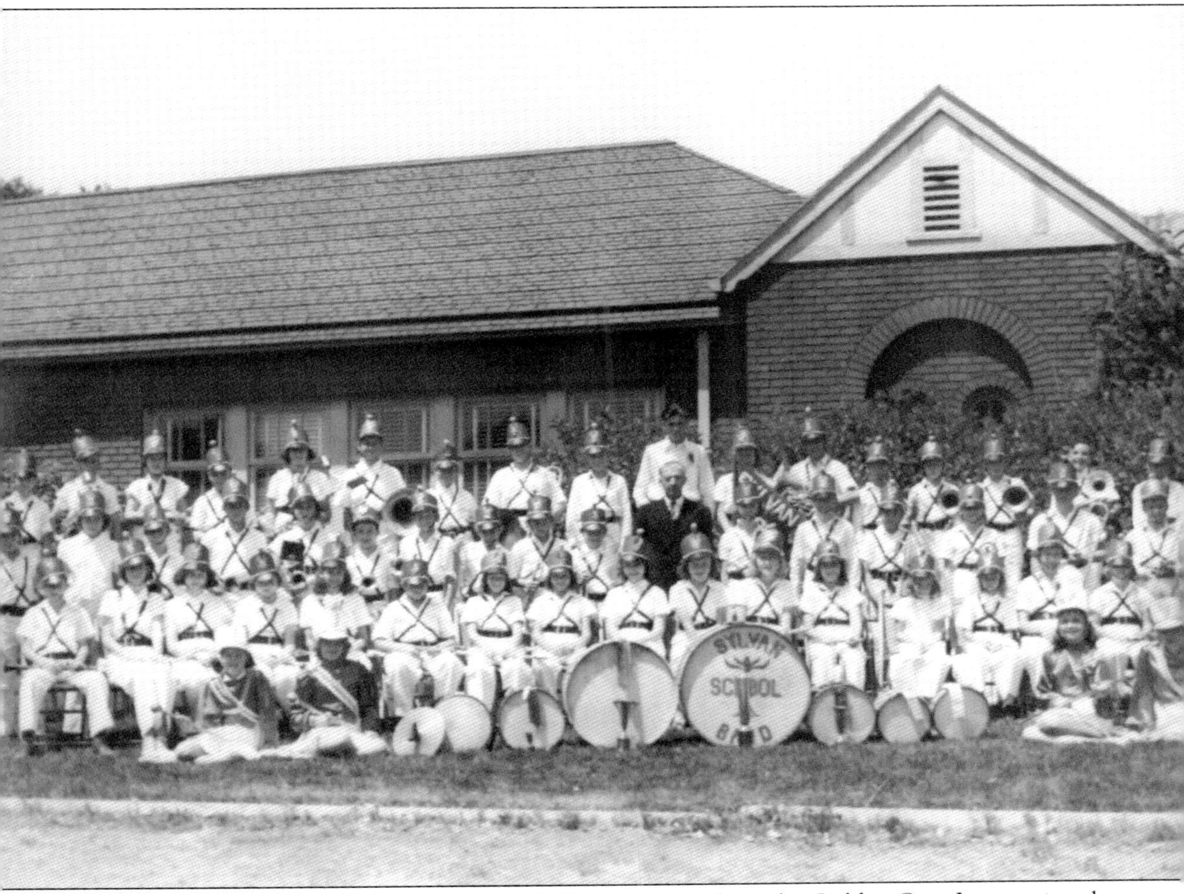

The Sylvan School Band was photographed after returning from the Golden Gate International Exposition (1939–1940) held at San Francisco's Treasure Island. The band competed with other schools. Trophies are displayed in front of the drums. (Courtesy Jim Van Maren.)

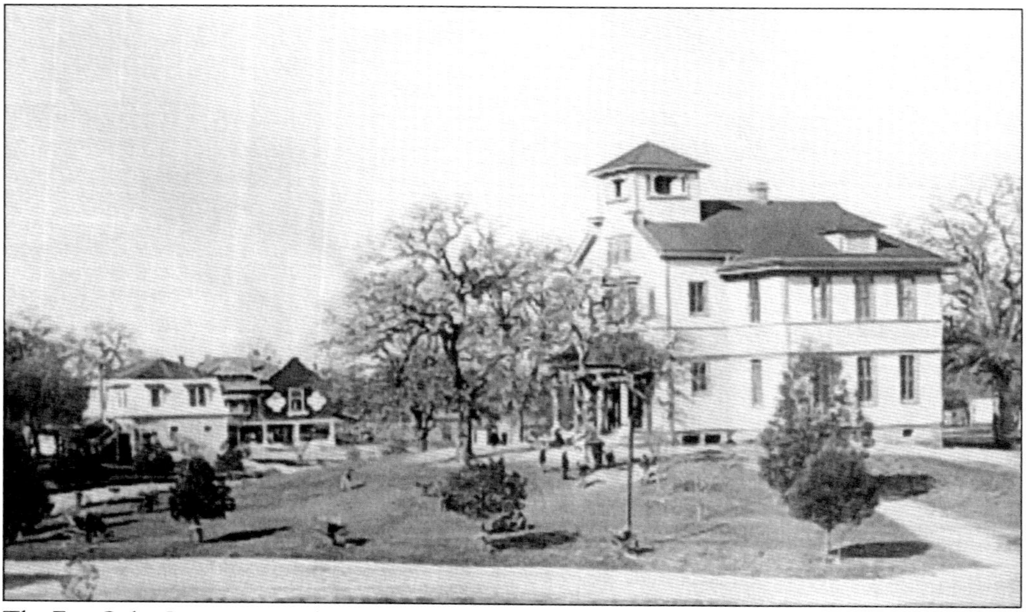

The Fair Oaks Community Club House served as the second San Juan High School in 1911 while the new San Juan High School was being built. This third high school was completed in 1913. The current San Juan High School is making preparations to celebrate its centennial. (Courtesy Fair Oaks Historical Society; Jim Van Maren.)

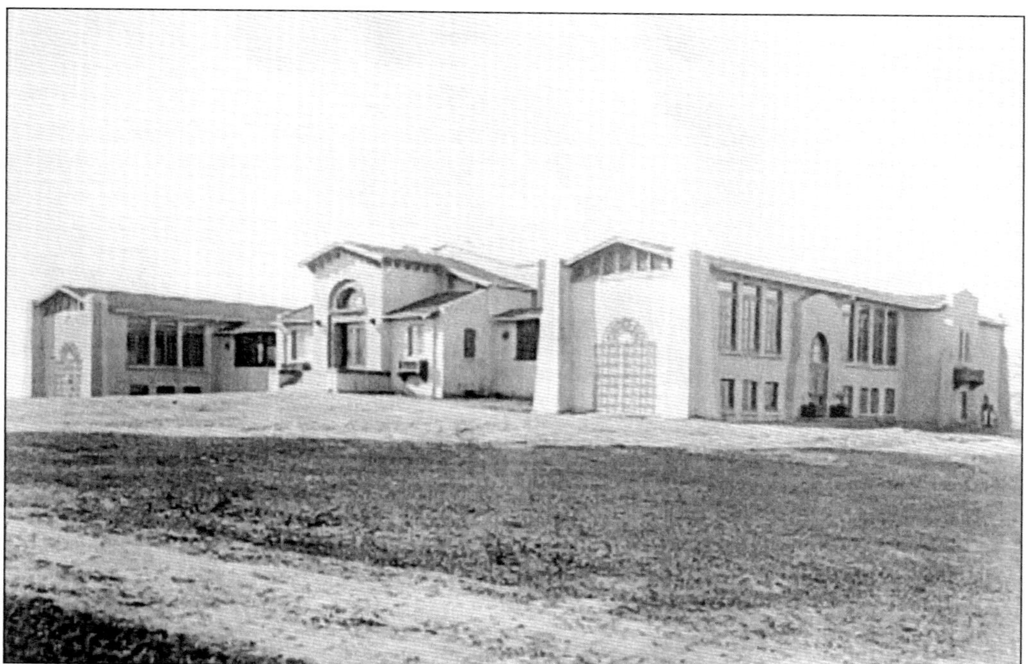

Note the lack of landscaping in this 1916 photograph of San Juan High School. (Courtesy San Juan High School Alumni Association.)

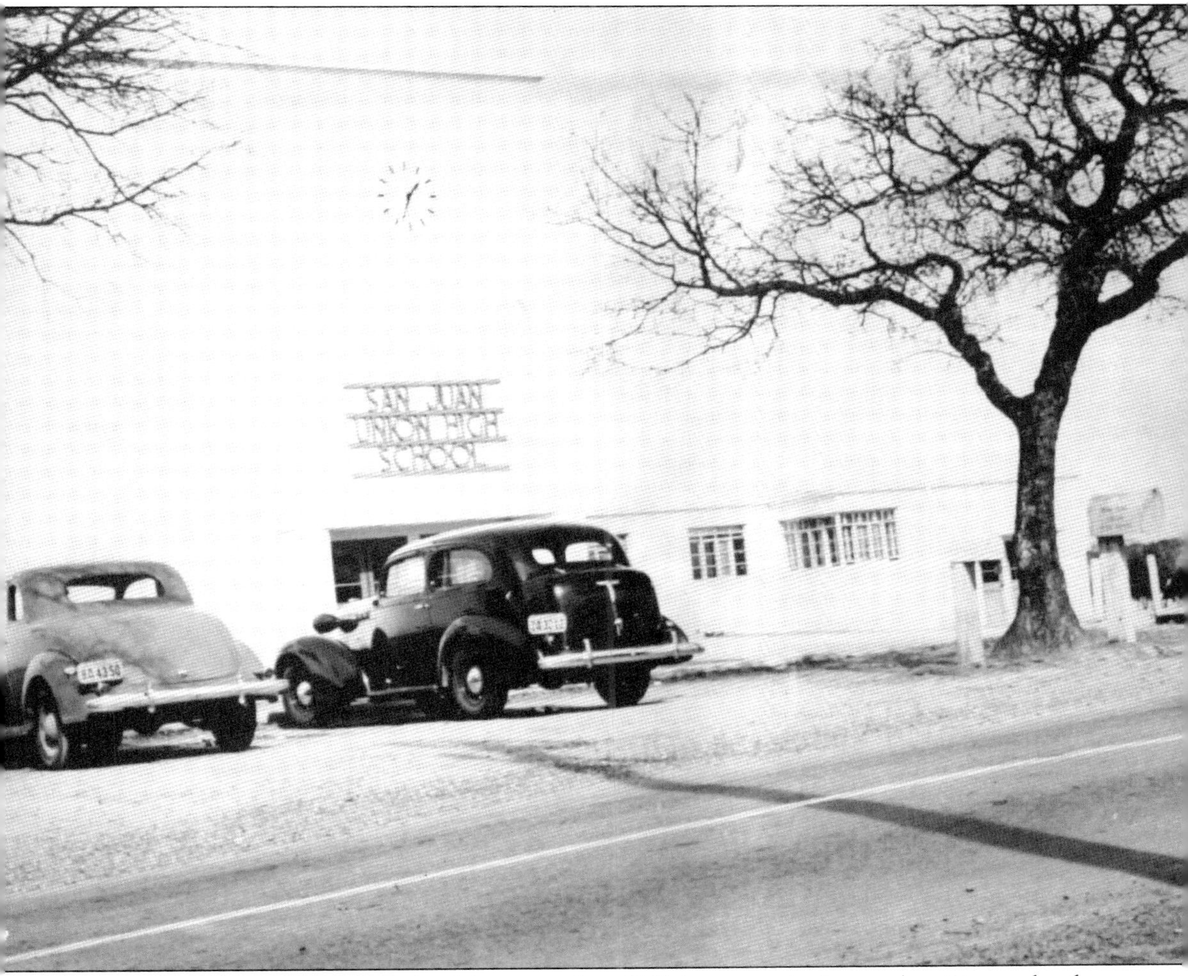

The school fronts onto Greenback Lane in this 1940 image, as it does today. Currently, the school is being remodeled with a new front that will simulate the original entrance. (Courtesy Jim Van Maren.)

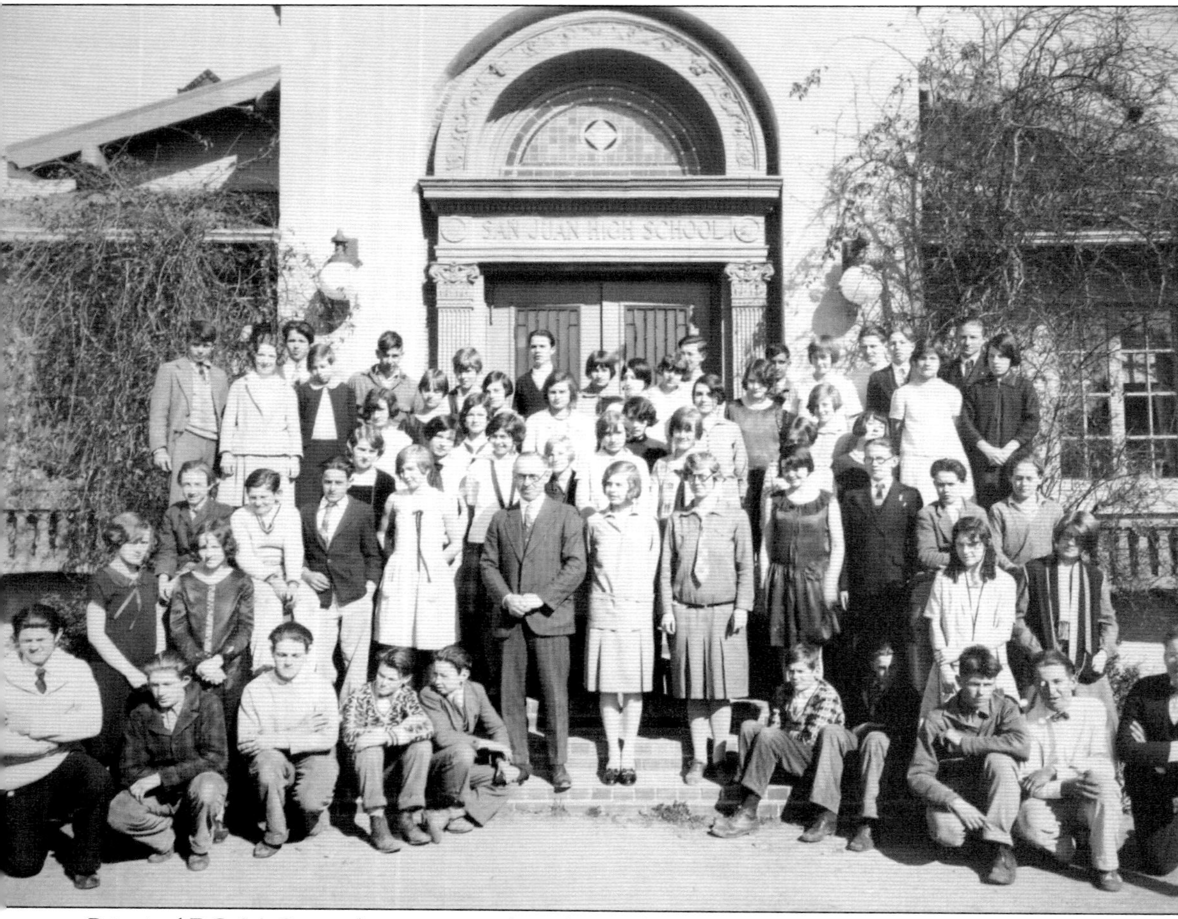

Principal E.O. McCormick, center, stands with a graduating class. McCormick was principal from 1922 to 1932. (Courtesy Jim Van Maren.)

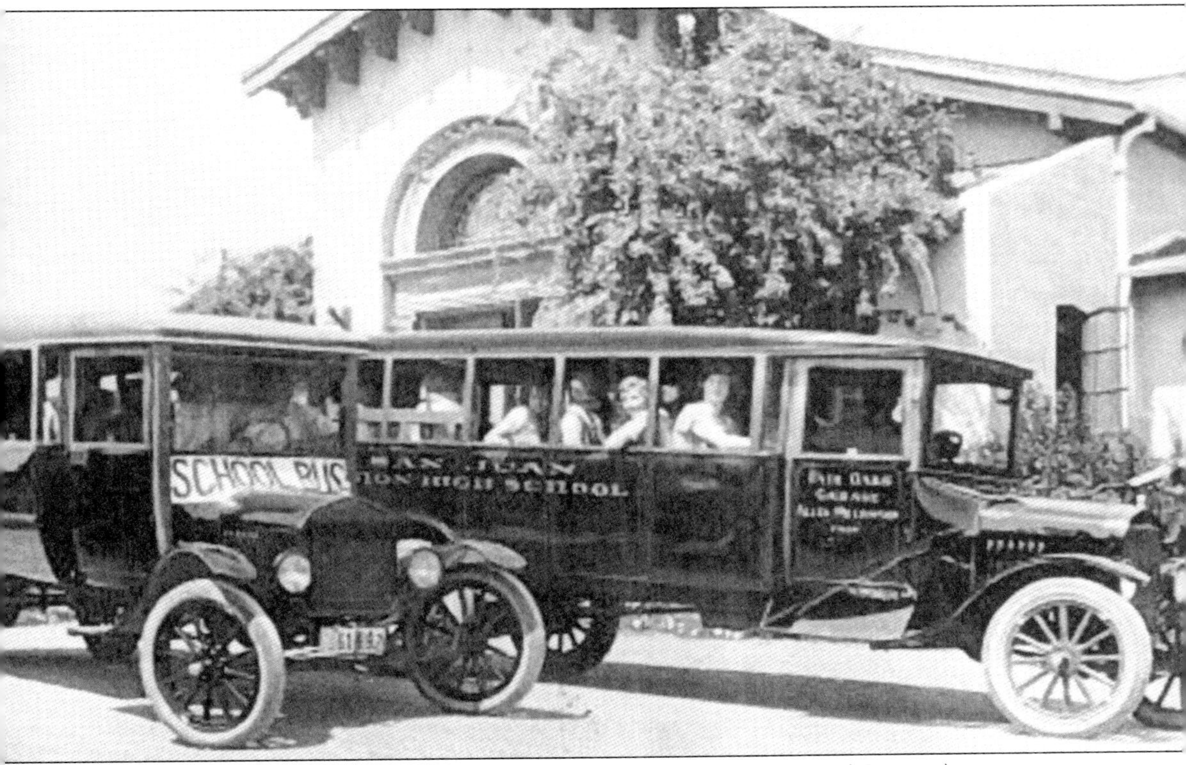

New school buses were obtained in 1921. (Courtesy Fair Oaks Historical Society.)

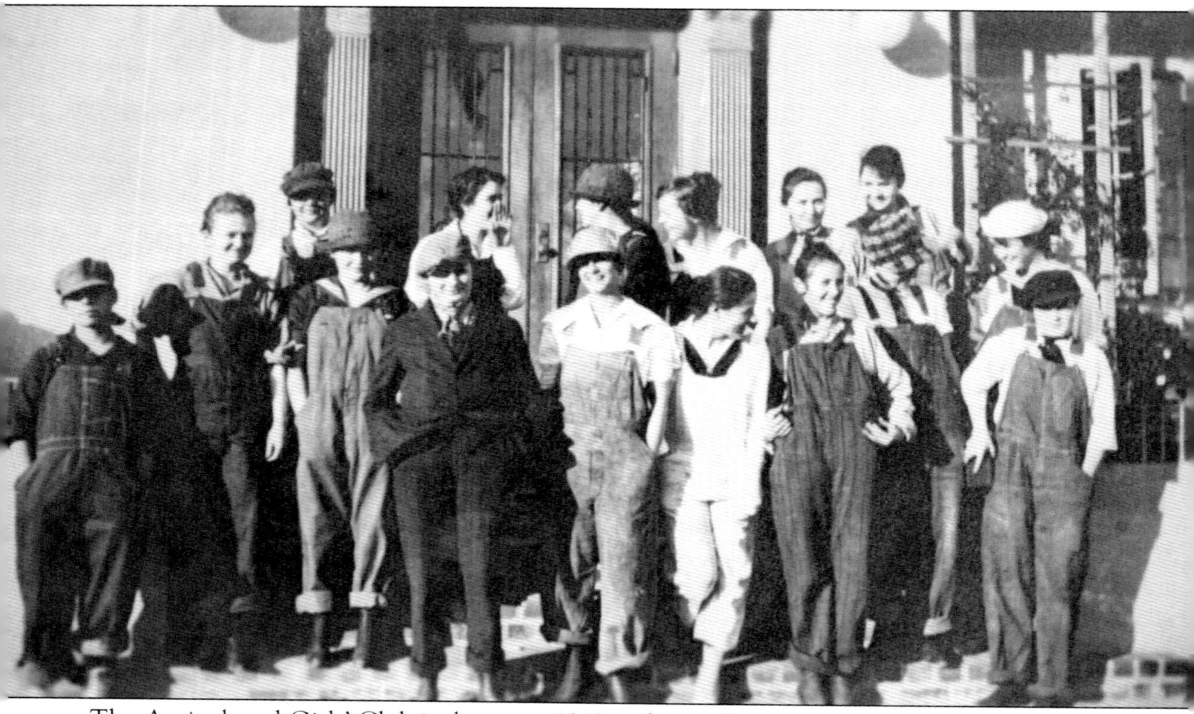

The Agricultural Girls' Club is shown in 1918 in front of San Juan High School. (Courtesy Jim Van Maren.)

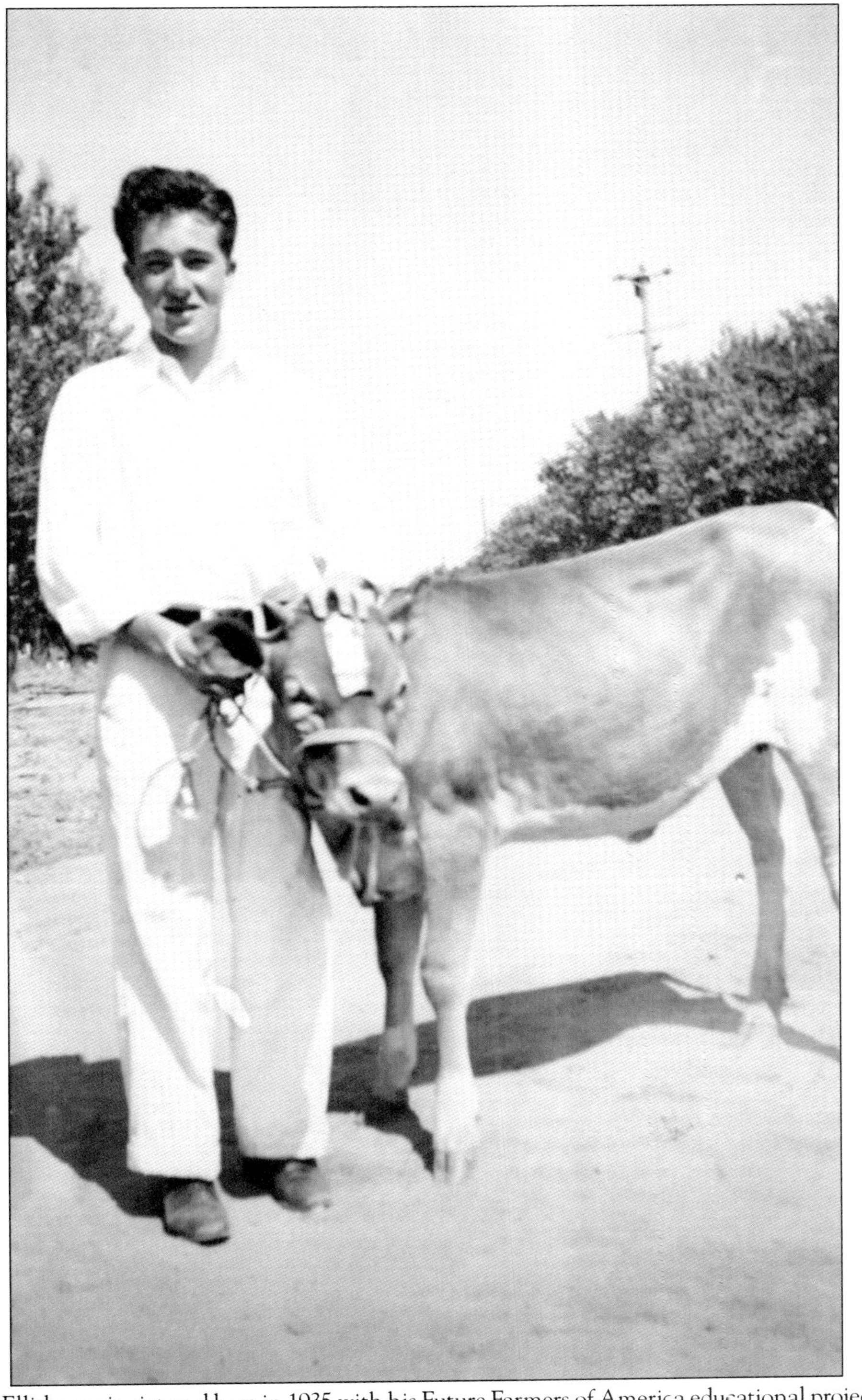

Bruce Ellithorpe is pictured here in 1935 with his Future Farmers of America educational project—a young heifer. (Courtesy Bruce Ellithorpe.)

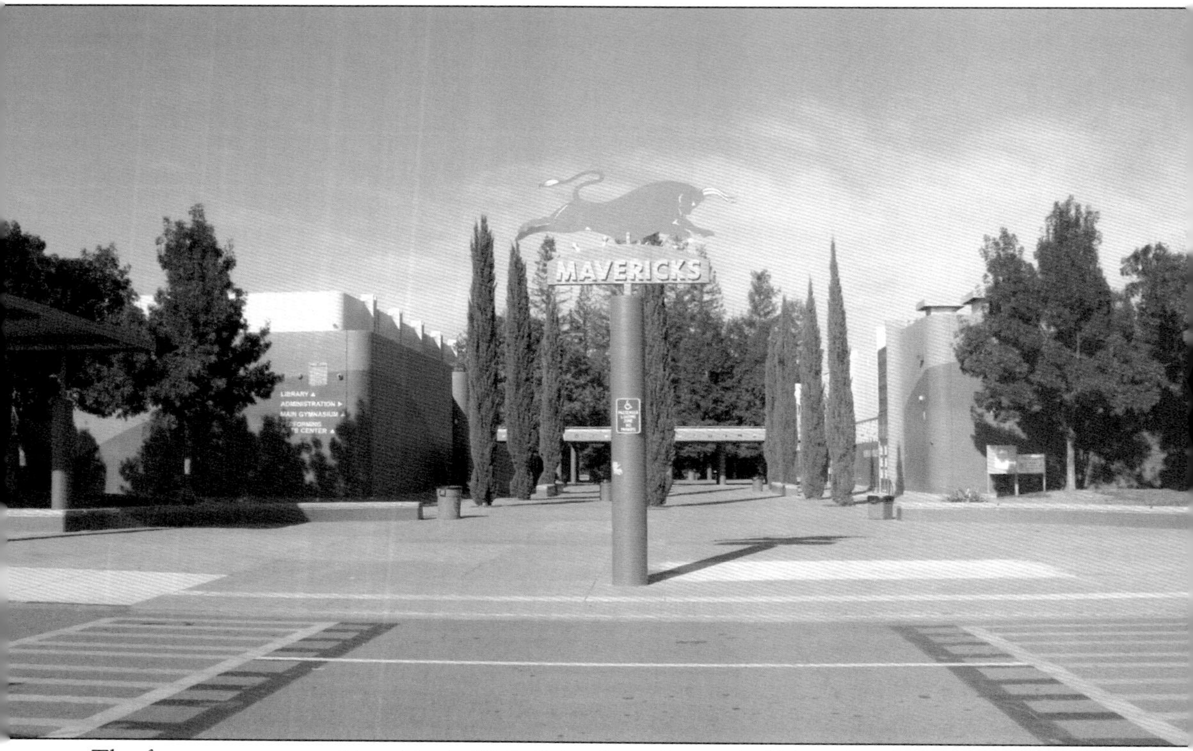

The front entrance to Mesa Verde High School was located off Antelope Road, Lauppe Lane, and Carriage Drive. (Courtesy Stephanie Cotter.)

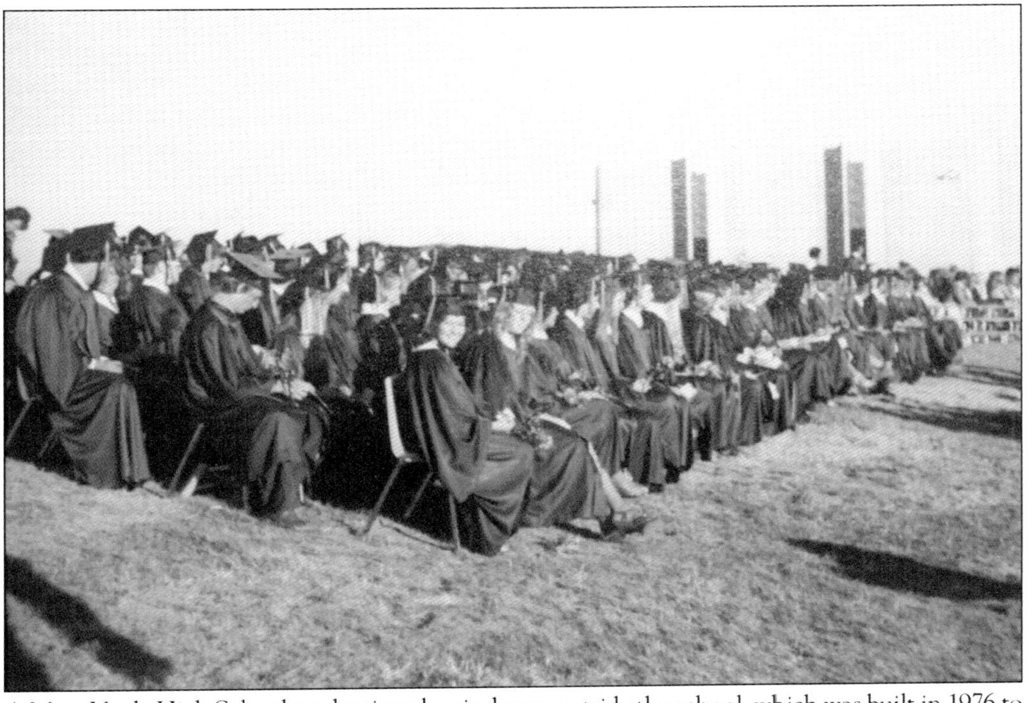

A Mesa Verde High School graduating class is shown outside the school, which was built in 1976 to relieve the increase in student population at San Juan High School. (Courtesy Dana Sauerland.)

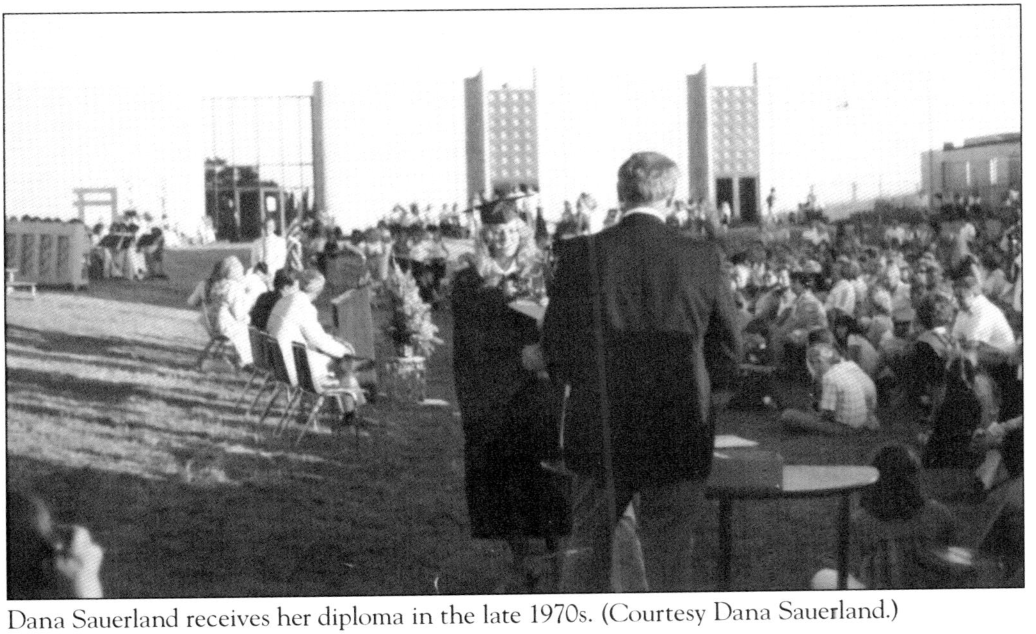

Dana Sauerland receives her diploma in the late 1970s. (Courtesy Dana Sauerland.)

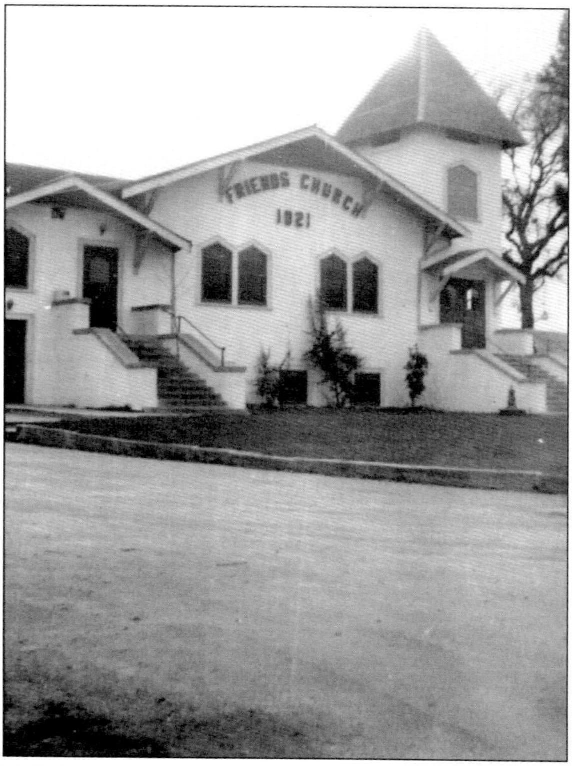

This 1921 photograph is of the Friends Church. It was the first religious edifice in Citrus Heights. In 1975, the Society of Friends moved to larger facilities and sold the property on Old Auburn Road to the Pioneer Baptist Church. (Courtesy Ernestine Botts Smith.)

The Pioneer Baptist Church is pictured here in 1975. (Courtesy Ernestine Botts Smith.)

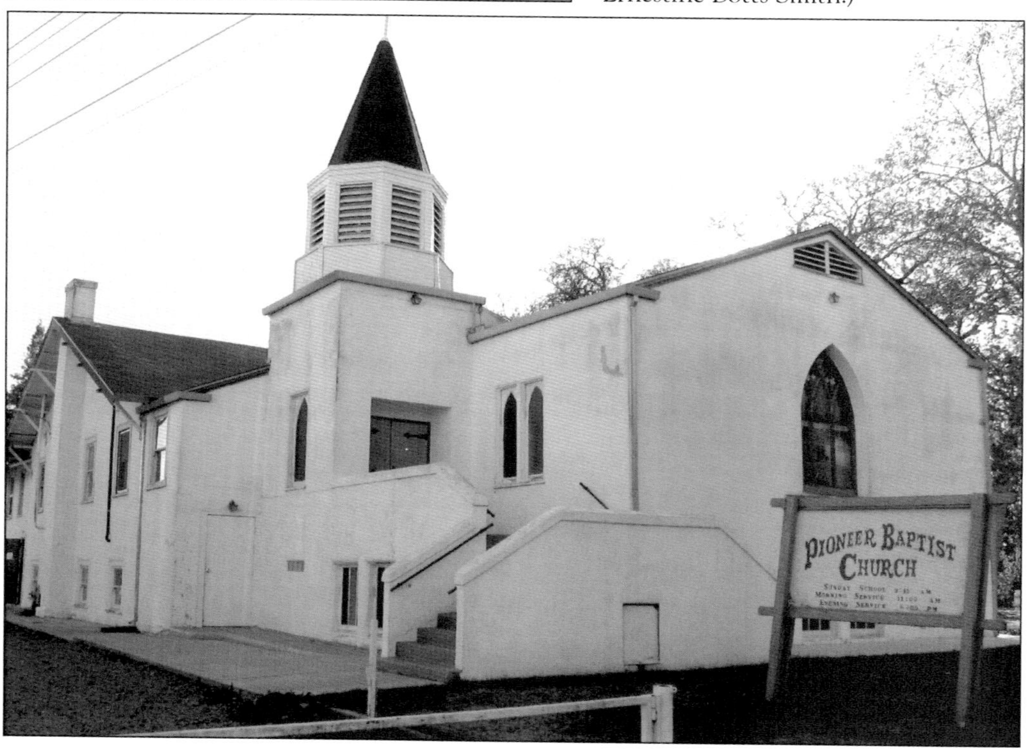

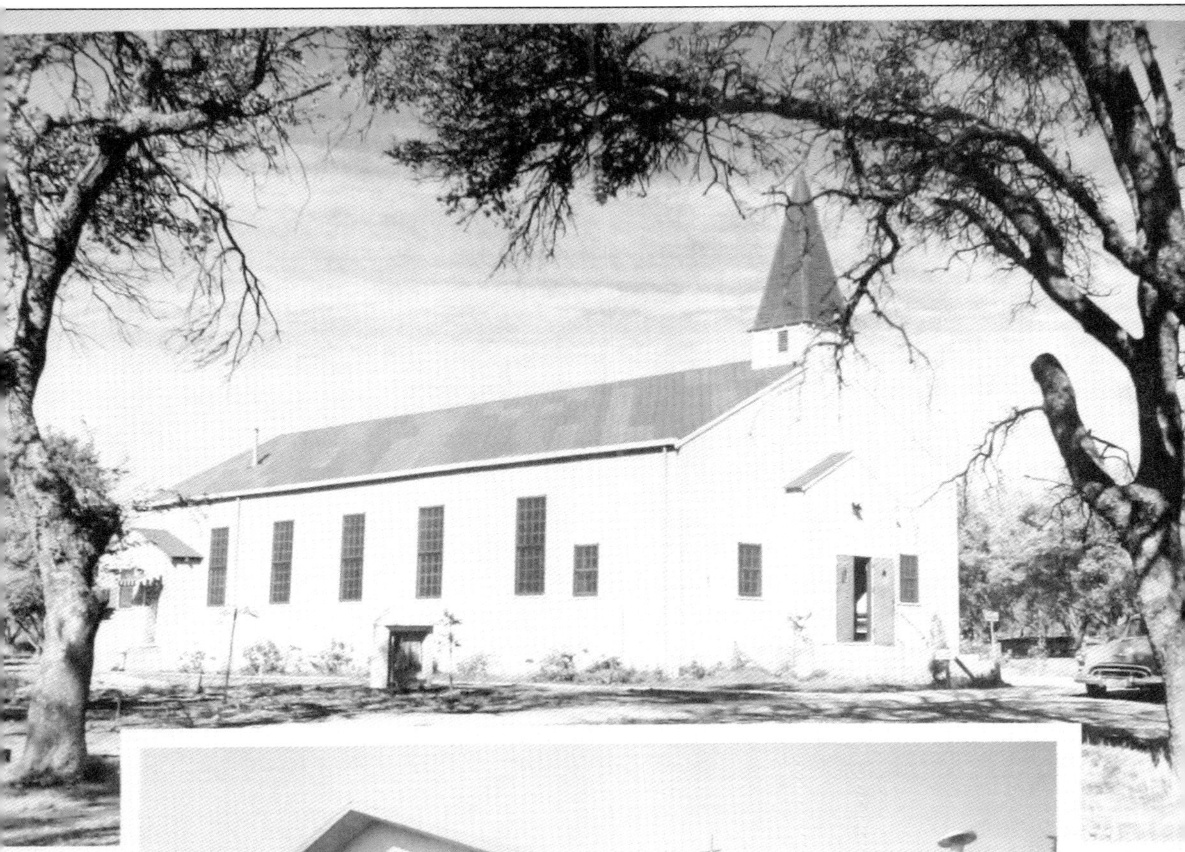

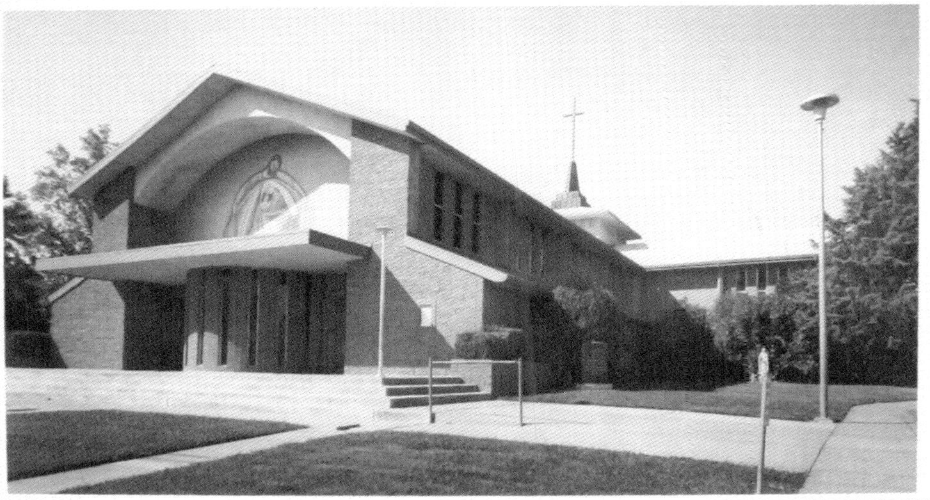

The Holy Family Catholic Church parish in Citrus Heights began in 1949. The Catholic Church originally held services in a Quonset hut (formerly a US Army chapel) that came from Camp Kohler. After 15 years of construction, Holy Family Catholic Church completed its new church in 1979. The design is in the form of a crucifix. (Courtesy Mitzi Valerio, Holy Family Catholic Church.)

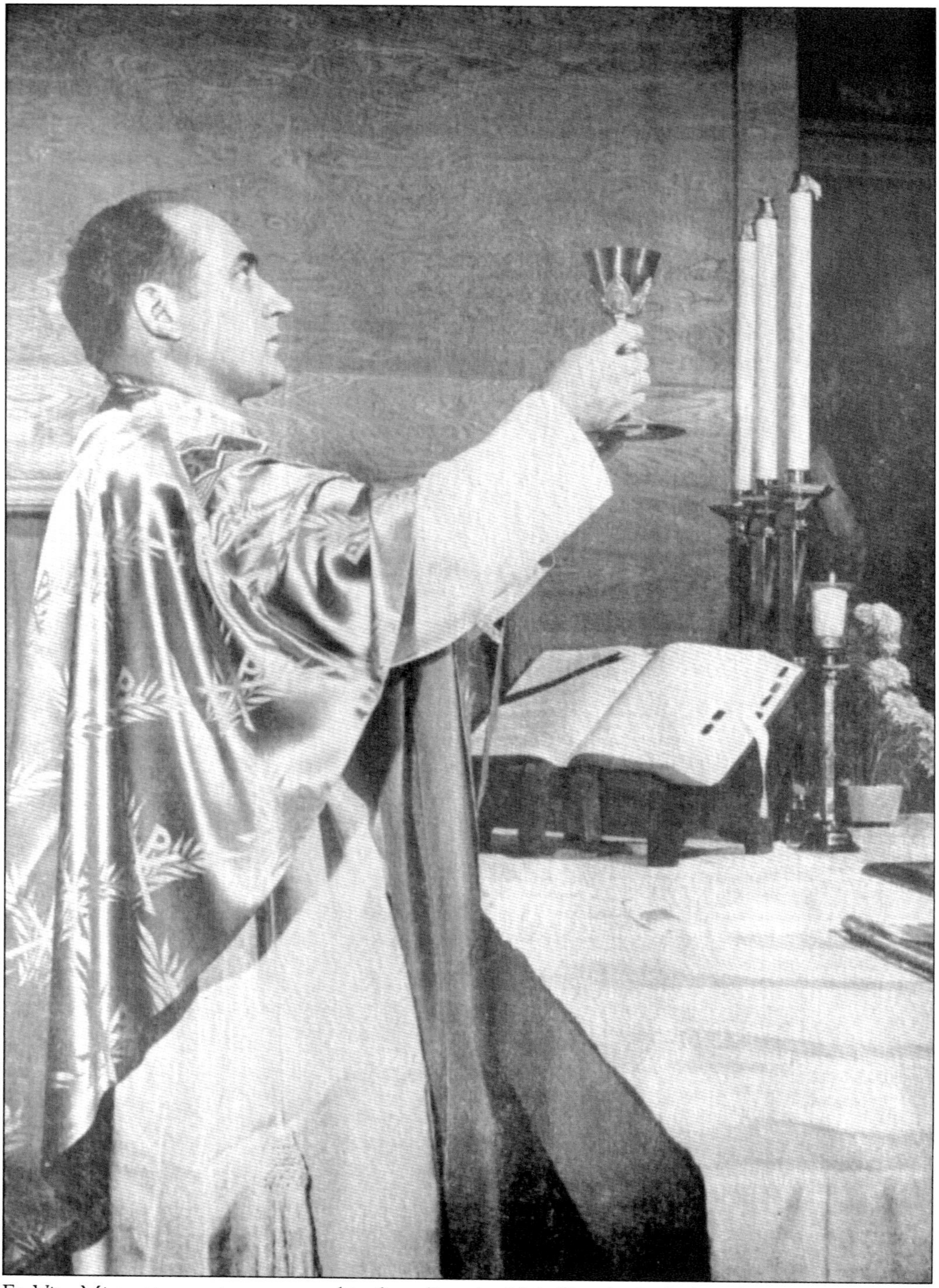

Fr. Vito Mistretta was instrumental in founding the Holy Family Catholic Church parish, which was located on three acres on Old Auburn Road. He served the local Catholic community from 1949 to 1990. (Courtesy Mitzi Valerio, Holy Family Catholic Church.)

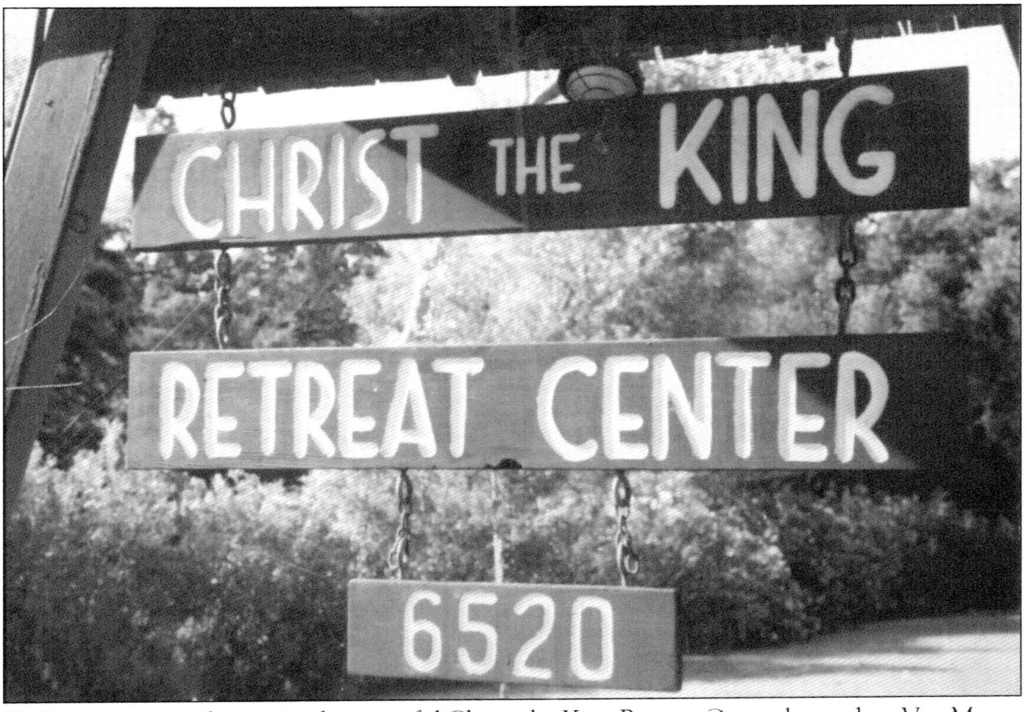

Under its canopy of trees sits the peaceful Christ the King Retreat Center located on Van Maren Lane. In 1946, the Passionists purchased this land from the Cross family estate in 1946. The retreat center itself was completed in 1950 and was expanded in 1957 when military barracks from Mather Air Base were moved onto the property to accommodate the growing need for space. (Both, courtesy Margaret Hinshaw and Brother Kirk, Christ the King Retreat Center.)

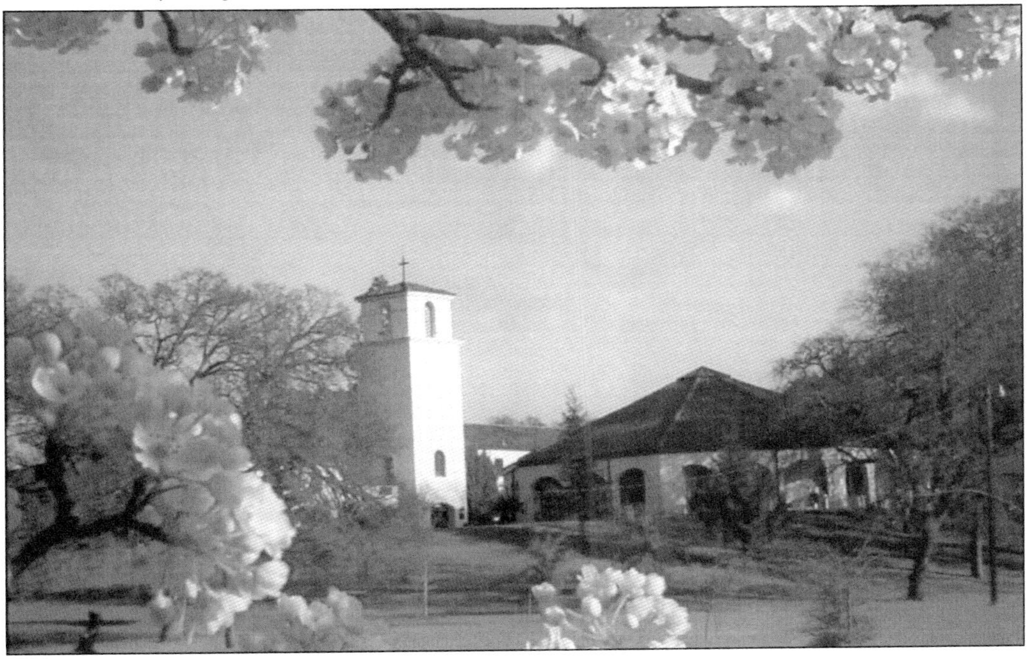

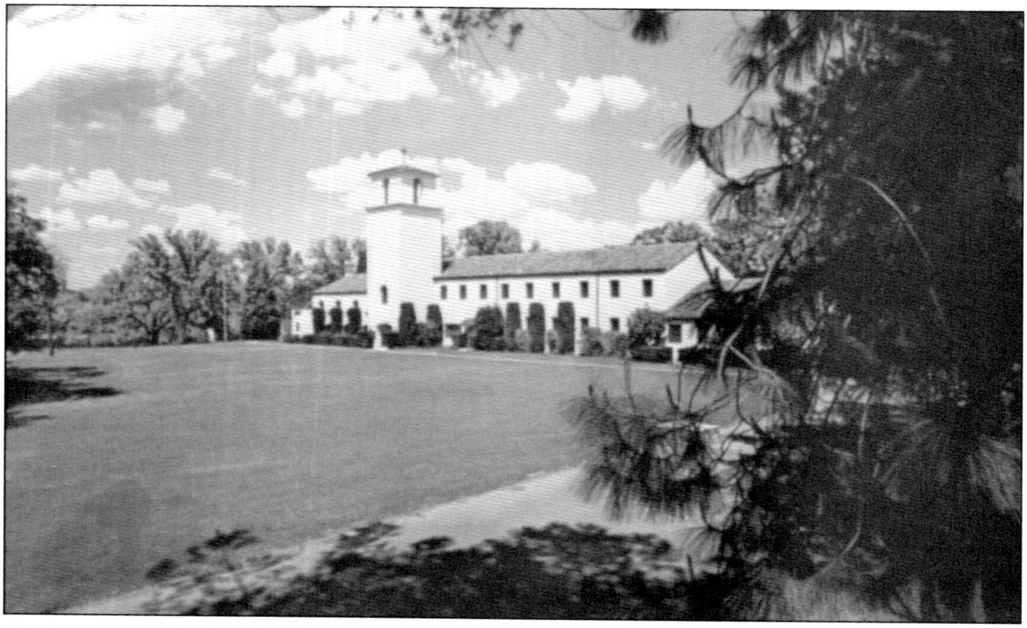

In 1987, a major expansion of the retreat center was undertaken, and the Holy Cross Building was constructed with 40 retreatant rooms, three small conference rooms, and a beautiful large assembly room. Each year, approximately 3,000 men and women attend the 31 weekend retreats, midweek retreats, and days of recollection. (Courtesy Christ the King Retreat Center; Margaret Hinshaw and Brother Kirk.)

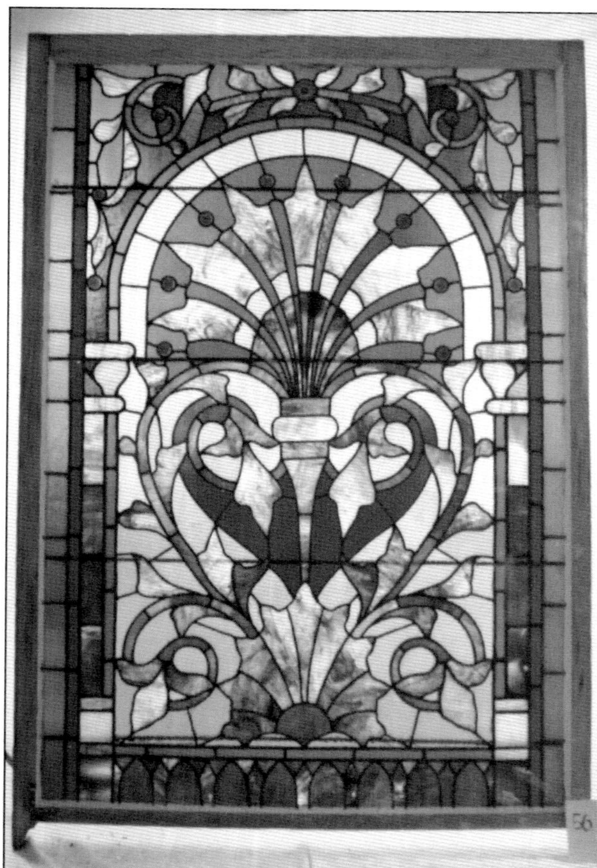

The 1895 stained-glass windows were created by the George Riordan Art Glass Studio in Kentucky, a company that exists to this day. Fred Moran donated funding to bring the beautiful windows to the center. (Courtesy Christ the King Retreat Center; Margaret Hinshaw and Brother Kirk.)

Six

Growth of the Community

The presence of the first Sacramento Valley Railroad between Sacramento and Folsom in 1856 and then the Central Pacific Railroad in 1864 placed the Sylvan District strategically between two major railroad routes. After the first national transcontinental railroad was completed in 1869, the nearby town of Roseville became a main shipping junction. Both the early thoroughfares, as represented by Auburn and Old Auburn Roads, and railroads played an integral part to regional growth. This transportation evolution within and around the Sylvan District contributed to the development of the area. With the help of other local farmers, Adolph Van Maren developed the Sylvan Telephone Company in 1901. It merged with the Roseville Rural Telephone Company in 1926 and continued rural telephone services through the 1930s. Today, the modern company is known as SureWest Communications and located in Roseville, California.

In 1910, real estate promoters Trainor-Desmond Company purchased large tracts of land in the Sylvan District. Walter Trainor was not satisfied with the name Sylvan, believing the area should be identified with citrus fruit. This would enhance his advertisement campaign for the land parcels he wished to sell. Therefore, he changed the name to Citrus Heights. The State Department of Highways undertook a major road-building program throughout California in 1912. They improved Auburn Boulevard to the intersection of Sylvan Road and turned it north to Roseville. This improved road became part of Lincoln Highway (Route 40), the first transcontinental highway.

In 1947, a post office was established. By 1974, it incorporated the area of what is Citrus Heights, and a new building was located at Old Auburn and Sylvan Roads. Here it remained until a larger facility was built on Fountain Square, across from the administrative offices of the City of Citrus Heights. The Sunrise Mall was built in 1970. It is a major urban shopping center featuring a variety of stores surrounding a concourse. In 1976, an open-style shopping center originally known as Birdcage Walk was developed with 100-plus shops across the street from Sunrise Mall. The entire area grew and is now called the Sunrise MarketPlace.

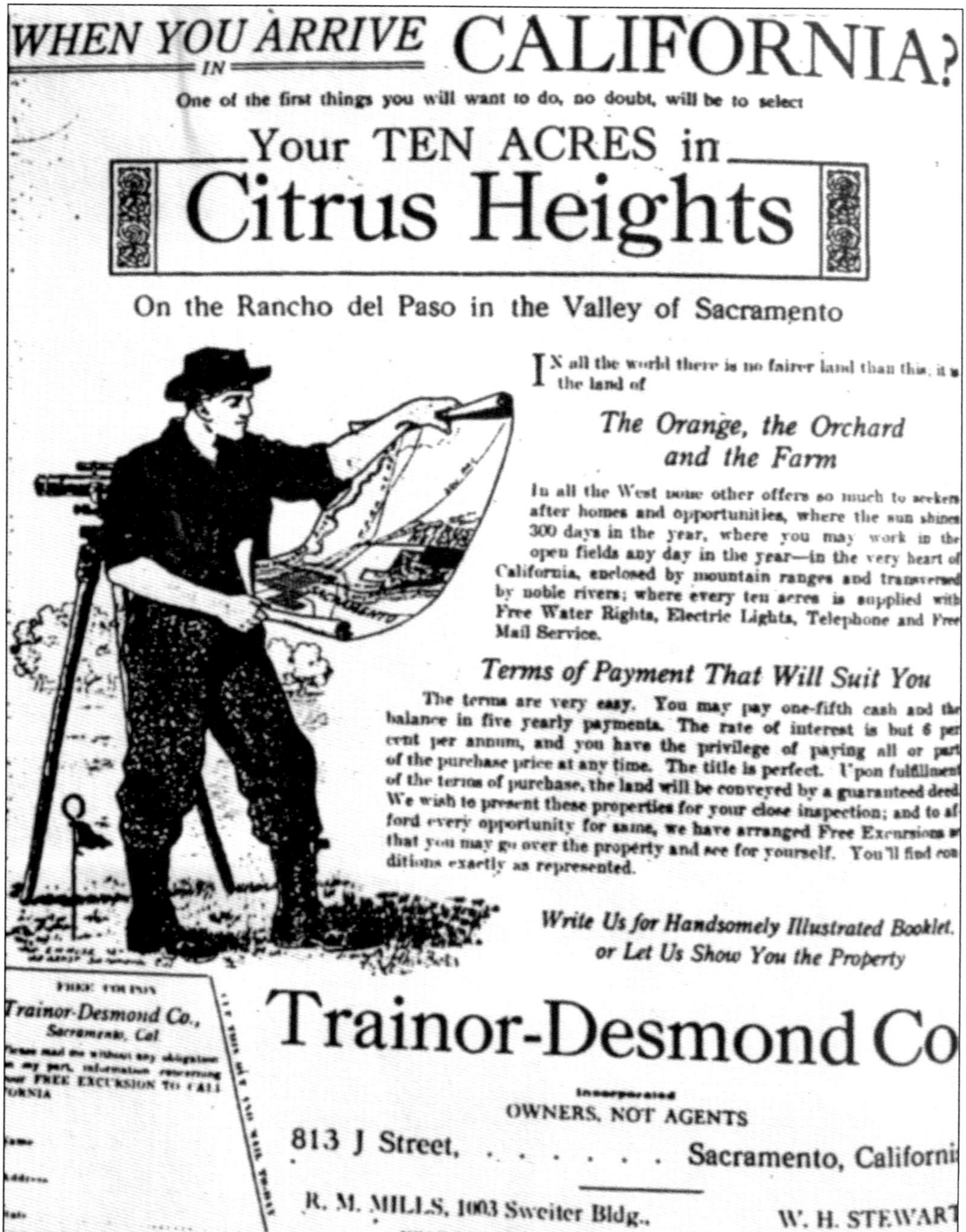

This promotional material by Trainor-Desmond Company for the sale of land in Citrus Heights was in a 1913 issue of *Sacramento Valley Monthly*. (Courtesy *Sacramento Bee*, 1987.)

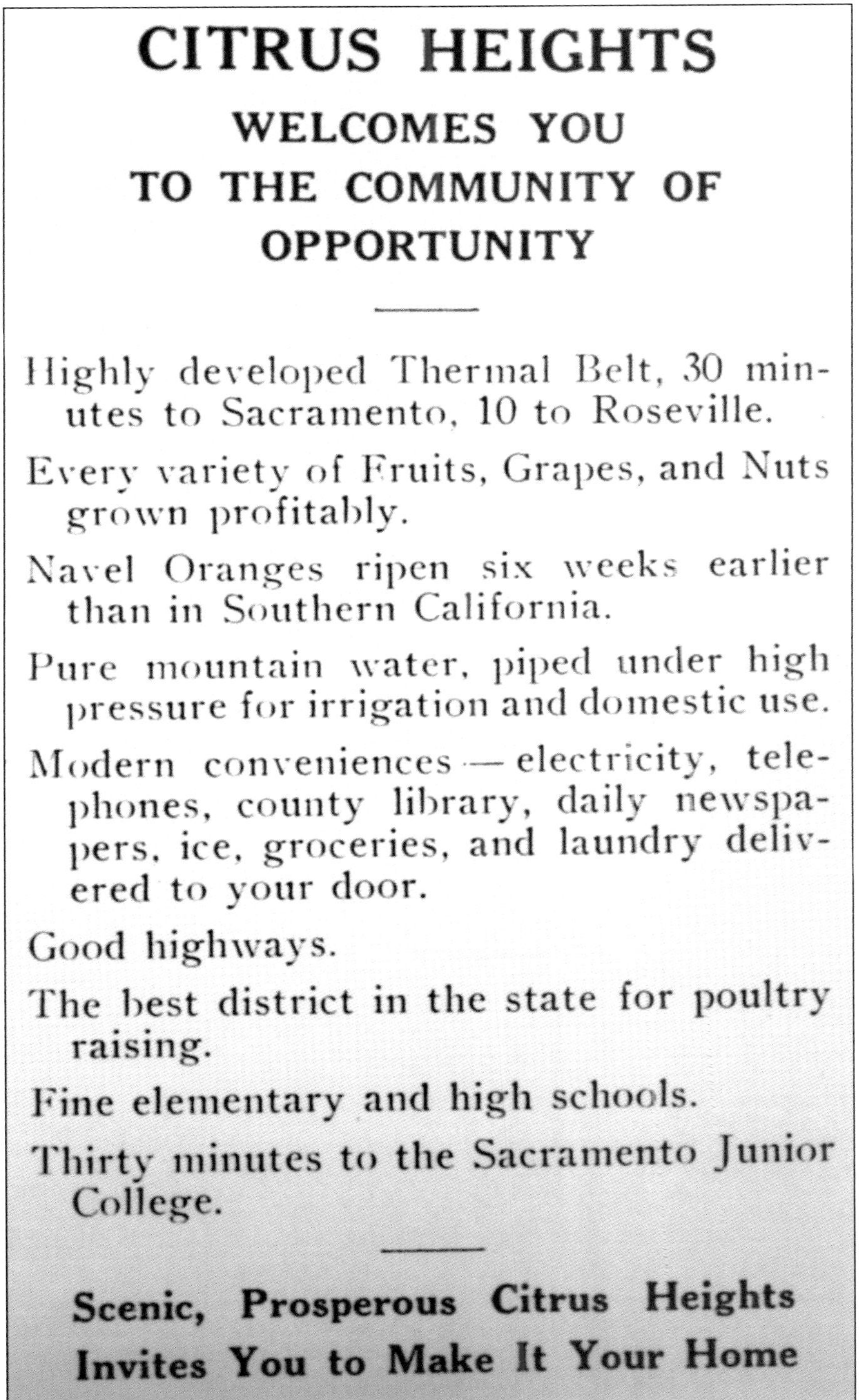

This 1937 promotional advertisement encourages potential new residents to come take advantage of the quality of life in Citrus Heights. (Courtesy *Citrus Heights Directory*, 1937.)

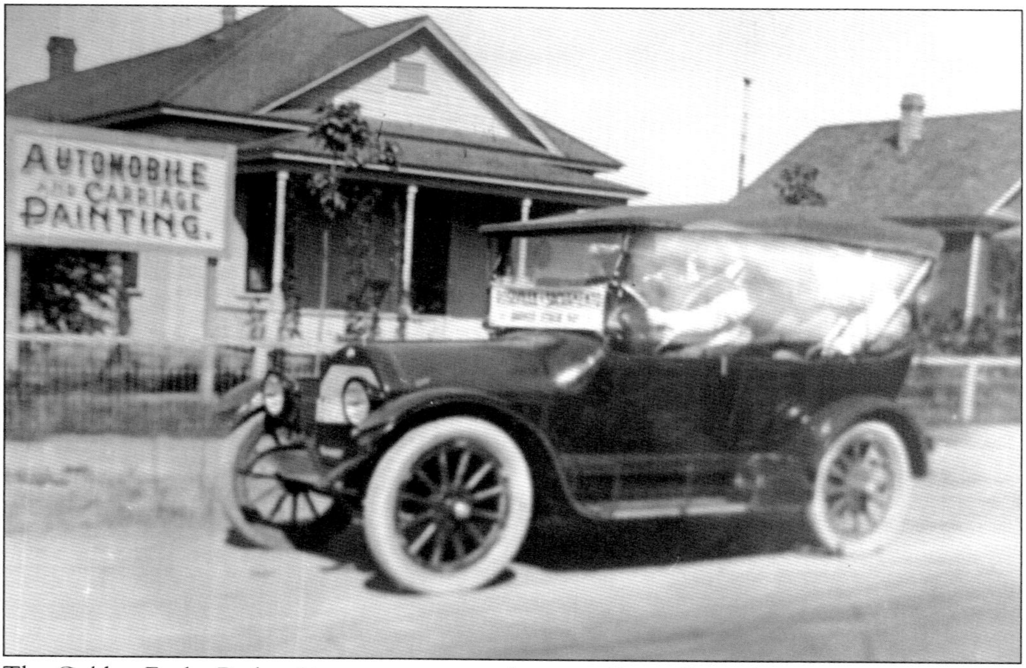

The Golden Eagle–Barker Line was operating between Roseville and Sacramento in 1914 via Citrus Heights. The fare was 50¢ per person. The line was replaced by California-Nevada Stages, Incorporated. It was later acquired by Beverly Gibson and renamed Gibson Bus Line until it was absorbed into the Continental Trailways Line. (Courtesy Leonard M. Davis.)

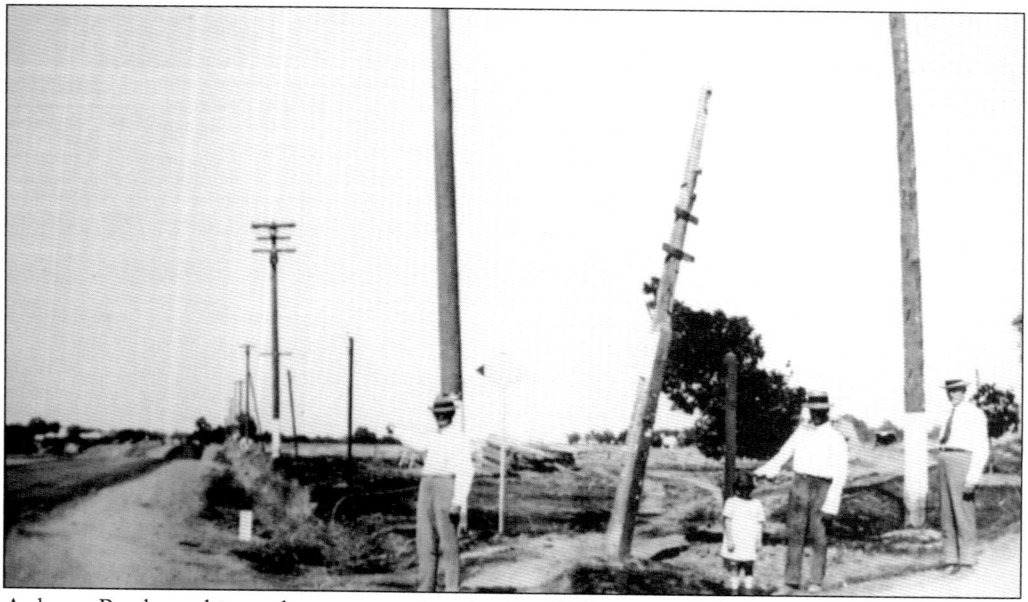

Auburn Boulevard is under construction in this 1920s image. The men are standing where Greenback Lane connects with Auburn Boulevard. (Courtesy Coldani family.)

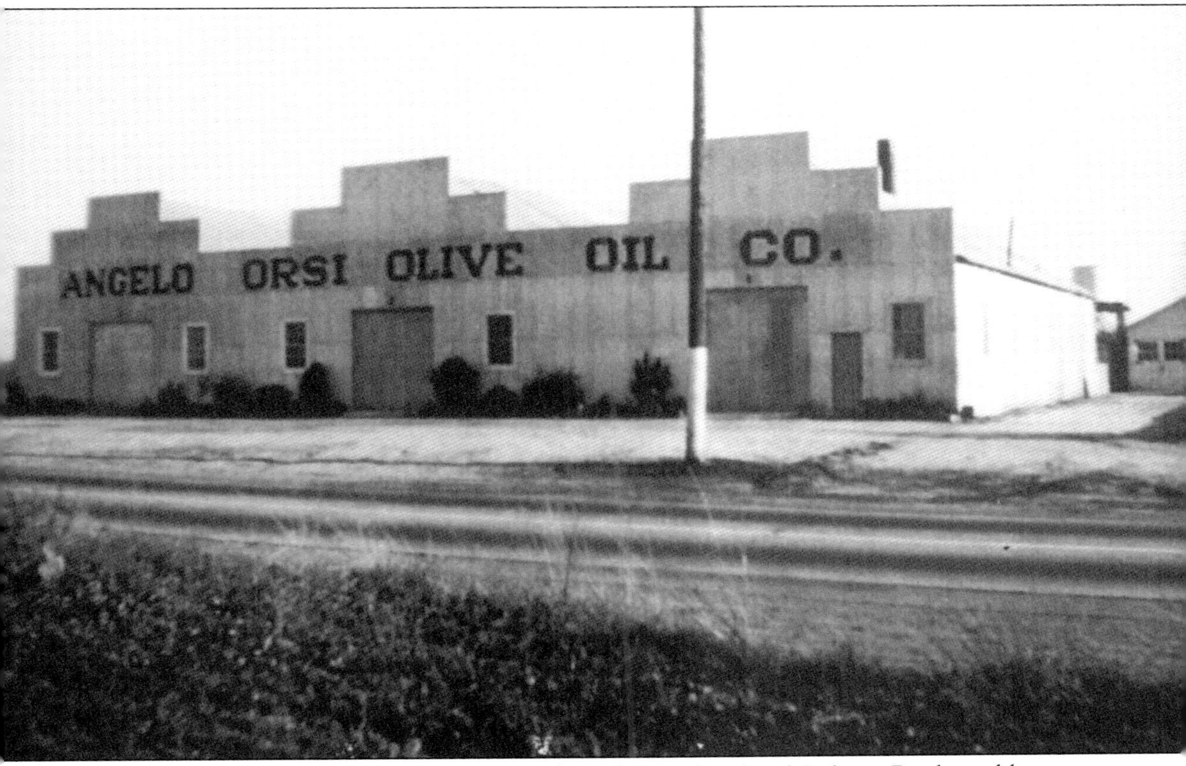

The Angelo Orsi Olive Oil Co. was located on the south side of Auburn Boulevard between Greenback Lane and Manzanita Avenue. The processing plant developed by Orsi was the first major facility of its kind in Citrus Heights. (Courtesy Coldani family.)

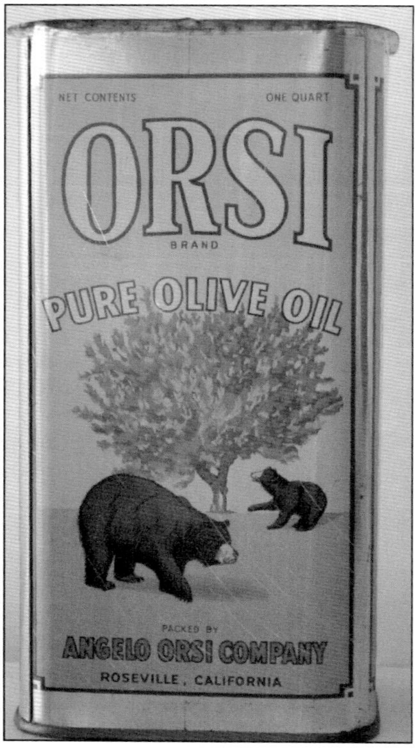

The Orsi logo was designed by April Orsi, Angelo's daughter, and the oil was sold exclusively in metal containers. (Courtesy Stephanie Cotter and Teena Stern.)

Seen here inside the processing plant is the equipment to separate the olives. (Courtesy April Orsi.)

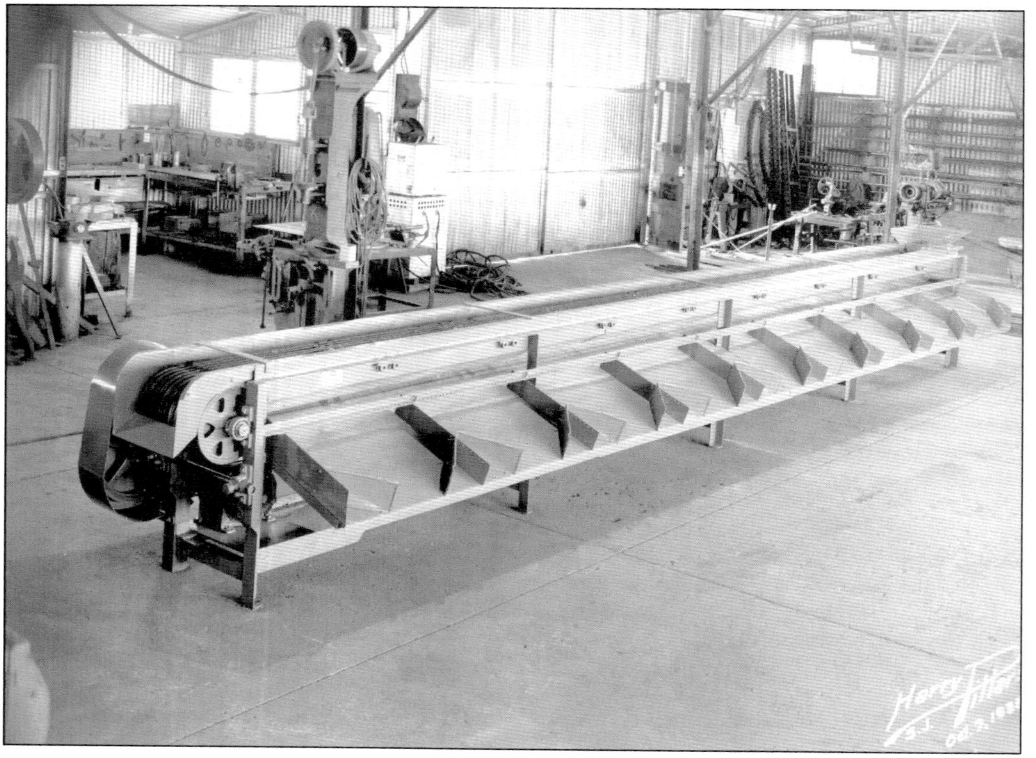

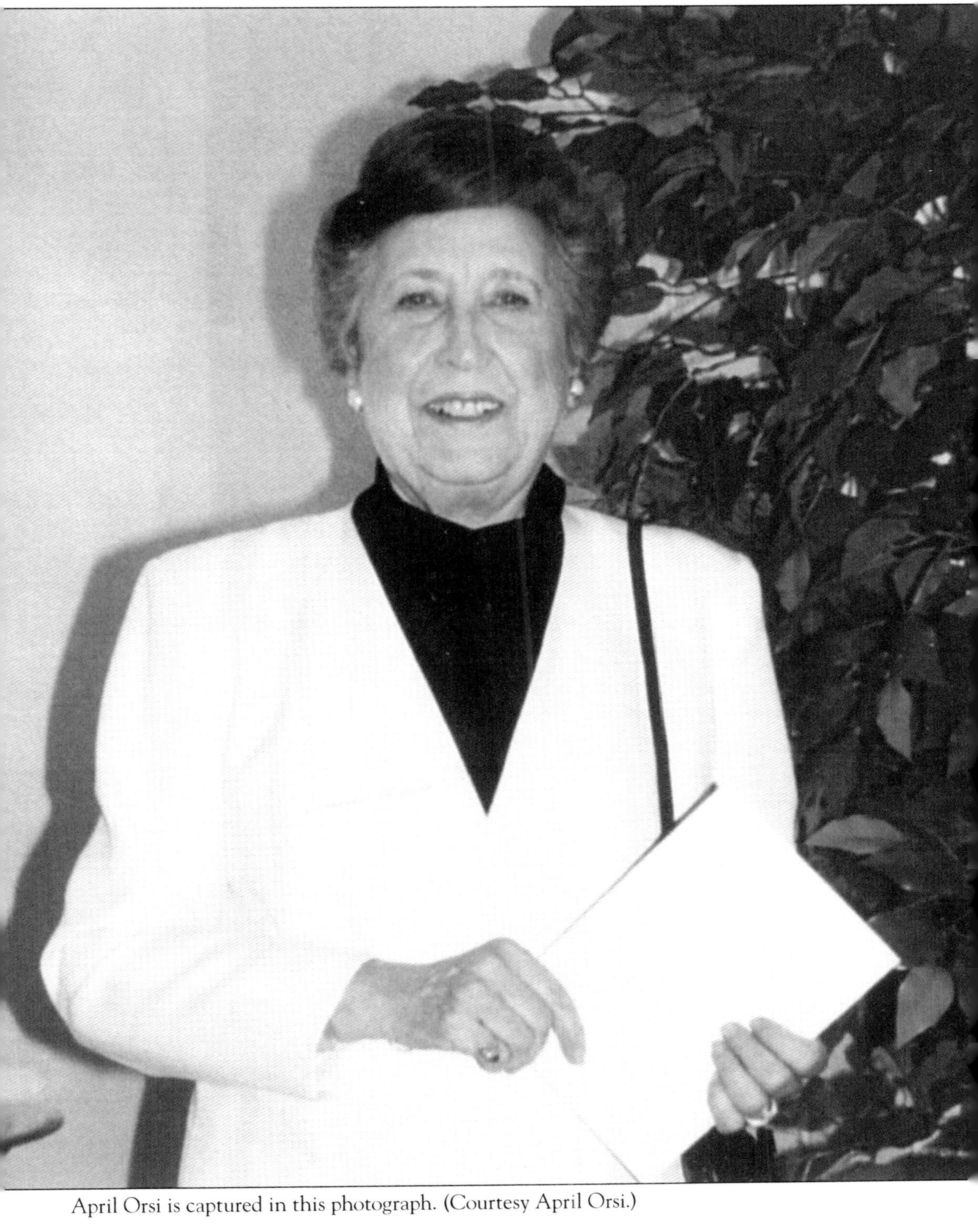

April Orsi is captured in this photograph. (Courtesy April Orsi.)

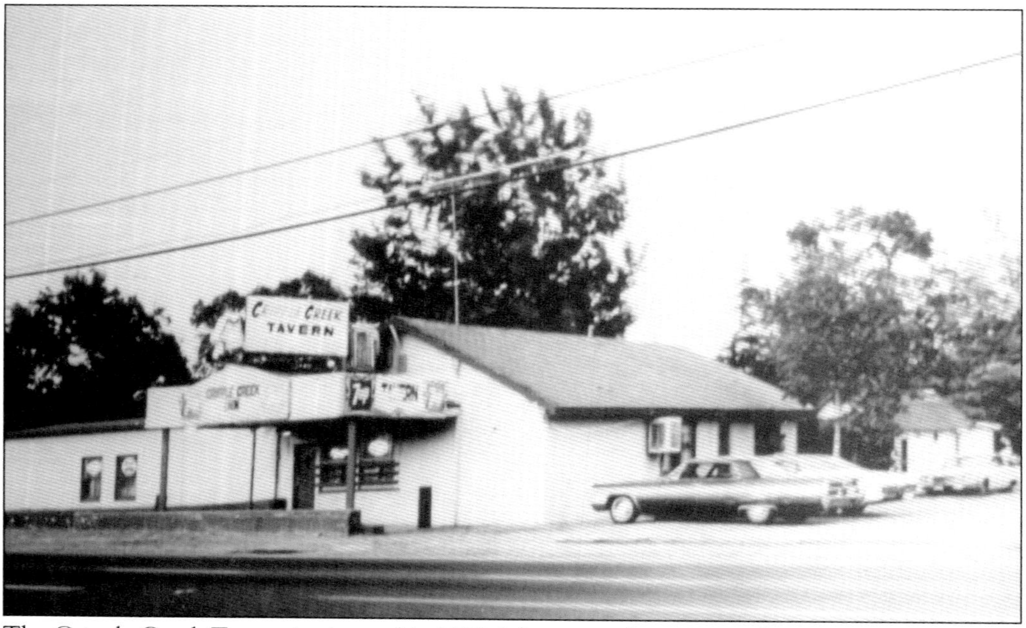

The Cripple Creek Tavern is pictured in 1939. It began in the 1920s and was later demolished to make way for development. (Courtesy Margrethe Law.)

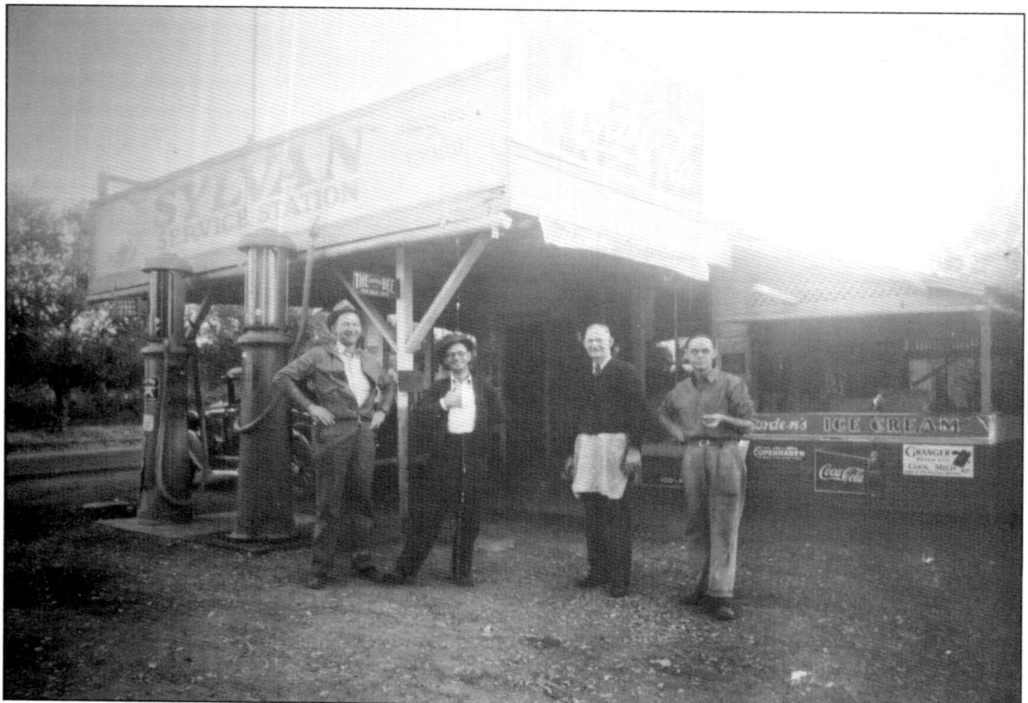

The Sylvan Service Station was located at the southwest corner of Sylvan Road and Auburn Boulevard. The station was owned by William Cobb, who is standing on the far right. Byron Myklebost, community constable from 1926 to 1960, is the first person on the left. Besides pumping gasoline, the station had a mini-mart. (Courtesy Jim Van Maren.)

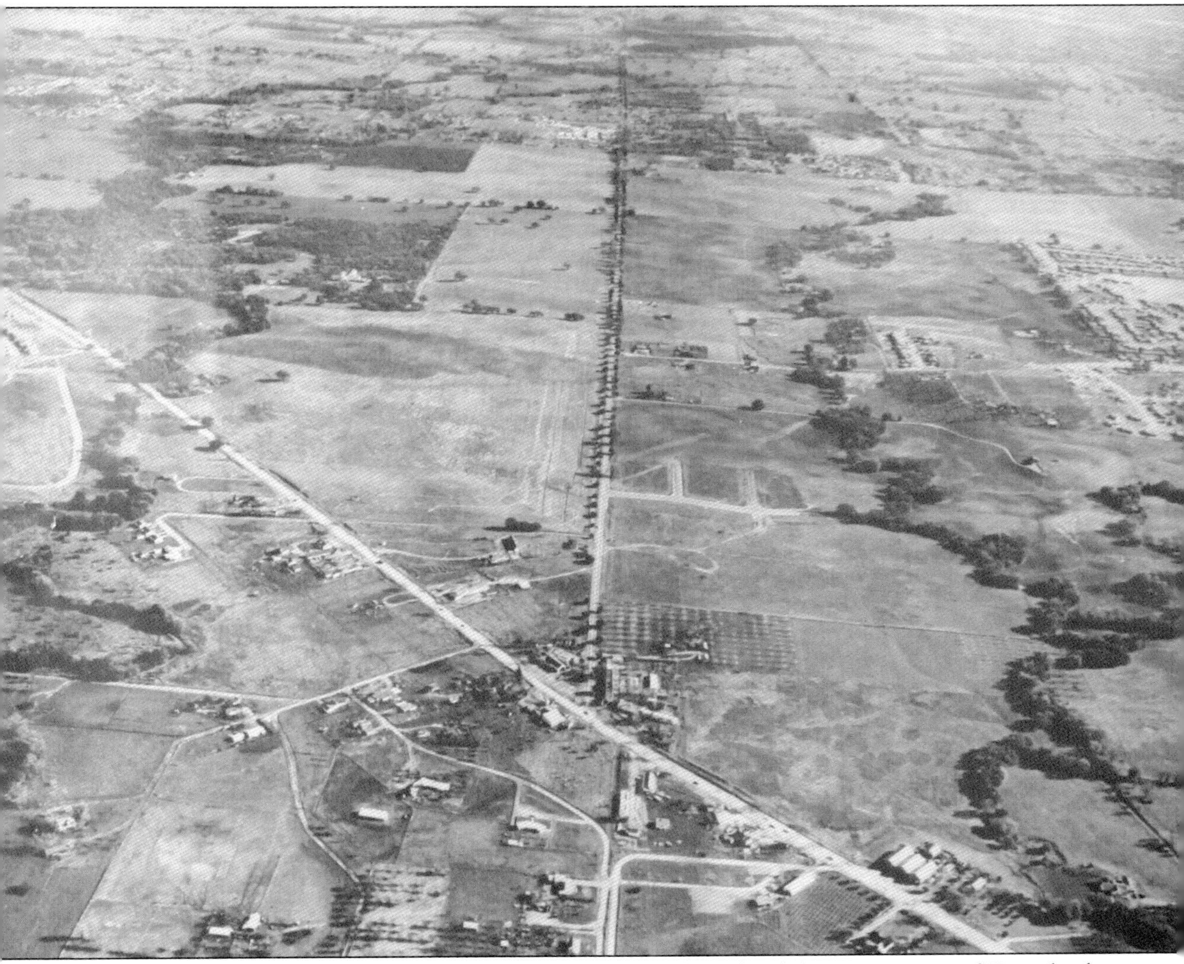

This aerial picture of open land in 1958 shows Auburn Boulevard and the intersection of Greenback Lane, which stopped at Auburn Boulevard. This includes undeveloped land, much of which was dedicated to farming. Near the top of the picture along Greenback Lane is San Juan High School. (Courtesy Jim Van Maren.)

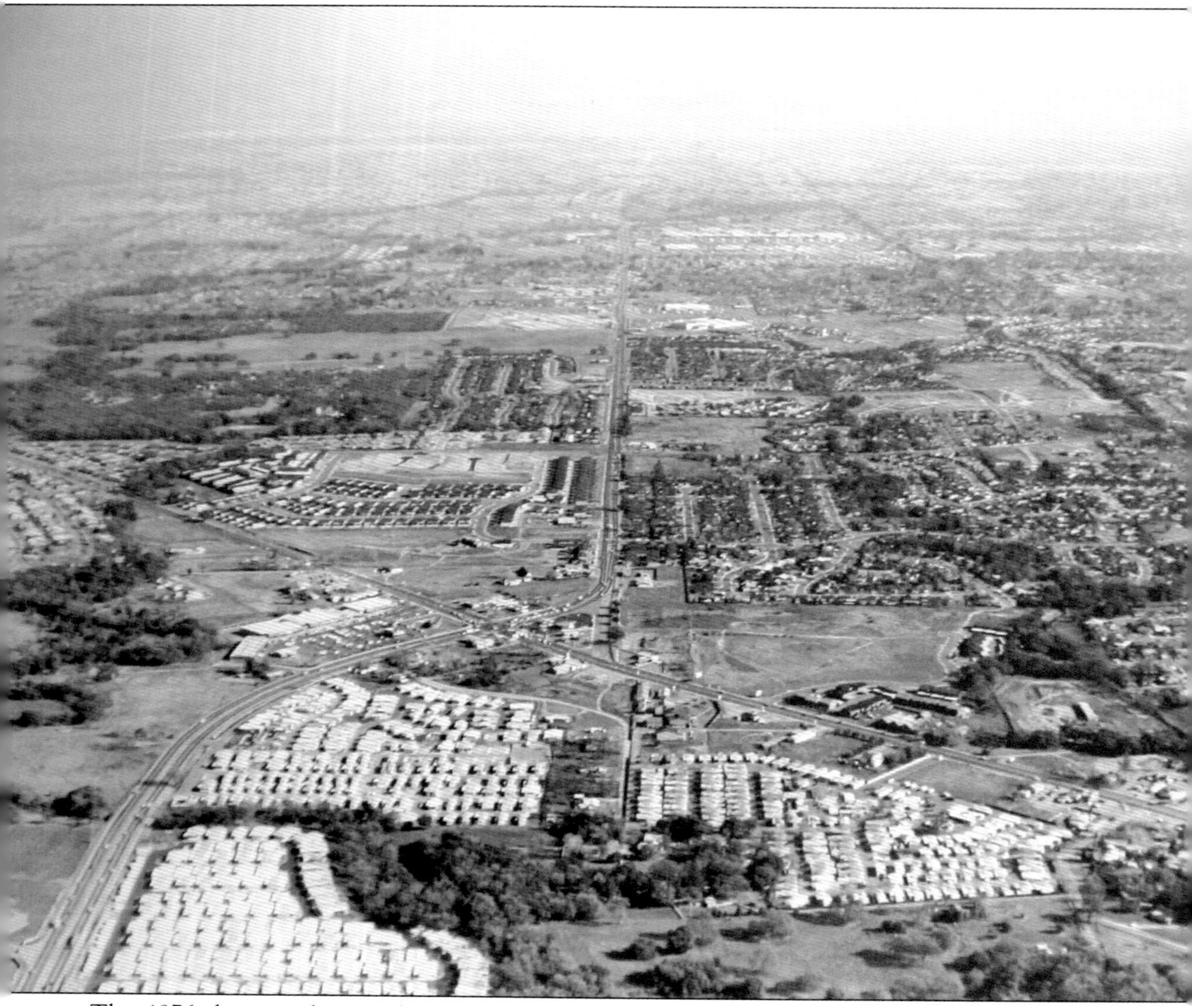

This 1976 photograph was taken from the same vantage point as the previous image. Both show the development of new homes being constructed on what was originally farmland. (Courtesy Jim Van Maren.)

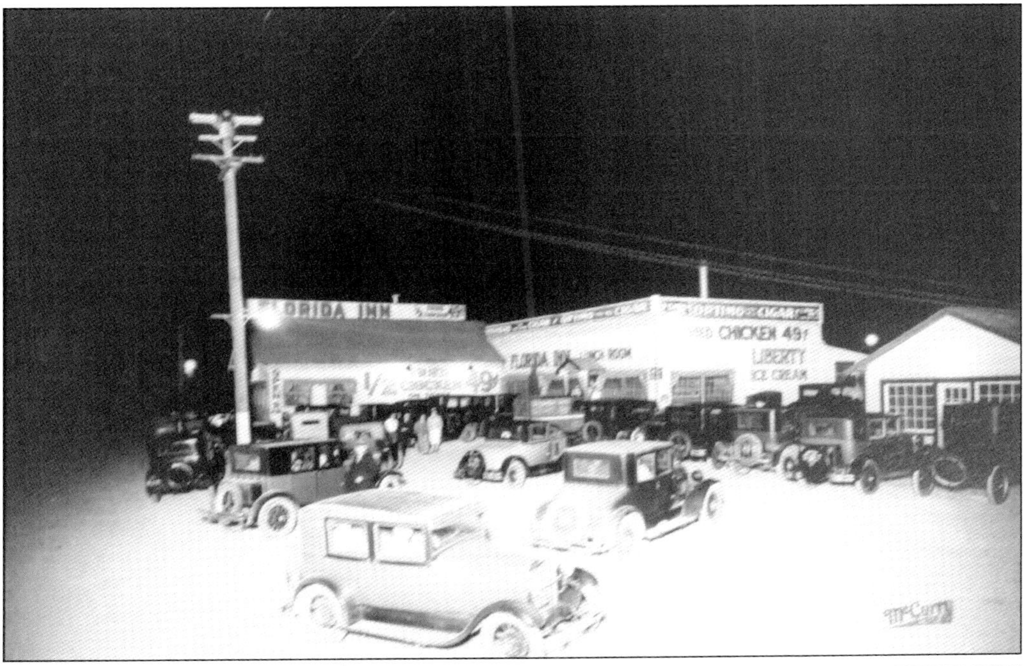

The Florida Inn Restaurant and Tavern, pictured here in 1929, was the first formal restaurant in Citrus Heights. It was located on Greenback Lane near Auburn Boulevard. (Courtesy Coldani family; photograph by McCurry.)

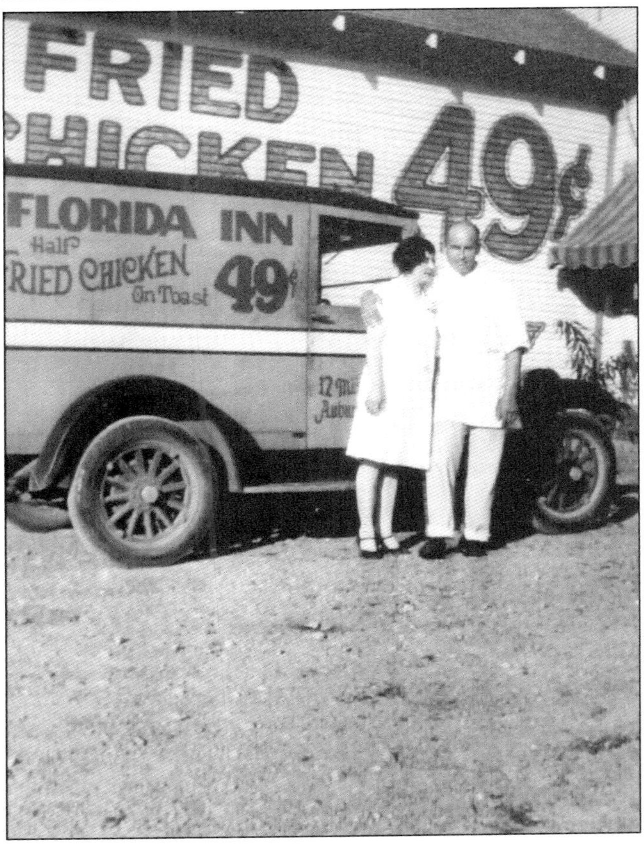

Owners Ann and Henry Coldani are seen standing in front of the Florida Inn. Note the advertisements on both the truck and restaurant wall. (Courtesy Coldani family.)

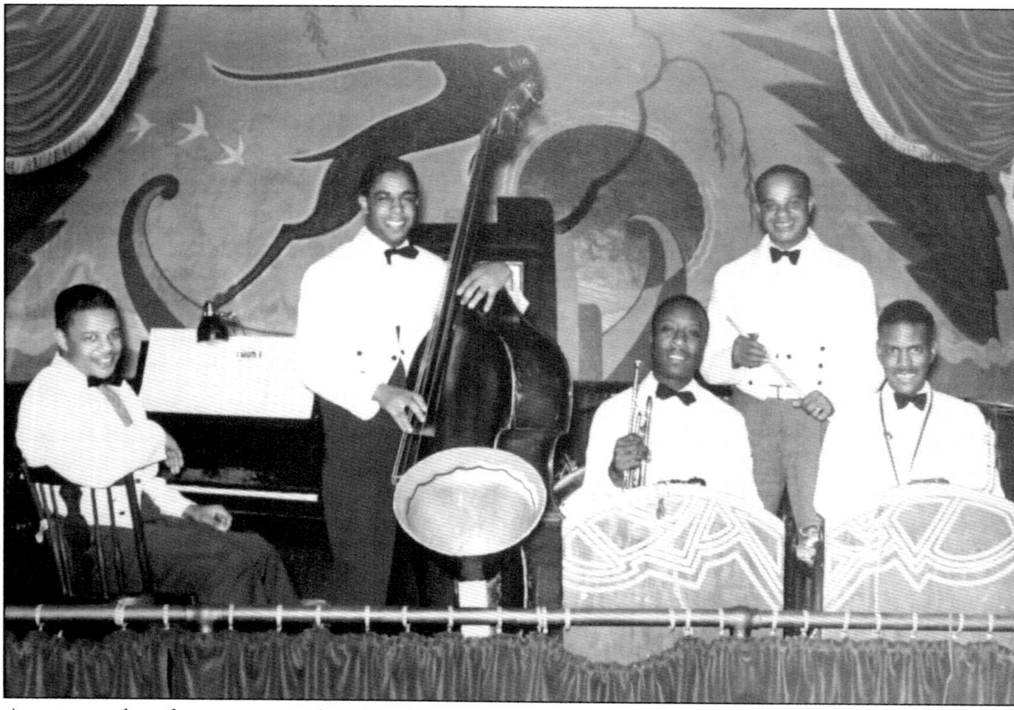

A quintet plays for patrons at the Florida Inn, a popular dinner and dancing destination. (Courtesy Coldani family.)

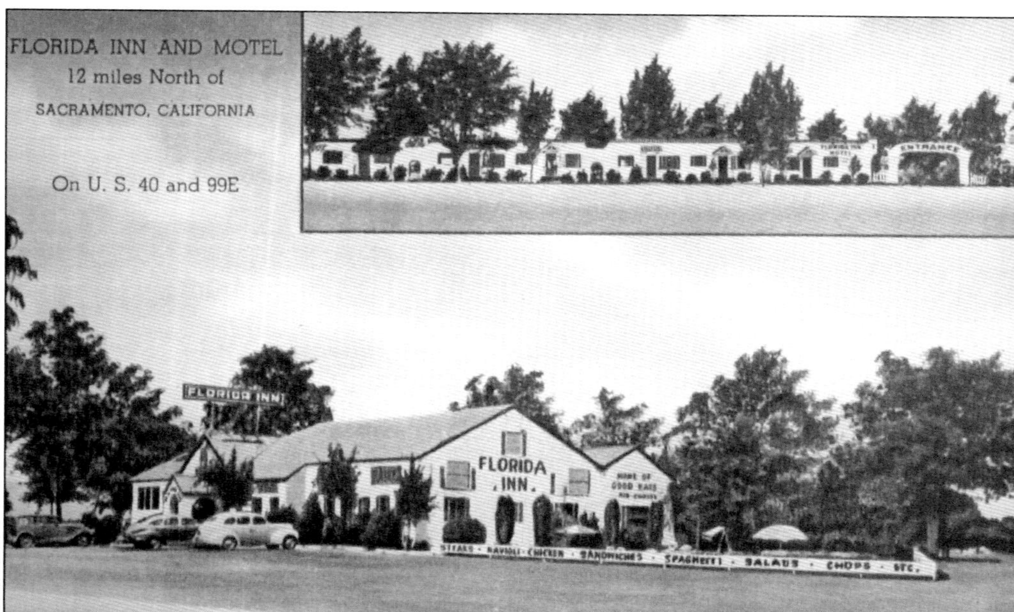

This postcard from 1939 advertises the Florida Inn as being 12 miles north of Sacramento on US 40 and 99E. (Courtesy Coldani family.)

The Sunrise Recreation and Park District operates 19 parks and associated facilities—such as playing fields, swimming pools, and picnic areas—within the city. It consistently offers varied and popular activities and high-quality classes for the community. Below is a student art show at Rusch Park, the city's largest park. (Above, courtesy Sunrise Recreation and Park District; below, courtesy Kiwanis Club of Citrus Heights.)

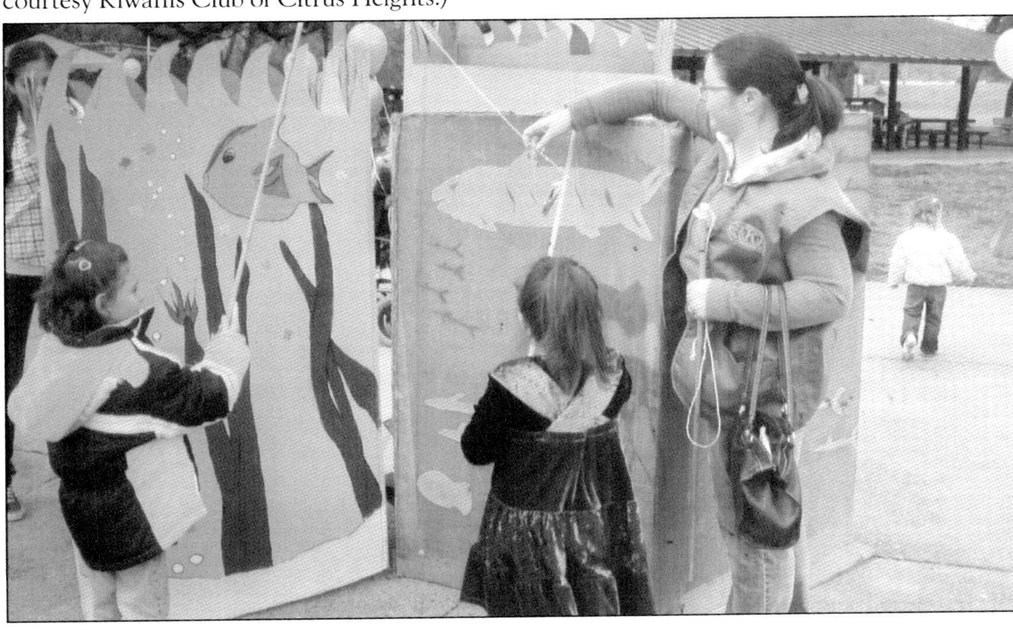

ACKNOWLEDGEMENTS

The following individuals and agencies are recognized for contributing to the development and dedication of Van Maren Park:

The staff of the City of Citrus Heights

The City of Citrus Heights Council Members:

Jeff Slowey, Mayor

Steve Miller, Vice Mayor

Jeannie Bruins, Council Member

Jayna Karpinski-Costa, Council Member

James Shelby, Council Member

The staff of Sunrise Recreation & Park District

The SRPD Advisory Board of Directors:

Jodi Tarr, Chairperson

David Sloan, Vice Chairperson

Alan Criswell

Ken Mitchell

John Padden

Mary Purvis and the Citrus Heights Queens

Ryland Homes

Land Architects

John Stock, Jr. and the Stock family

Jim Van Maren and five generations of the Van Maren family

VAN MAREN PARK DEDICATION

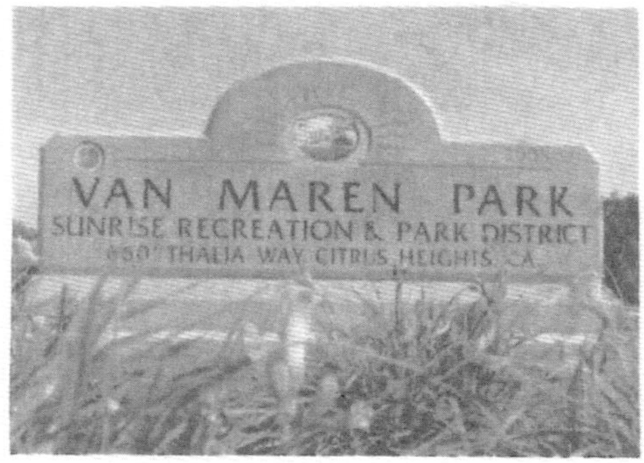

SATURDAY, JUNE 30TH

11:30 A.M.

VAN MAREN PARK
6601 THALIA WAY

Event hosted by:

Dedicated in 2007, Van Maren Park is just one of the open green spaces scattered throughout the city. Comprising 32 acres, it is located on farmland that once belonged to the Van Maren family. Their ranch was approximately 1,000 acres and harvested wheat, oats, and barley. The Van Maren Ranch also grew a fair amount of grapes, almonds, and olives. (Courtesy Jim Van Maren.)

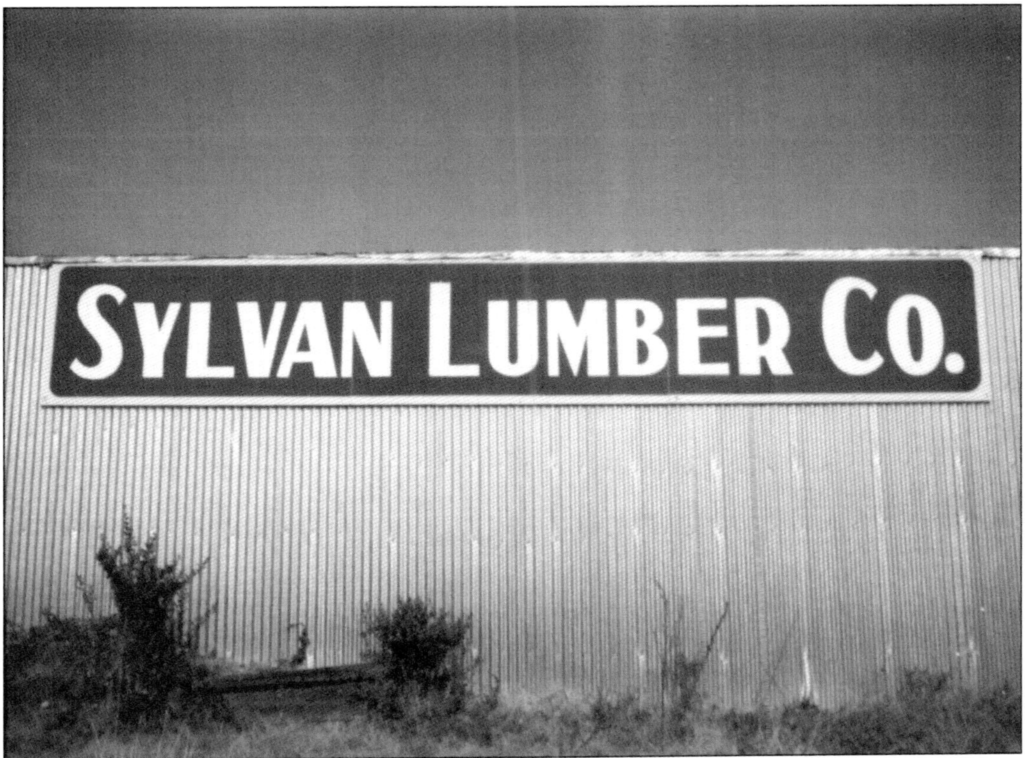

Established in the early 1930s, the Sylvan Lumber Co. was one of the area's primary suppliers for lumber products until the 1990s. It was located on Auburn Boulevard across from Sylvan Middle School. (Courtesy Leineke family.)

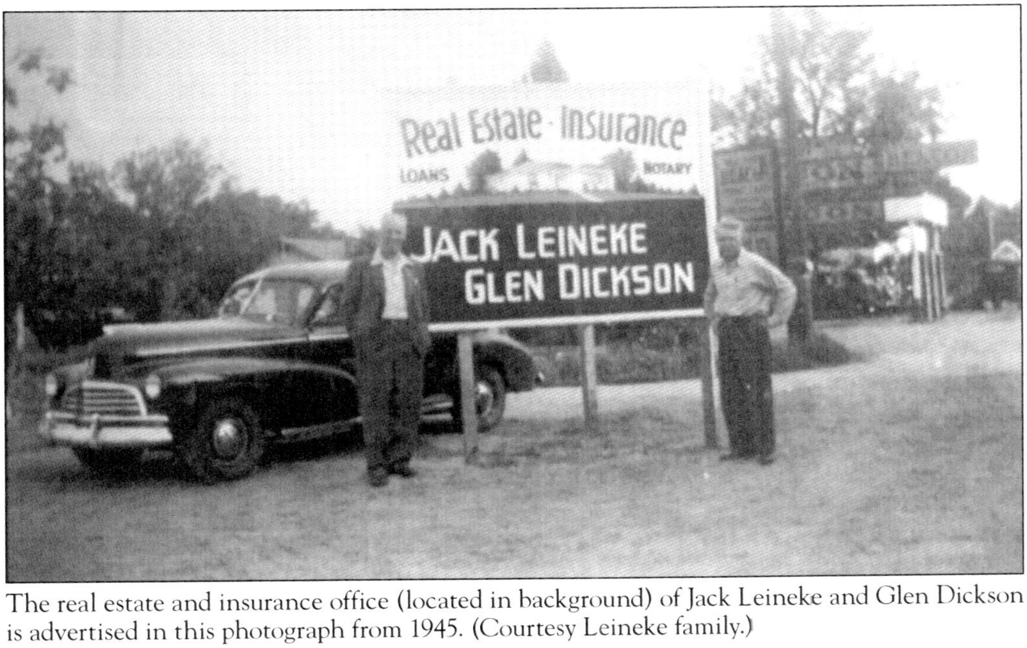

The real estate and insurance office (located in background) of Jack Leineke and Glen Dickson is advertised in this photograph from 1945. (Courtesy Leineke family.)

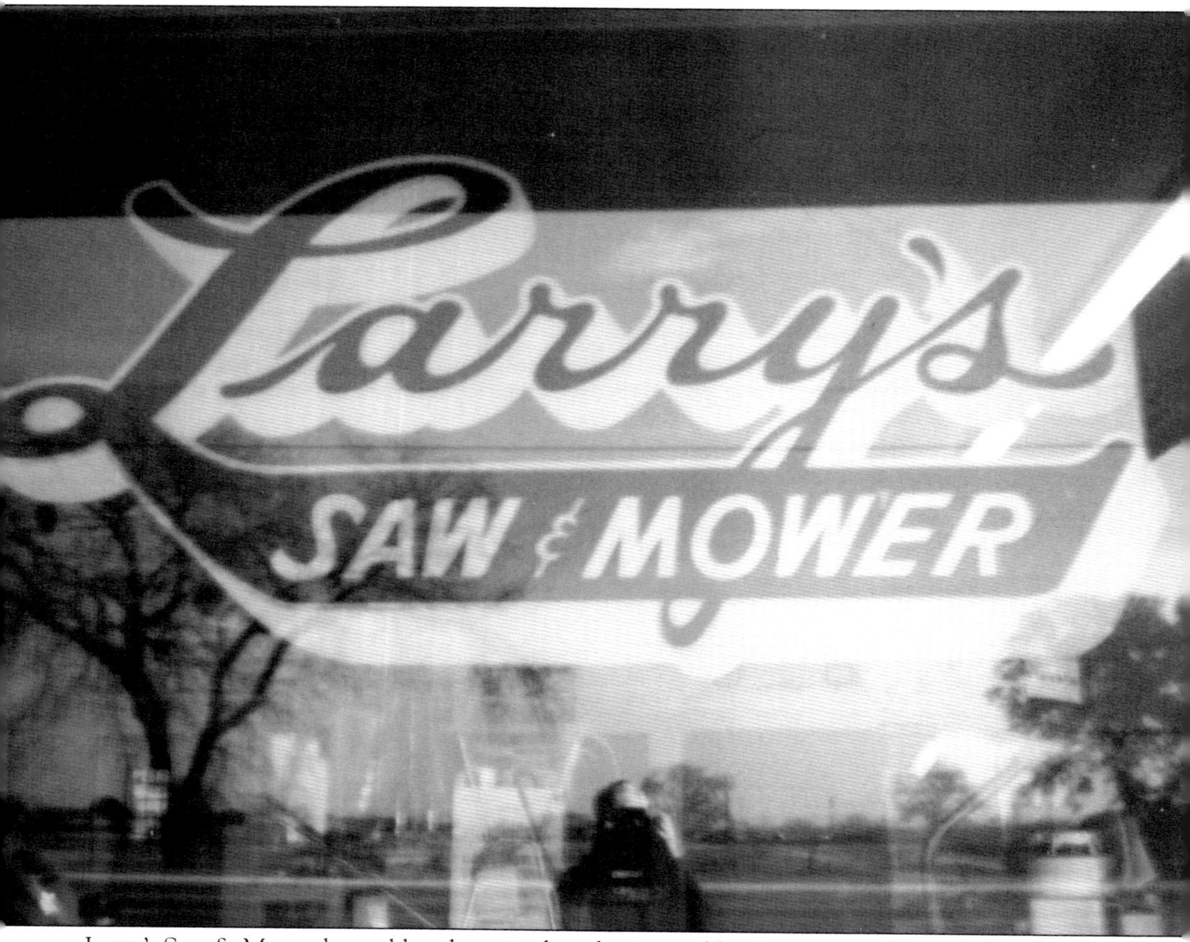

Larry's Saw & Mower has sold and repaired gardening and landscaping tools since the 1940s. It remains in business today on Auburn Boulevard, across from Sylvan Middle School. (Courtesy Leineke family.)

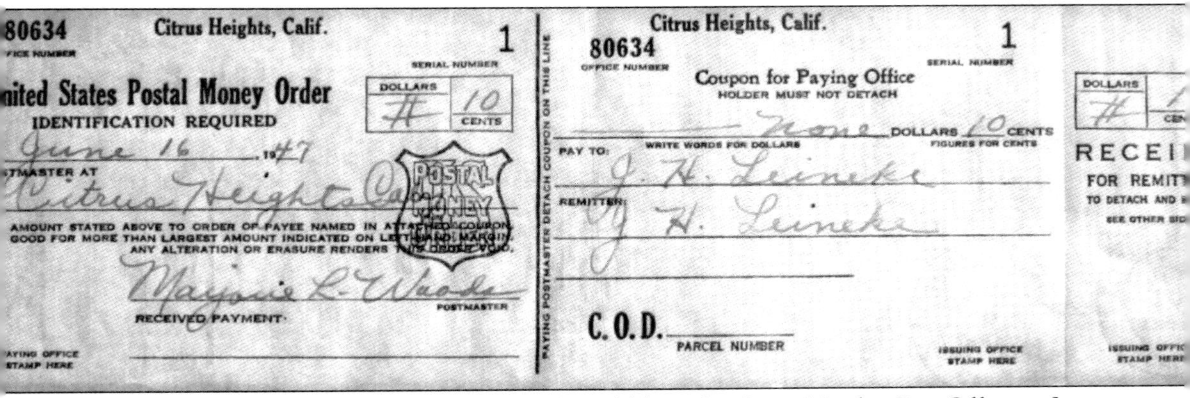

80634 Citrus Heights, Calif. 1
[OF]FICE NUMBER SERIAL NUMBER
[U]nited States Postal Money Order
IDENTIFICATION REQUIRED
DOLLARS # 10 CENTS
June 16 1947
[POS]TMASTER AT
Citrus Heights Cal.
AMOUNT STATED ABOVE TO ORDER OF PAYEE NAMED IN ATTACHED COUPON, GOOD FOR MORE THAN LARGEST AMOUNT INDICATED ON LEFT-HAND MARGIN. ANY ALTERATION OR ERASURE RENDERS THIS ORDER VOID.
POSTAL MONEY ORDER
Marjorie L. Woods
POSTMASTER
RECEIVED PAYMENT
[P]AYING OFFICE STAMP HERE

PAYING POSTMASTER DETACH COUPON ON THIS LINE

Citrus Heights, Calif.
80634 1
OFFICE NUMBER SERIAL NUMBER
Coupon for Paying Office
HOLDER MUST NOT DETACH
None DOLLARS 10 CENTS
WRITE WORDS FOR DOLLARS FIGURES FOR CENTS
PAY TO: J. H. Leineke
REMITTER: J. H. Leineke
C.O.D.
PARCEL NUMBER
ISSUING OFFICE STAMP HERE

DOLLARS #
RECEI[PT]
FOR REMIT[TER]
ISSUING OFFI[CE] STAMP HERE

This is a copy of the first US postal money order sold from the Citrus Heights Post Office on June 16, 1947. The money order was purchased by Jack Leineke for 10¢ and was signed by Marjorie L. Woods, postmaster. (Courtesy Leineke family.)

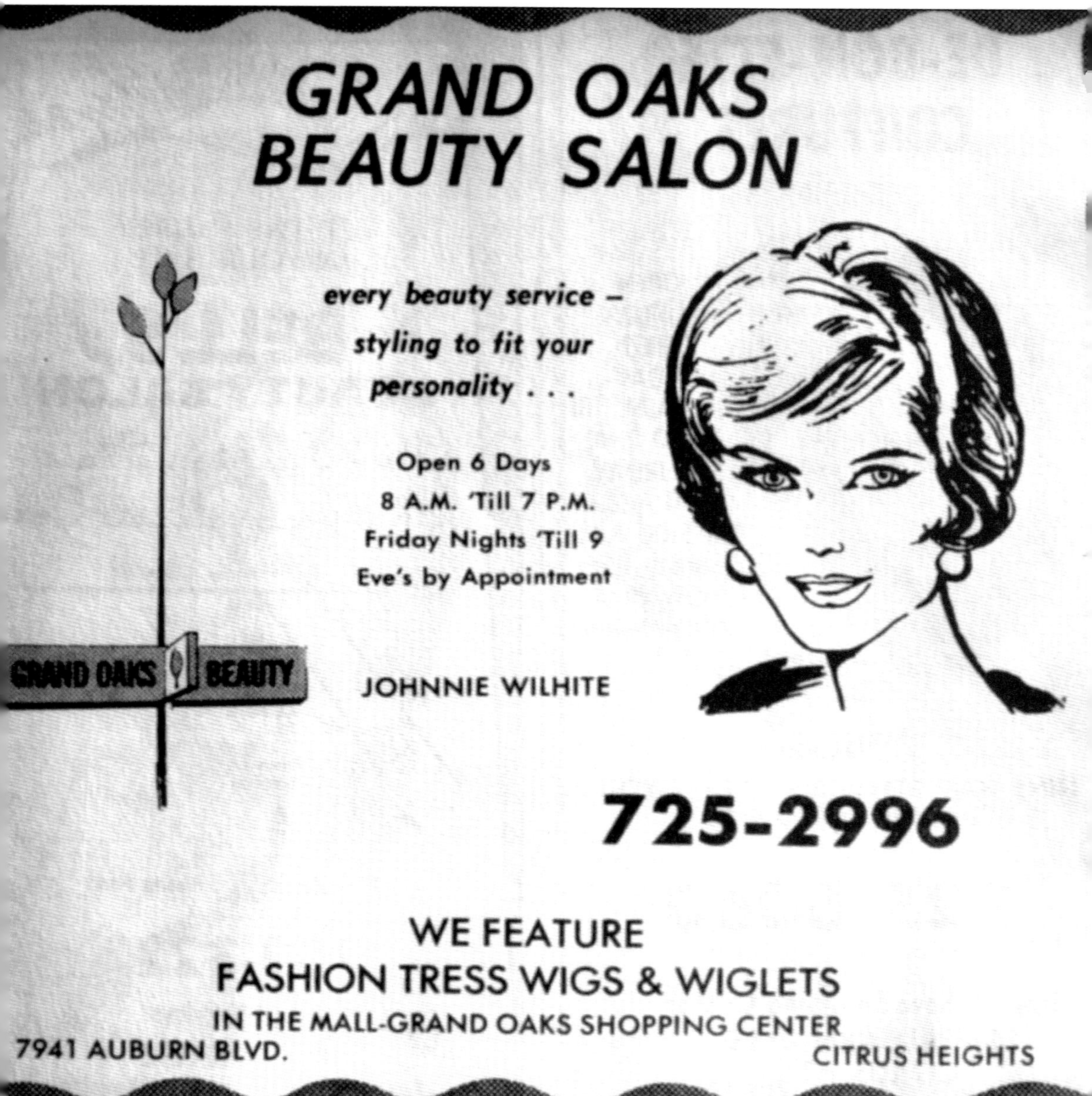

The first major retail area in Citrus Heights was the Grand Oaks Shopping Plaza, which was built in the 1960s on Auburn Boulevard north of the Sylvan Cemetery. The Grand Oaks Beauty Salon is still offering services in the shopping plaza. (Courtesy Roseville-Citrus Heights phone book, 1965; Andrew Felsenstein.)

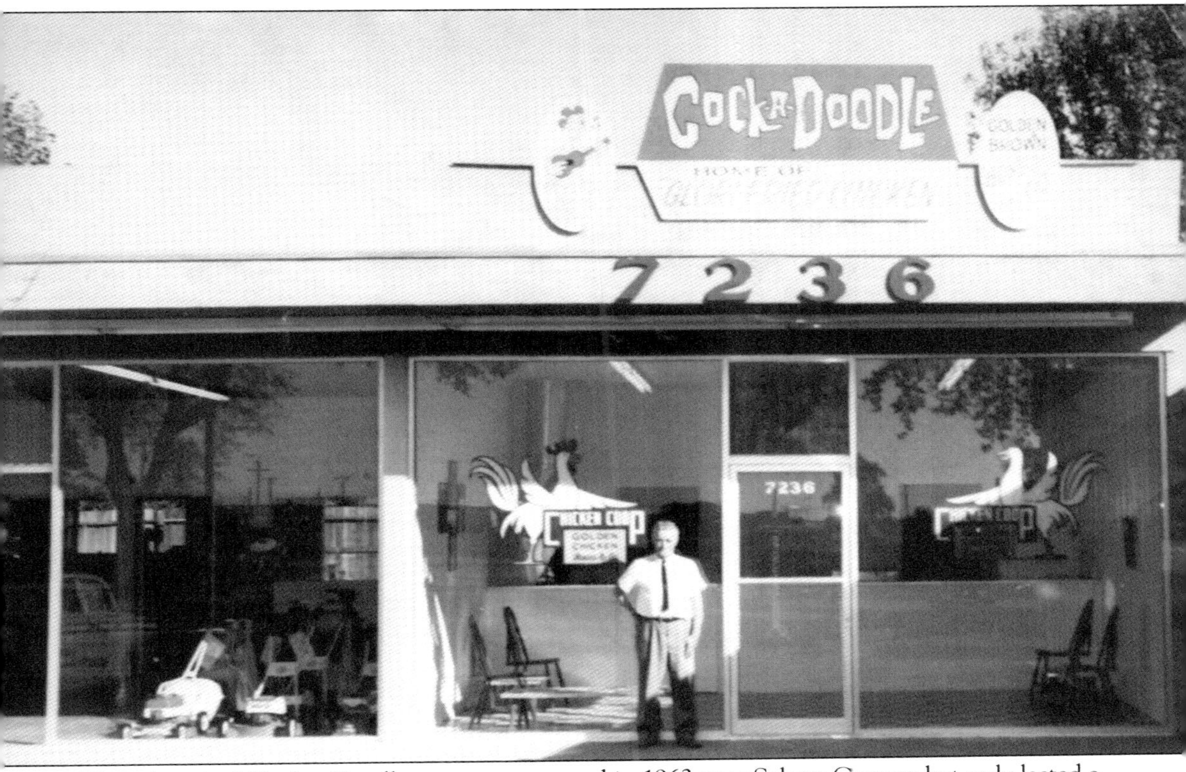

The whimsical Cock-a-Doodle restaurant opened in 1963 near Sylvan Corners but only lasted a few years. (Courtesy Leineke family.)

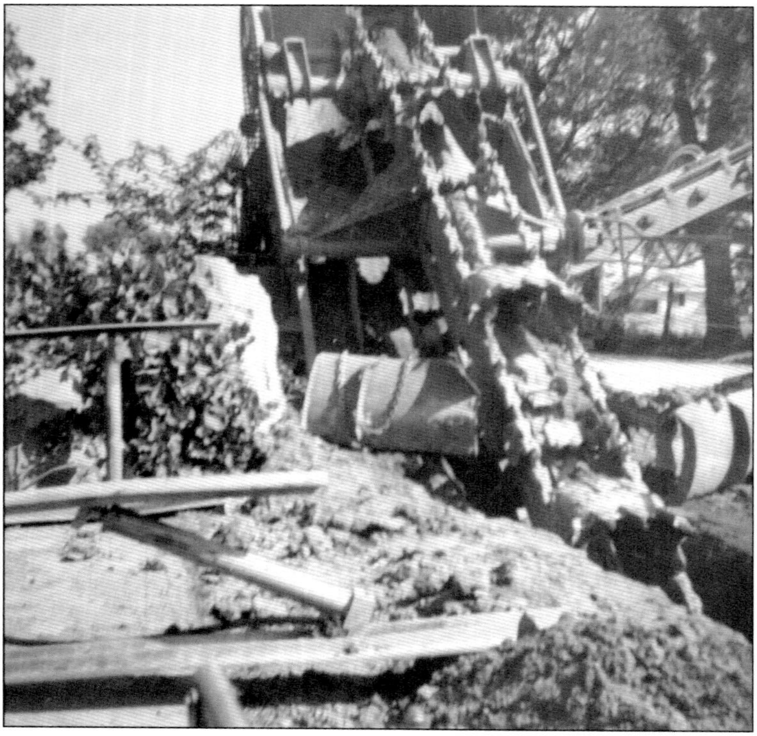

Public sewage disposal became available in the 1960s. At left, a sewer trench is dug on Highland Avenue. The photograph below is of Charles Camilleri in front of his Highland home. He is digging a trench to facilitate service and discontinue use of his sewer tank and line. Meanwhile, his three-year-old son Dan is watching him dig. (Both, courtesy Wilma Camilleri.)

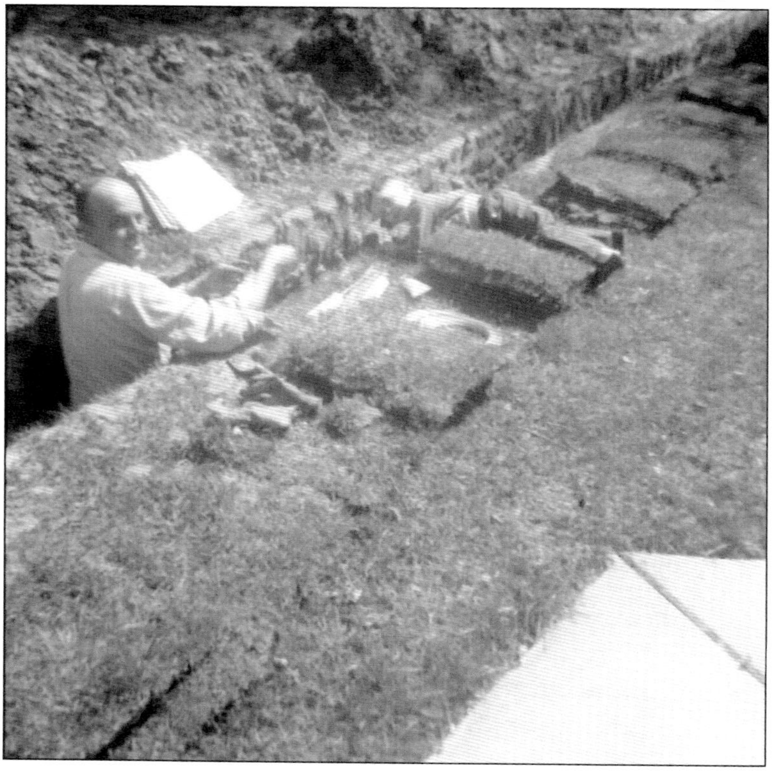

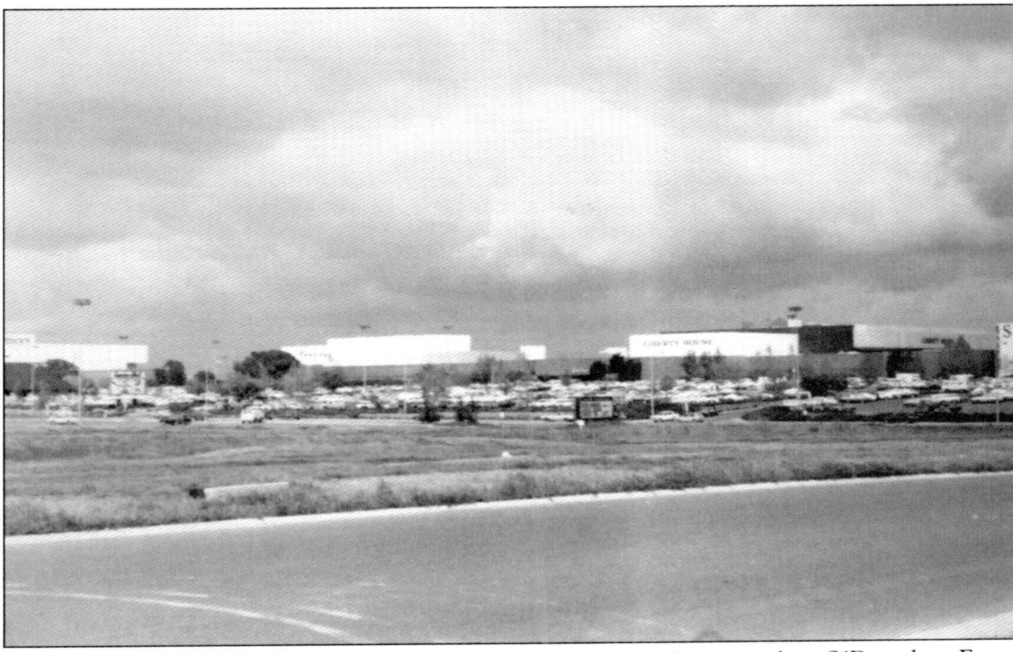

The Sunrise Mall (above) was built on land that had been the Cornelius O'Donahue Farm, which had grown almond trees. This enclosed mall was the beginning of a large retail district for Citrus Heights (below). Directly across the street on the same land is the open-air Marketplace at Birdcage, which was built in 1976. Both malls have been remodeled and border Greenback Lane and Sunrise Boulevard. Other retail centers in the area include Sunrise Village and Grand Oaks Plaza. (Both, courtesy Chuck and Joy Engvall.)

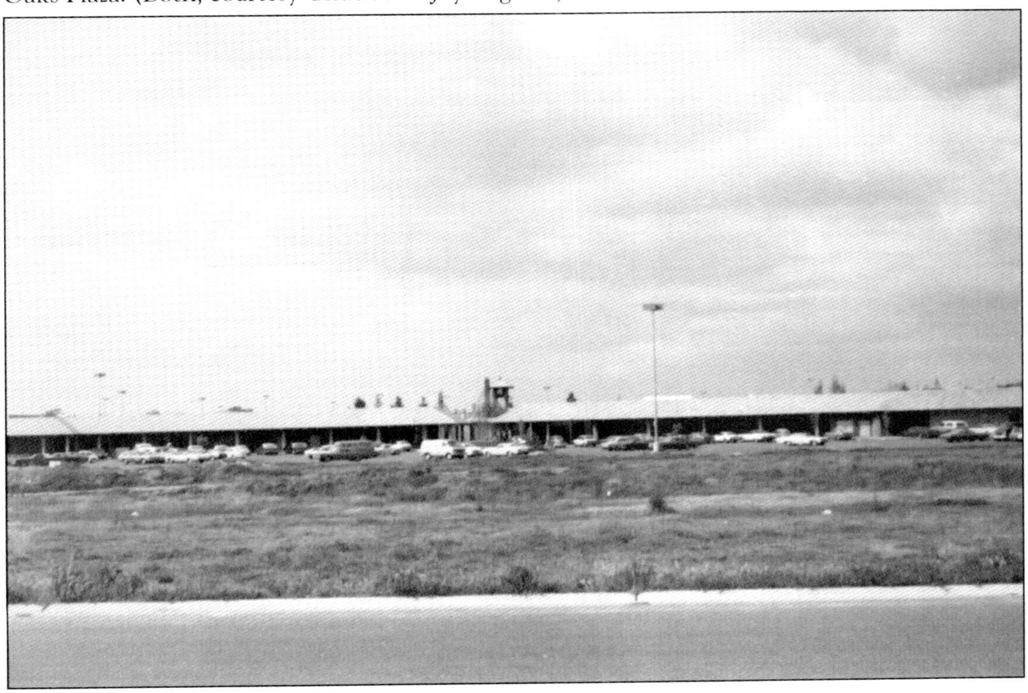

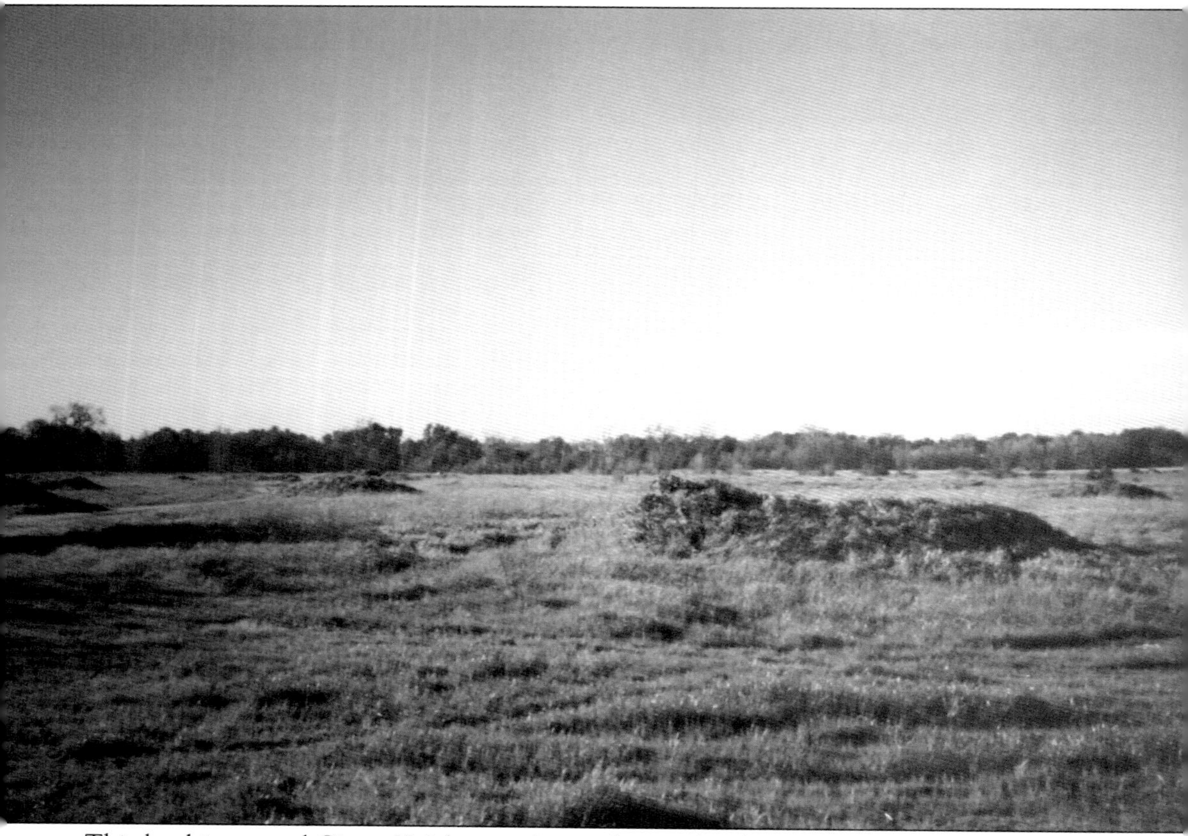

This land in central Citrus Heights on the southern side of Auburn Boulevard was formerly owned by Adolph and Catherine Van Maren. It was inherited by their daughter May (Stock) Corlett and eventually passed down to John Stock in the late 1970s. Presently, Stock Ranch, a portion of which is still owned by John Stock, houses Costco and Wal-Mart, over 43 acres of residential development, and 32 acres of open space. This open space is one of the last remaining undeveloped areas in the city. (Courtesy Jim Van Maren.)

Seven

WAR YEARS

World War II brought many changes to Citrus Heights. One of the first local actions was to organize a surveillance corps. The purpose of the Ground Observer Corps was to alert the community in case of an air attack. Surveillance went on 24 hours a day, seven days a week between December 1941 and October 1942. Sylvan School students were recruited to work during the day while at school. They used the school phone to report any aircraft. A 15-foot tower was soon built that included a platform and phone. By the end of 1942, the Air Force operated a radar detection system, and the community-manned observation station was no longer needed.

A number of young men and woman were either drafted into or enlisted in the military. The government mandated rationing, using food and gasoline stamps for this purpose. During World War II, many of the Citrus Heights volunteer firefighters were called to war. Formed in 1942 by fire chief Eugene Desimone, the Ladies Auxiliary helped fight fires in the local area and beyond. It was one of the country's earliest all-female firefighting crews.

In the midst of the war, a Signal Corps Replacement Center, called Camp Kohler, was constructed in the Sacramento Valley in 1943. The facility served a number of purposes. It was used as an Army and Air Force basic training and advanced communication training site. It also housed the Walerga Collection Center, an interim detention facility for Japanese Americans. In June 1947, a passing train ignited a grass fire. The Ladies Auxiliary responded to the fire, and a limited area of the camp was destroyed. While the members continued to fight fires afterwards, 1947 marked the end of the Ladies Auxiliary.

There are two monuments dedicated to veterans in the Citrus Heights area. The one at the Sylvan Cemetery honors veterans from all military conflicts. It was placed there by the Veterans of Foreign Wars. The second monument is located in the Rose Garden at Rusch Park. It lists the names of 272 men and women from Citrus Heights who were in World War II.

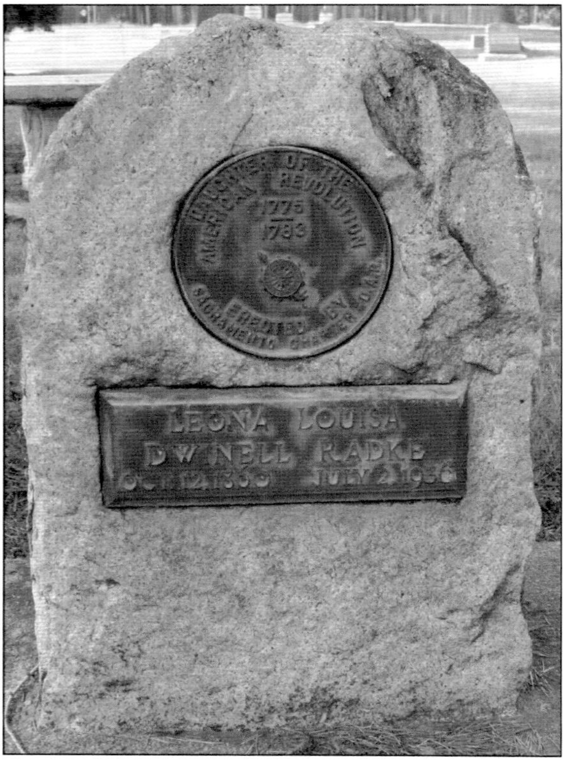

The Daughters of the American Revolution are responsible for this gravestone at Sylvan Cemetery. It honors veteran Dwinell Parke, who died in 1800. (Courtesy Stephanie Cotter.)

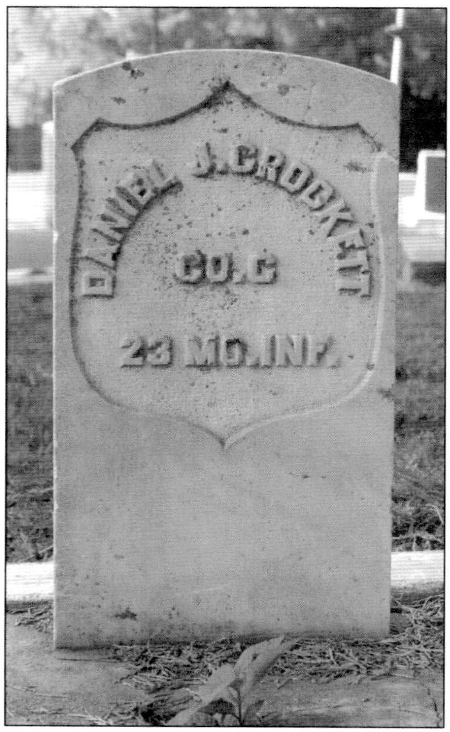

Civil War veterans Richard A. Astill, Alvin E. Farnham, Daniel J. Crockett, and Amos McGee are buried in Sylvan Cemetery. The Astill family lives in the area. (Courtesy Wilma Camilleri and James Monteton.)

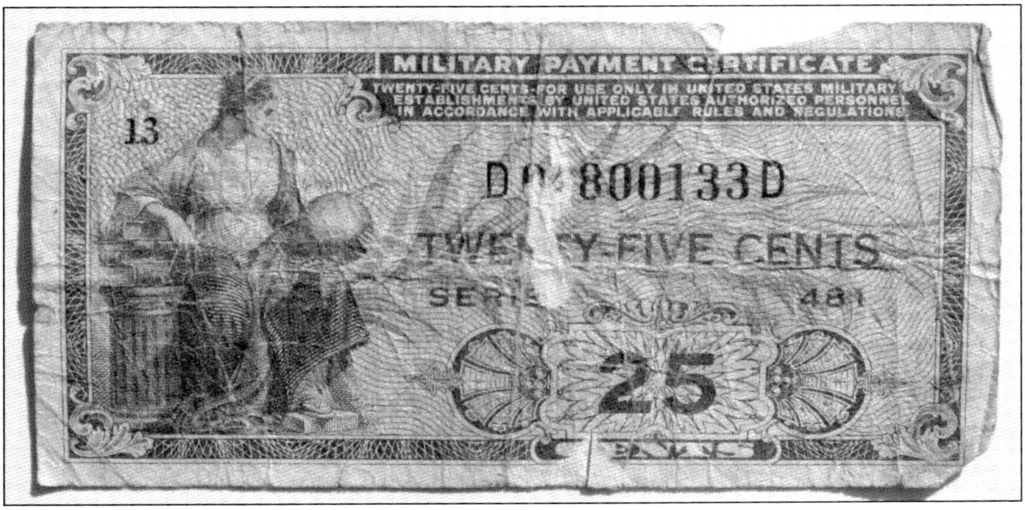

During World War II, servicemen and women on military bases used notes like this 25¢ military payment certificate. (Courtesy Jim Van Maren.)

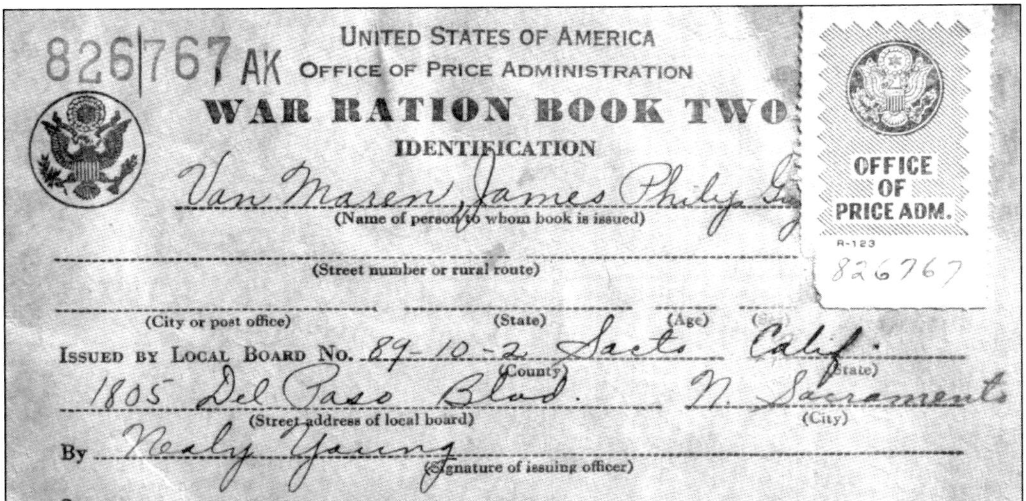
826767 AK

UNITED STATES OF AMERICA
OFFICE OF PRICE ADMINISTRATION

WAR RATION BOOK TWO

IDENTIFICATION

Van Maren, James Philip G
(Name of person to whom book is issued)

(Street number or rural route)

(City or post office) (State) (Age) (Sex)

OFFICE OF PRICE ADM.
R-123
826767

ISSUED BY LOCAL BOARD No. 89-10-2 Sacto Calif.
(County) (State)
1805 Del Paso Blvd. N. Sacramento
(Street address of local board) (City)

By Nealy Young
(Signature of issuing officer)

SIGNATURE
(To be signed by the person to whom this book is issued. If such person is unable to sign because of age or incapacity, another may sign in his behalf)

WARNING

1 This book is the property of the United States Government. It is unlawful to sell or give it to any other person or to use it or permit anyone else to use it, except to obtain rationed goods for the person to whom it was issued.
2 This book must be returned to the War Price and Rationing Board which issued it, if the person to whom it was issued is inducted into the armed services of the United States, or leaves the country for more than 30 days, or dies. The address of the Board appears above.
3 A person who finds a lost War Ration Book must return it to the War Price and Rationing Board which issued it.
4 PERSONS WHO VIOLATE RATIONING REGULATIONS ARE SUBJECT TO $10,000 FINE OR IMPRISONMENT, OR BOTH.

OPA Form No. R-121 16—30853-1

Issued to James Philip Guy Van Maren and used during World War II, this war ration book contained stamps. Each stamp authorizes the person to whom the book is issued to purchase rationed goods in the quantities and at times designated by the US Office of Price Administration. Without the stamps, citizens were unable to purchase those specific goods. (Courtesy Jim Van Maren.)

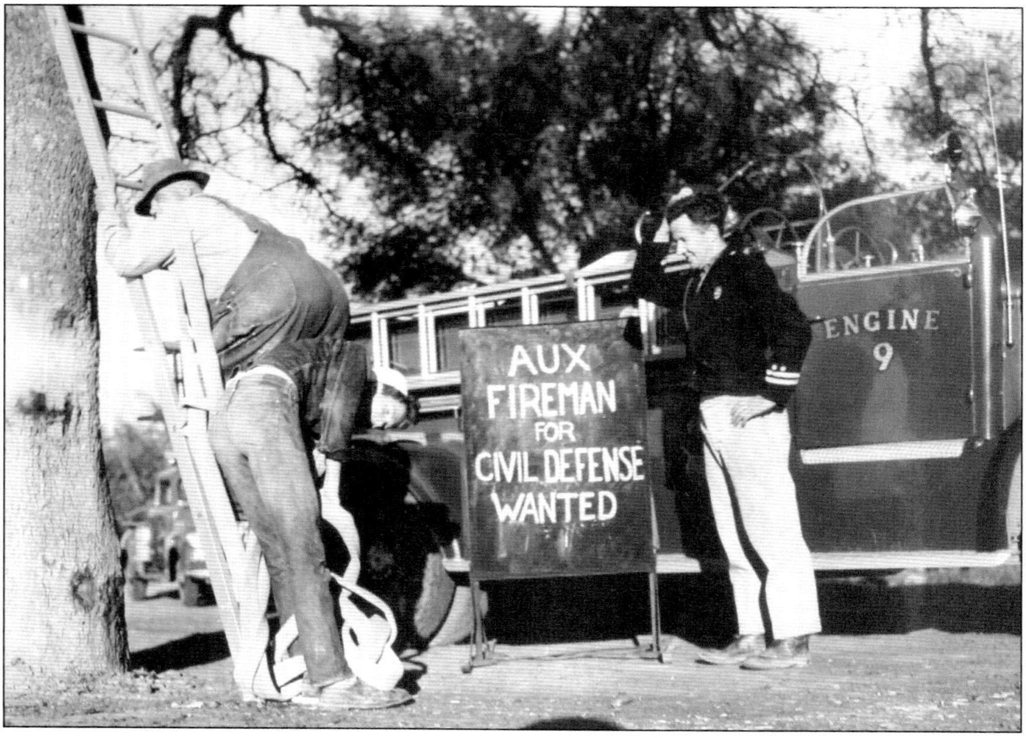

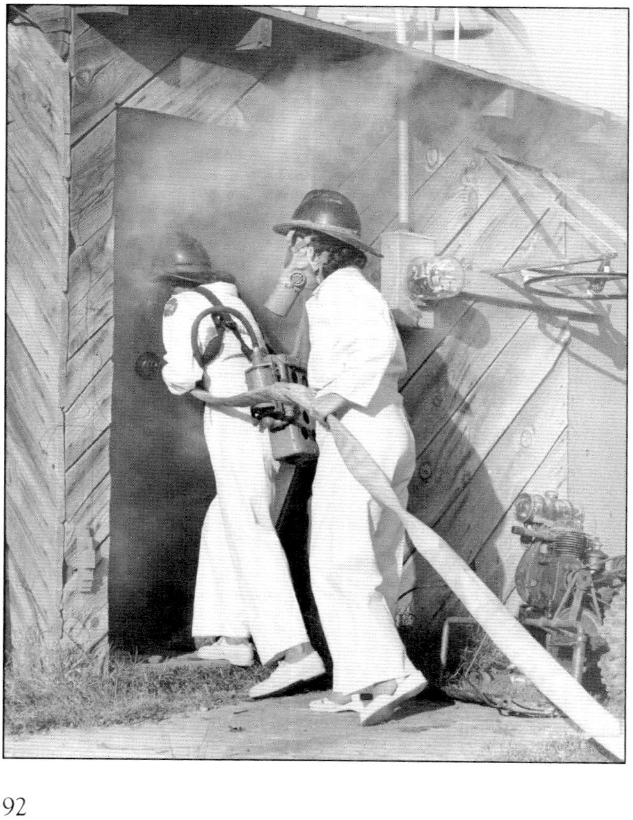

During World War II, California governor Earl Warren noted, "Women . . . respond patriotically to the call to relieve men needed elsewhere in war activities." (Courtesy Warren Desimone collection, City of Citrus Heights.)

Members of the Ladies in White are seen responding to a building fire. (Courtesy Warren Desimone collection, City of Citrus Heights.)

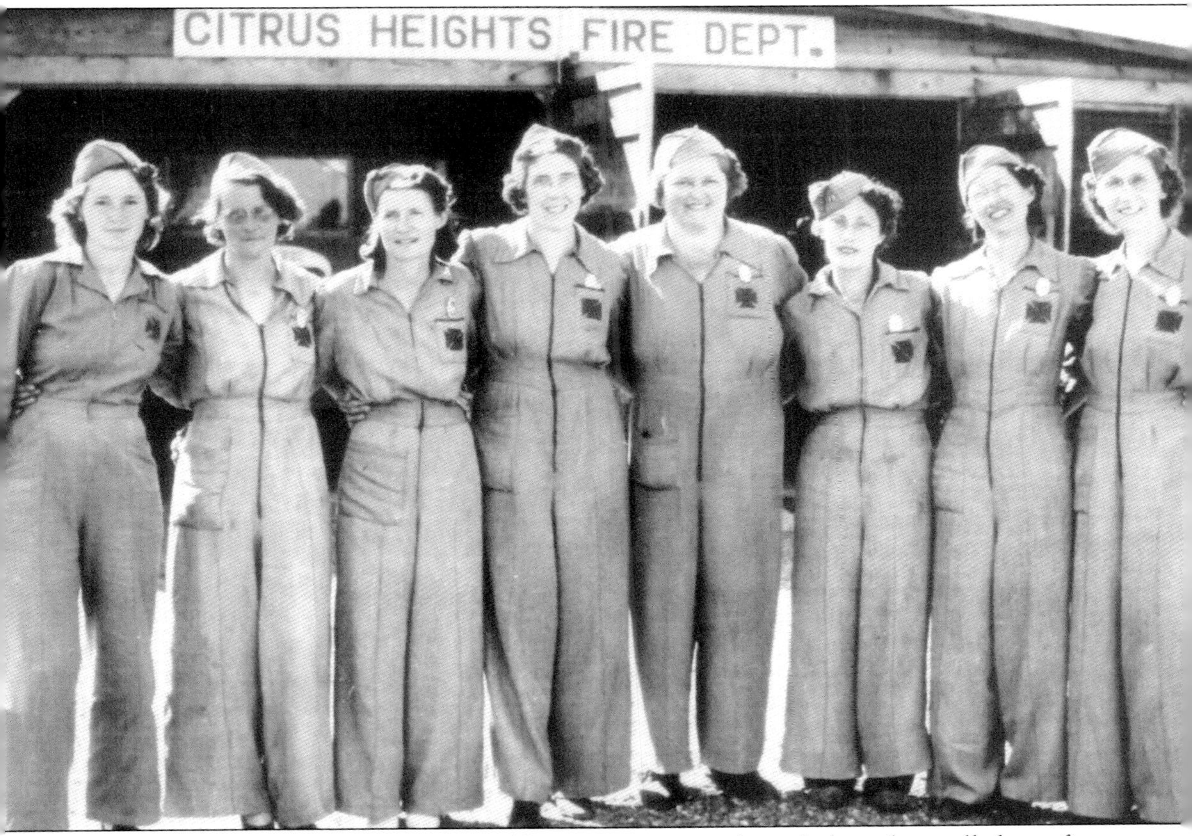

Members of the Ladies Auxiliary wore blue jumpsuits over their clothes when called to a fire. Posing in front of the Citrus Heights Fire Department are, from left to right, Oneta Harper, Elisabeth Stoddard, Lola Oldham, Verda Taylor, Palmyra Ravinale, Mary Bost, Zella Desimone, and Estaline Mulch. (Courtesy Warren Desimone collection, City of Citrus Heights.)

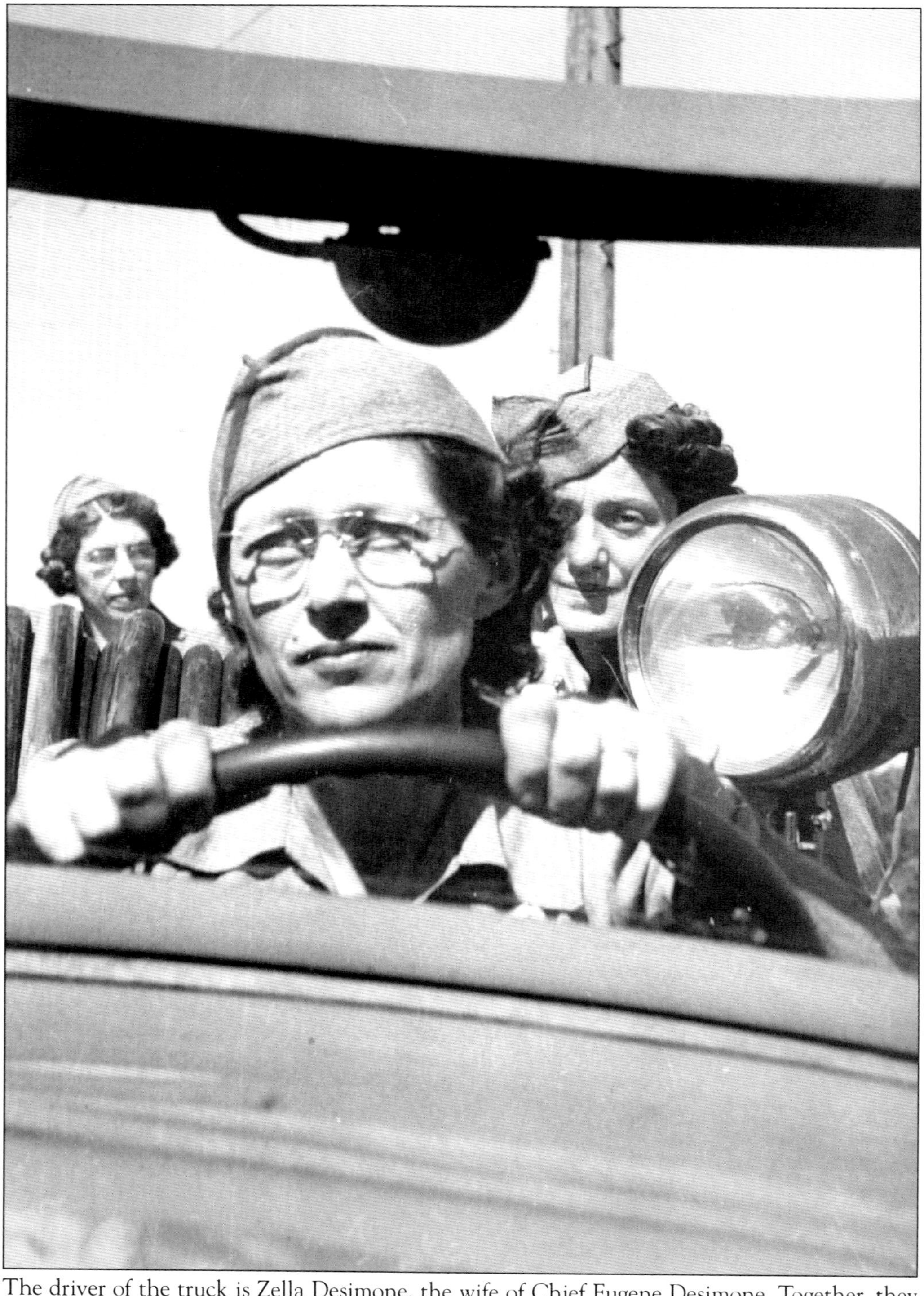

The driver of the truck is Zella Desimone, the wife of Chief Eugene Desimone. Together, they formed the Ladies Auxiliary to help fight fires during the war years. Also shown are Verda Taylor (left) and Mary Bost. (Courtesy Warren Desimone collection, City of Citrus Heights.)

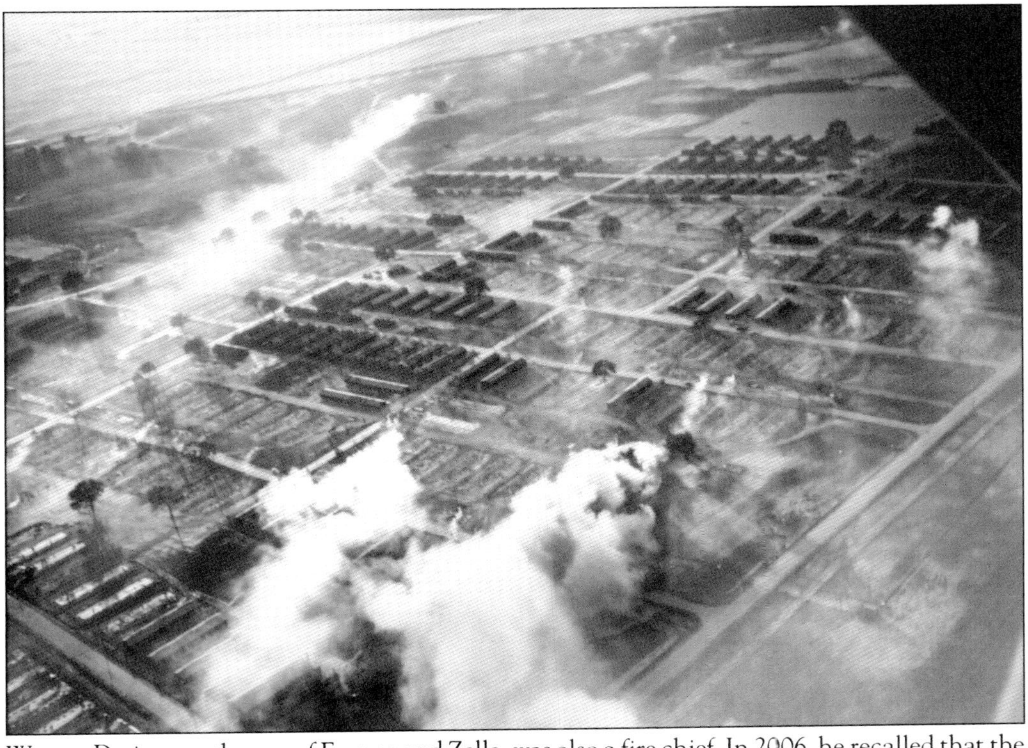

Warren Desimone, the son of Eugene and Zella, was also a fire chief In 2006, he recalled that the "Camp Kohler fire was the worst that we ever had—a real whopper." Reed Jordan, a *Sacramento Bee* reporter, noted that "viewed from the air, the burned area looked not unlike a battlefield." (Courtesy *Sacramento Bee*.)

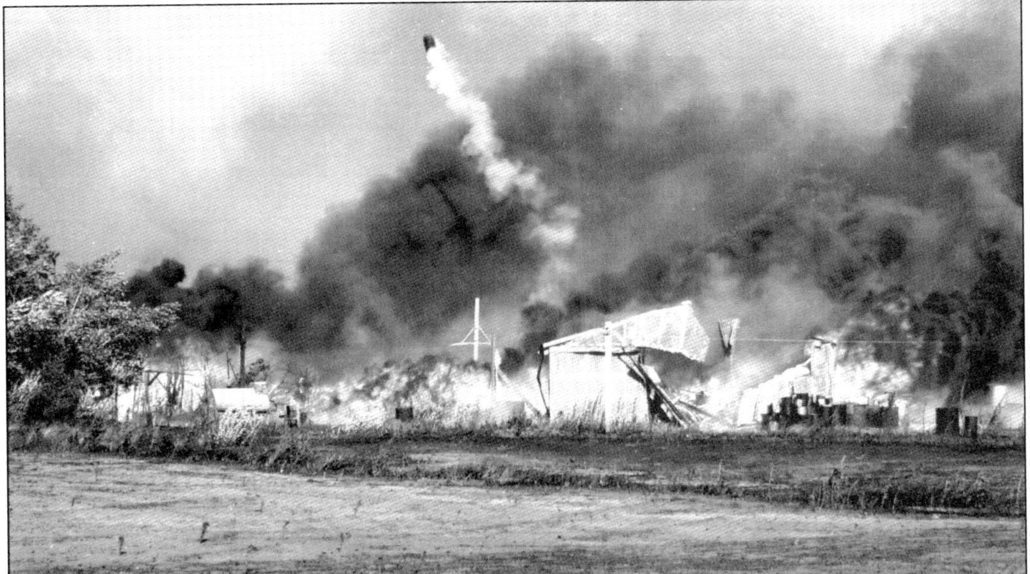

An oil drum skyrockets into the air as flames lick at the oil tanks of the Earl Oil Company plant. (Courtesy *Sacramento Bee*; photograph by Irving Camp.)

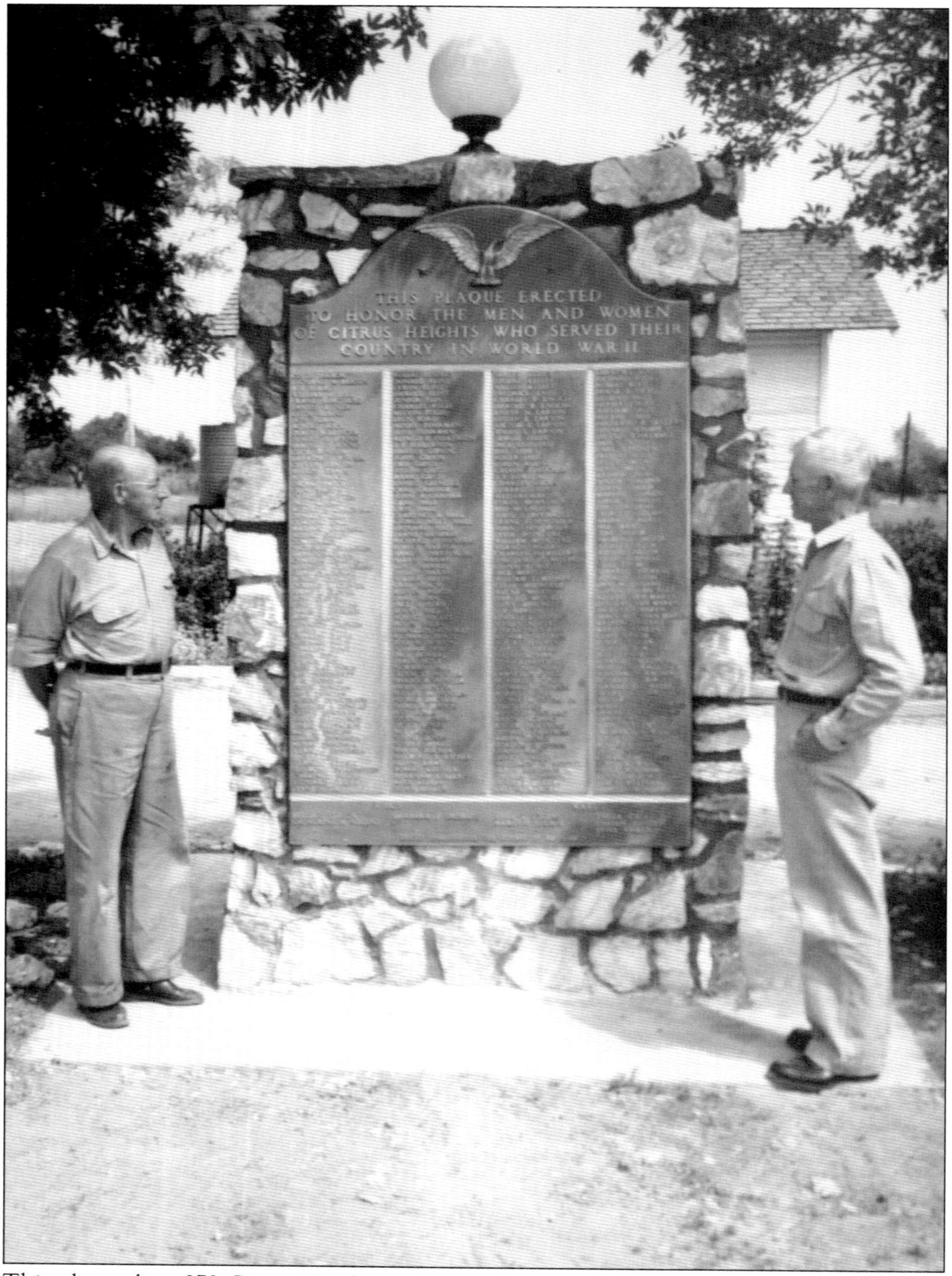

This plaque lists 272 Citrus Heights residents who served during World War II. The 1948 monument was originally located in front of the first library on Sylvan Road, which was on land donated by William Cobb. It was relocated to the Rusch Park rose garden in 1976. (Courtesy Roseville Historical Society Collection, City of Citrus Heights.)

Eight

Compassion

Compassion was strong among early settlers, particularly in their desire to educate their children. Schools needed to be constructed. There was no government program to support educational ambitions, so the farmers gave time and funds to this purpose. They pooled their money to build a grammar school, hire teachers, and procure school supplies, including pencils and paper.

Respecting health concerns, the settlers, most of whom were from Europe, used their old family remedies to care for the ill. Since there were no doctors to serve families, some women became midwives. There was no hospital other than the one in Sacramento. As time passed, doctors became available.

In the 1930s, priorities were jobs, food, and funds for basic necessities and to pay the bills. In 1924, residents organized the Citrus Heights Community Club, a nongovernmental association where the residents could come together to resolve social and infrastructure issues, helping those in need and making the community a better place to live. This was the forerunner of the service clubs in Citrus Heights.

Through their benevolence, the outstanding service organizations of Citrus Heights commit their time and funds to help others. The clubs have benefitted many families from more than just a financial standpoint, including consolation in times of grief and pain. The compassion of these clubs shows they are warmhearted, sincere, and enthusiastic. Above all, they care about the people. The clubs invest a lot of time and effort to make fundraising a success so that they can provide food, pay health care bills, assist in paying living expenses, provide Christmas baskets, and otherwise gather funds to help those less fortunate to improve their lives. The Rotary Club, Kiwanis Club, Lions Club, Regional Chamber of Commerce, Women's Club, Soroptimist Club, Hearts for Parks, Relay for Life, and others are present in Citrus Heights. These organizations are an example of what democracy is all about. Citrus Heights is a proud and spirited city. In a study of these service organizations, close to $122,000 was donated to charity in 2010. It is estimated that there could be an equal amount of money contributed by other groups, including local churches.

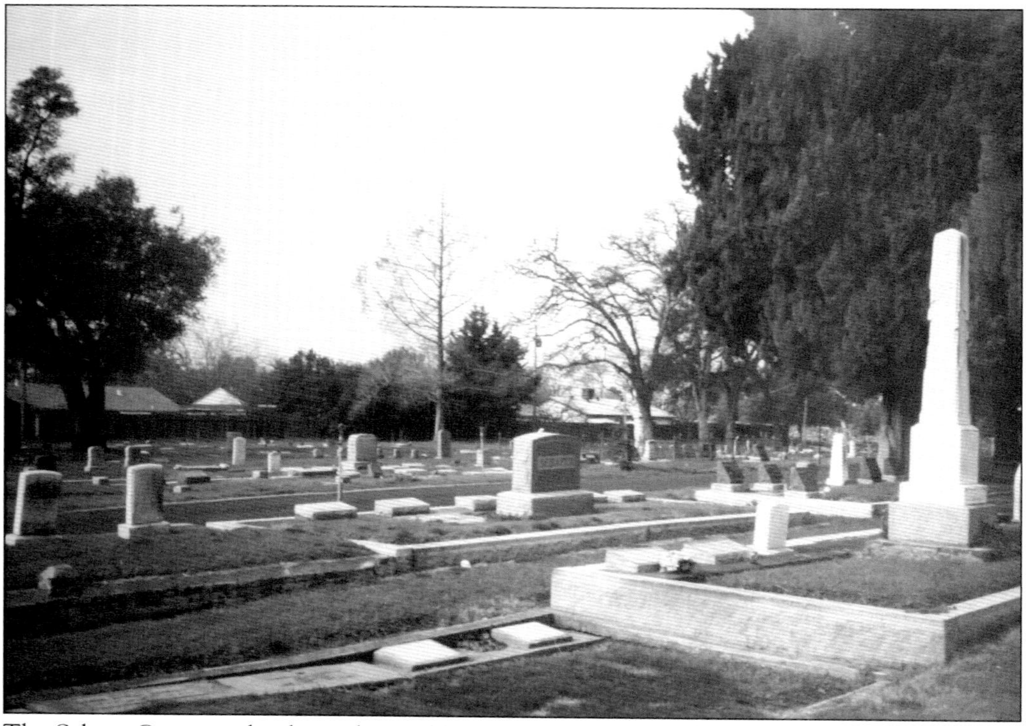

The Sylvan Cemetery land was donated by Daniel Lewis in 1863. Originally only half an acre, today the cemetery comprises in excess of 20 acres along Auburn Boulevard. Shown below is the cemetery's first grave marker, that of John Horton, whose death made the cemetery necessary. Horton was a laborer at the J.F. Cross Farm. (Above, courtesy City of Citrus Heights; below, courtesy Stephanie Cotter.)

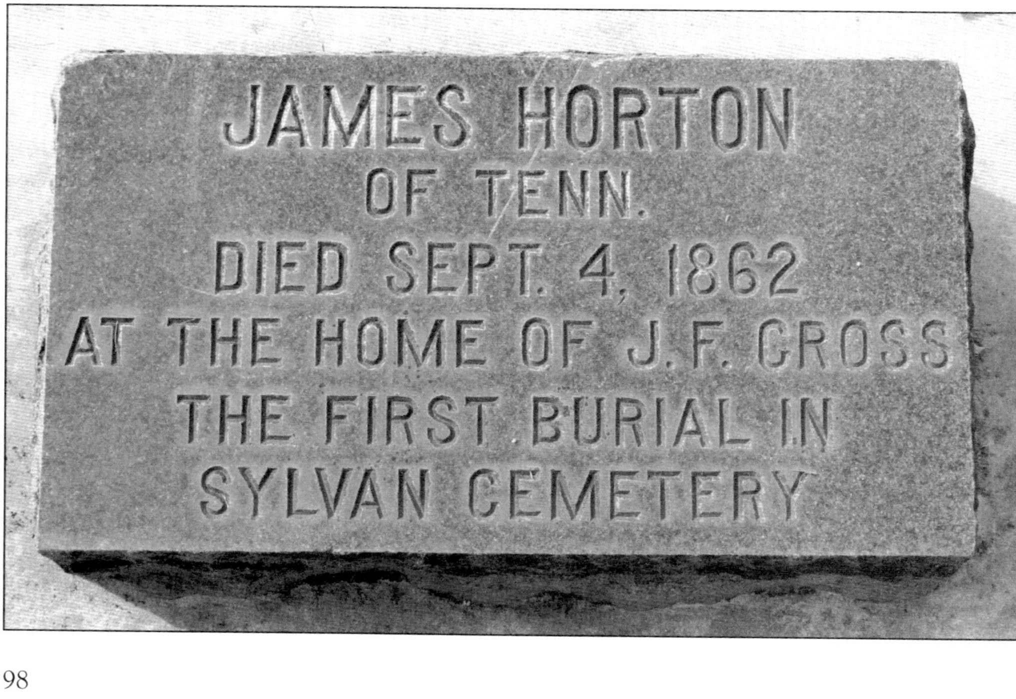

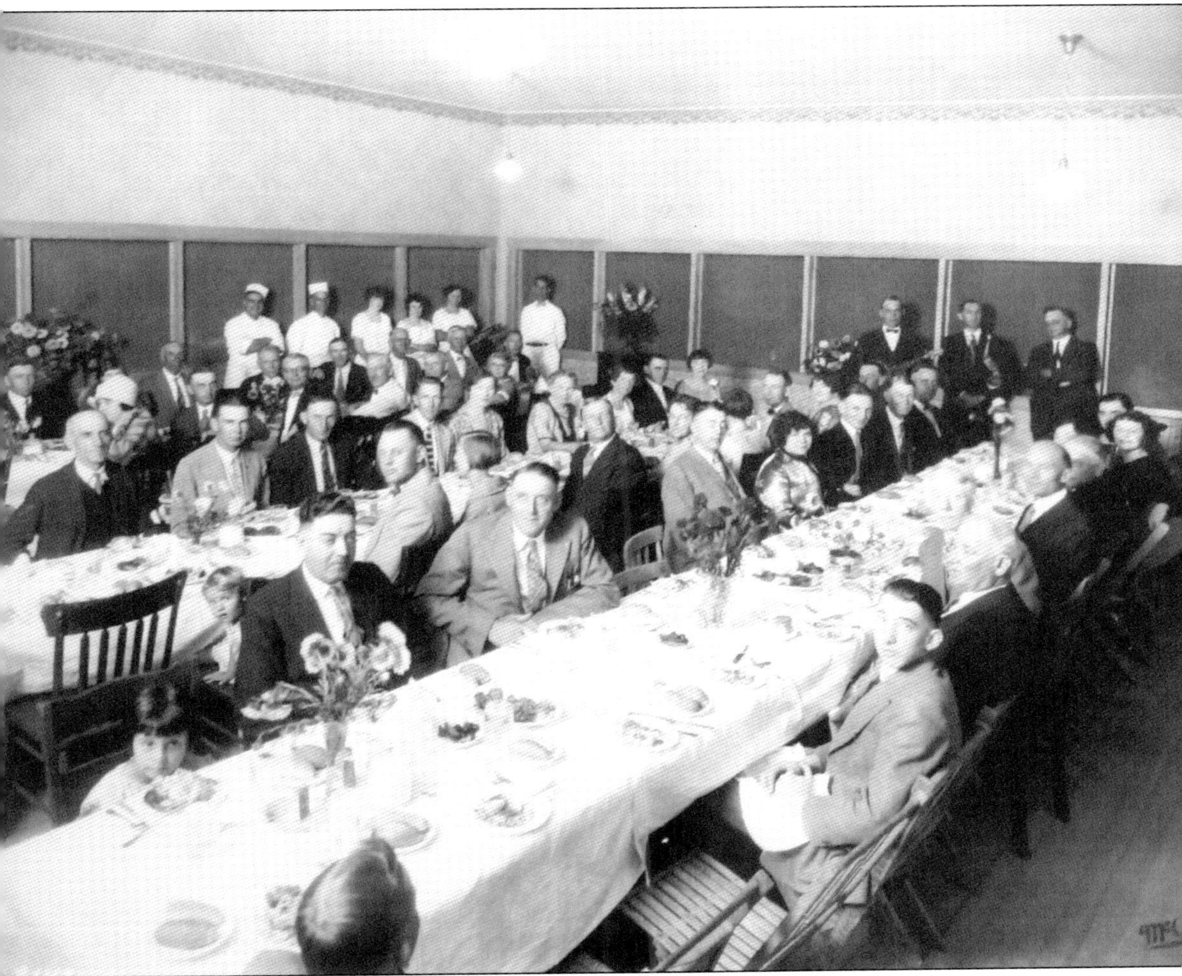

In this image, a service club dines at the Florida Inn. These clubs have contributed dramatically to the quality of life for many in Citrus Heights. (Courtesy Coldani family.)

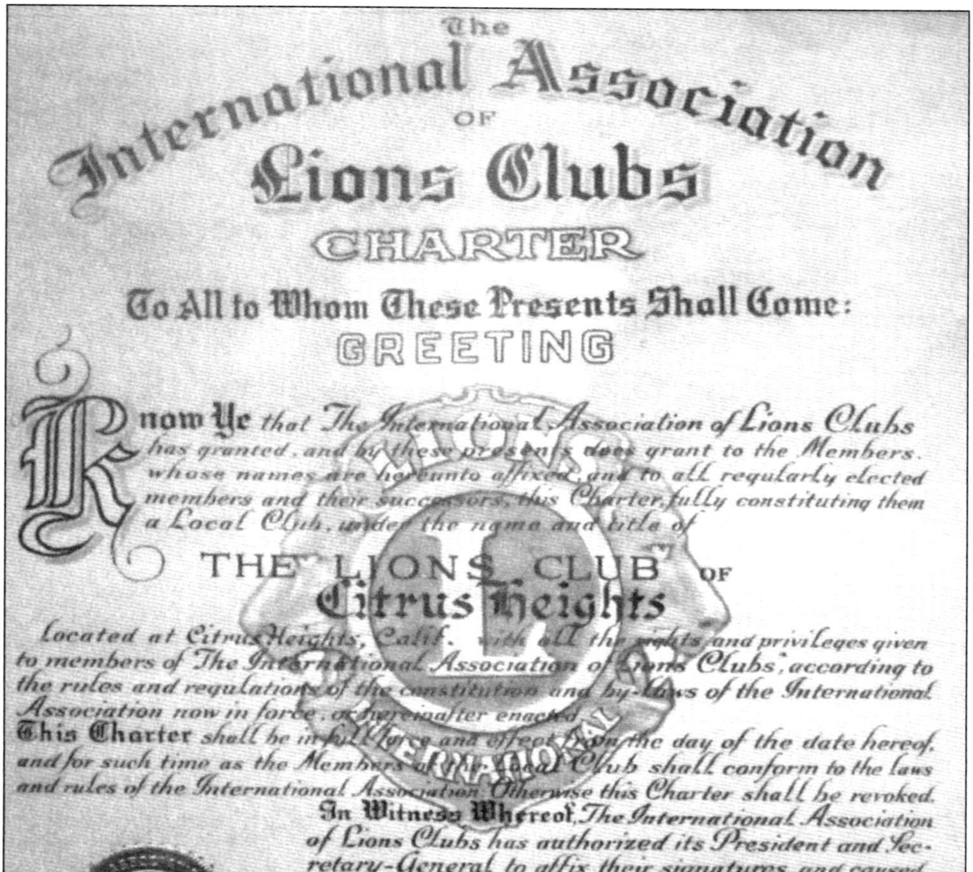

The International Association of Lions Clubs

CHARTER

To All to Whom These Presents Shall Come:

GREETING

Know Ye that The International Association of Lions Clubs has granted, and by these presents does grant to the Members, whose names are hereunto affixed, and to all regularly elected members and their successors, this Charter, fully constituting them a Local Club, under the name and title of

THE LIONS CLUB OF Citrus Heights

located at Citrus Heights, Calif. with all the rights and privileges given to members of The International Association of Lions Clubs, according to the rules and regulations of the constitution and by-laws of the International Association now in force, or hereafter enacted.

This Charter shall be in full force and effect from the day of the date hereof, and for such time as the Members of the Local Club shall conform to the laws and rules of the International Association. Otherwise this Charter shall be revoked.

In Witness Whereof, The International Association of Lions Clubs has authorized its President and Secretary-General to affix their signatures, and caused the seal of the Association to be hereunto affixed this 13th day of October in the year of our Lord 1949

Charter Members

This is the charter for the International Association of Lions Clubs, October 13, 1949. It was the first service club in Citrus Heights, with headquarters located on Sylvan Road across from the Community Clubhouse. (Courtesy Rebekkah McCurry.)

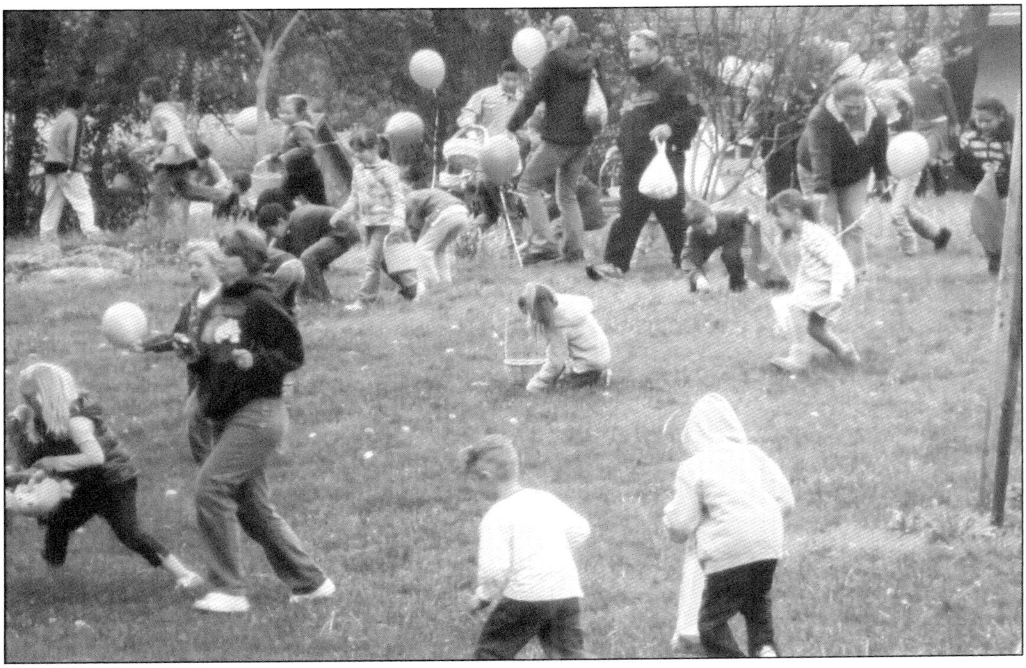

The Kiwanis Club of Citrus Heights is involved in a number of charitable works, both locally and internationally. Above, local children enjoy an Easter egg hunt that was sponsored by the Kiwanis Club at Rusch Park. Below, some of the medical supplies gathered by club members for a Bulgarian orphanage are pictured in 2008. (Both, courtesy Bill Hooper, Kiwanis Club of Citrus Heights.)

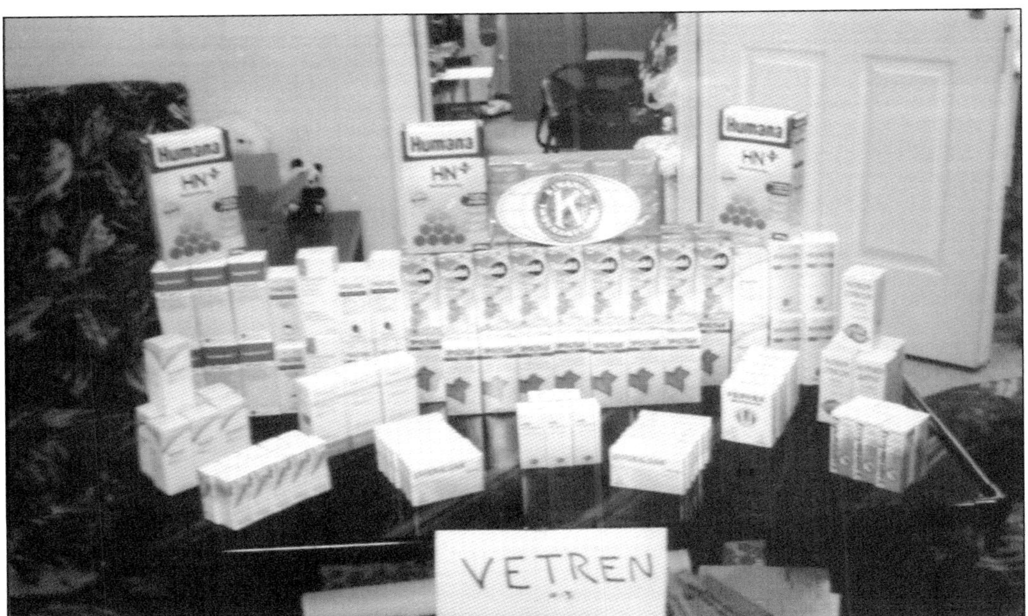

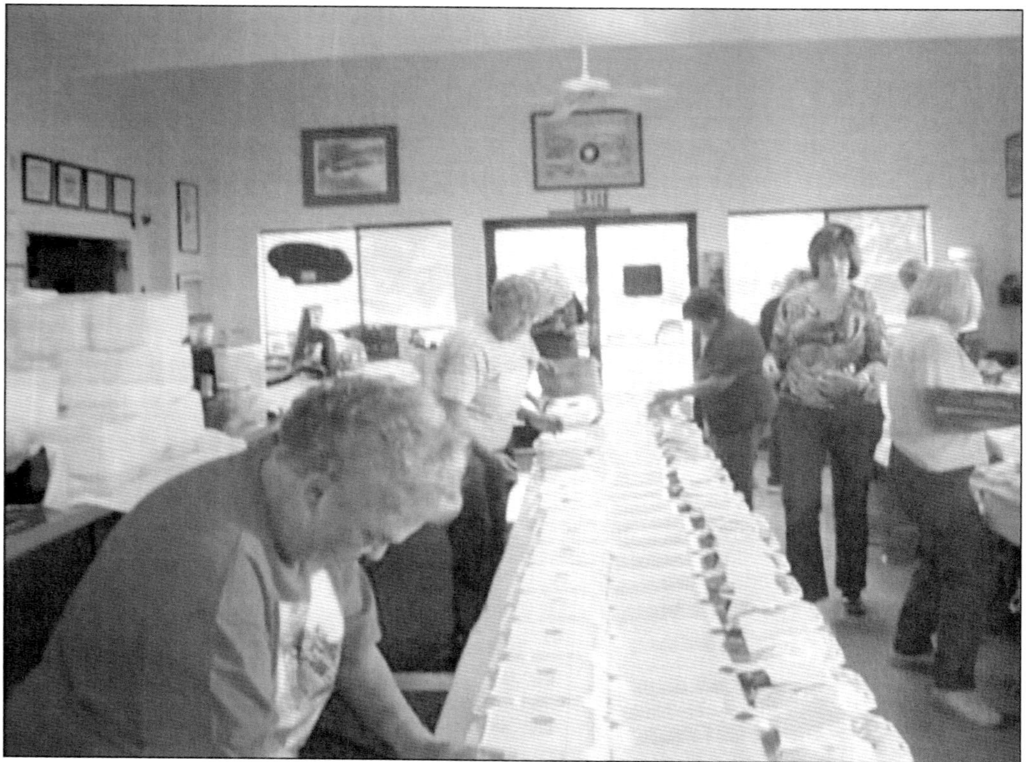

The Soroptimist Club is an international volunteer organization of women who work to improve the lives of others. In the photograph above, club members are preparing lunch boxes to be sold as a fundraiser to help families in need. Costumed members (below) have just won the Mayor's Award for their float at the City's Red, White, and Blue Parade. (Both, courtesy Bonnie Hart, Soroptimist Club of Citrus Heights.)

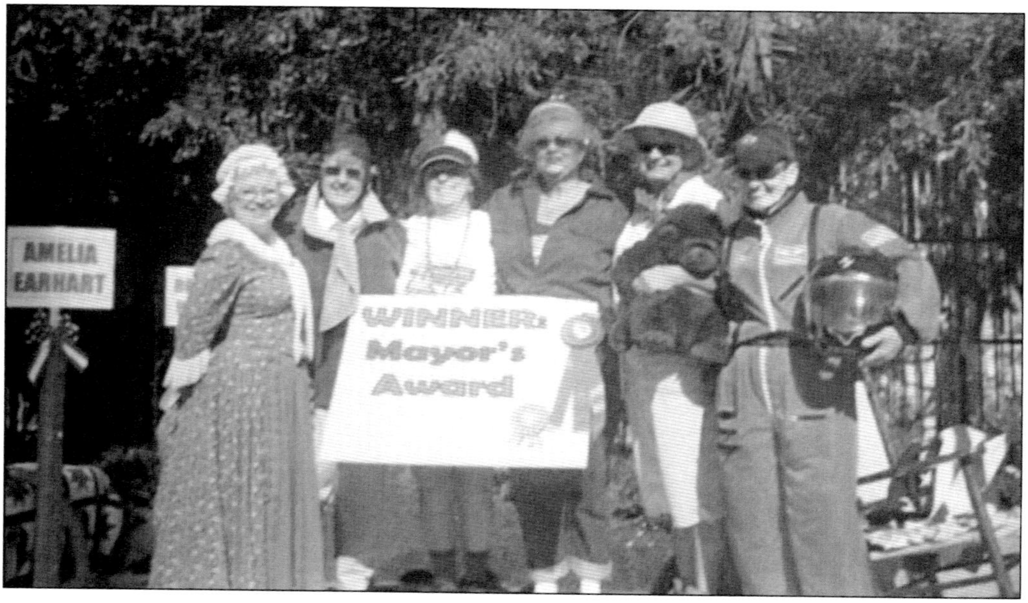

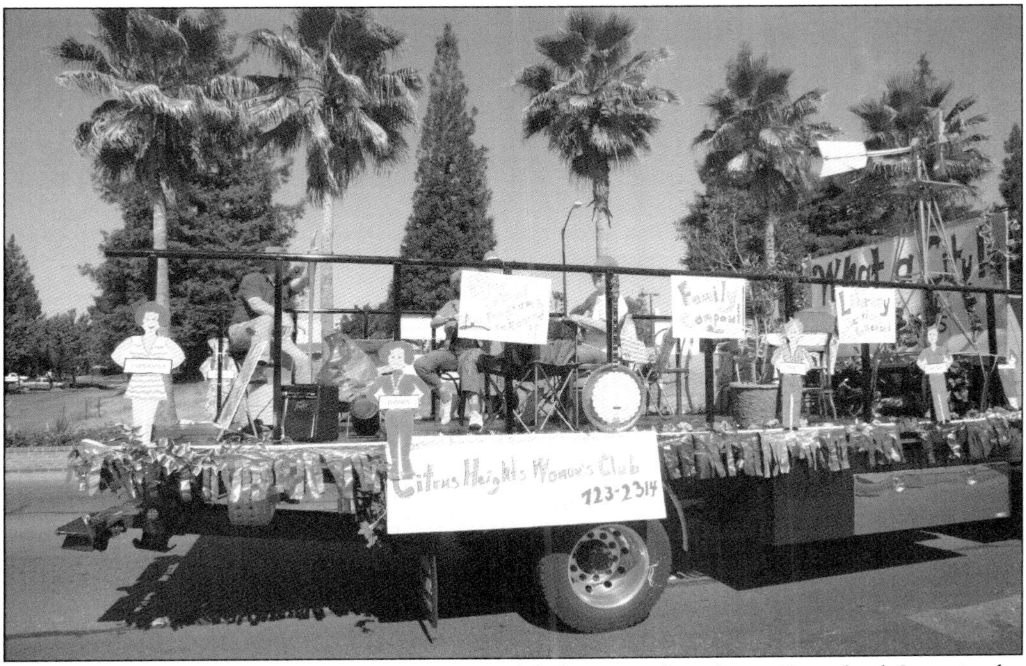

Pictured above is the Citrus Heights Women's Club float traveling down Greenback Lane in the annual Red, White, and Blue Parade sponsored by the City of Citrus Heights. (Courtesy City of Citrus Heights.)

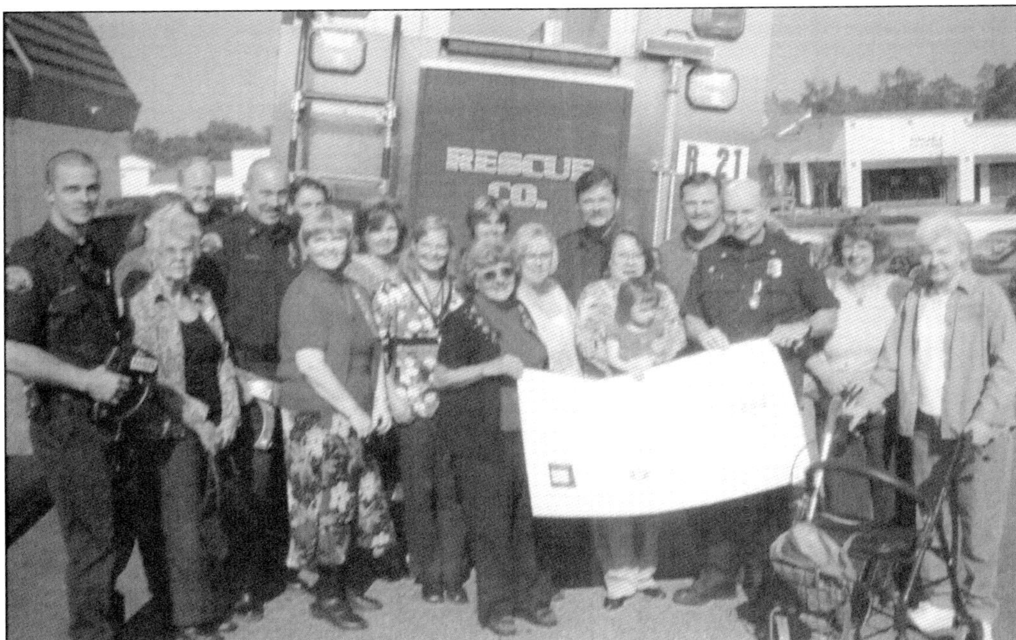

The Women's Club donated $3,000 to the Sacramento Metropolitan Fire District to purchase a thermal imaging scanner, which improves emergency response. (Courtesy Emily Neeland, Citrus Heights Women's Club.)

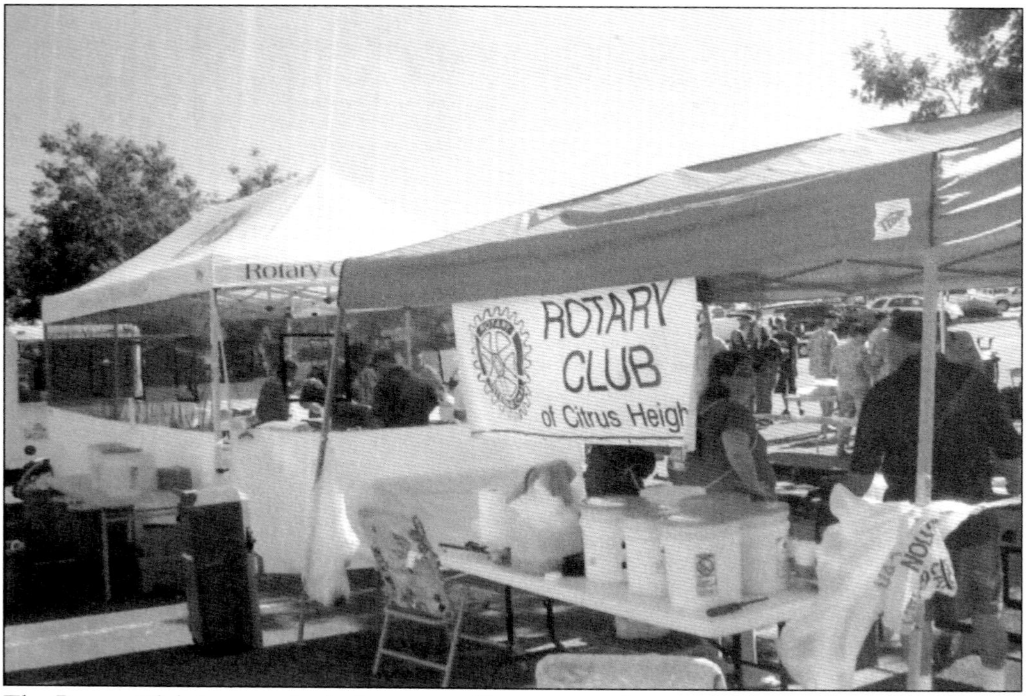

The Rotary Club is comprised of a group of businesspeople engaged in various local activities, including charitable causes. The Citrus Heights Rotary, above, is at the Red, White, and Blue Parade with refreshments for parade-goers. Below, members work hard to cook and serve pancakes to help support the club's many charitable undertakings. (Both, courtesy Rotary Club of Citrus Heights.)

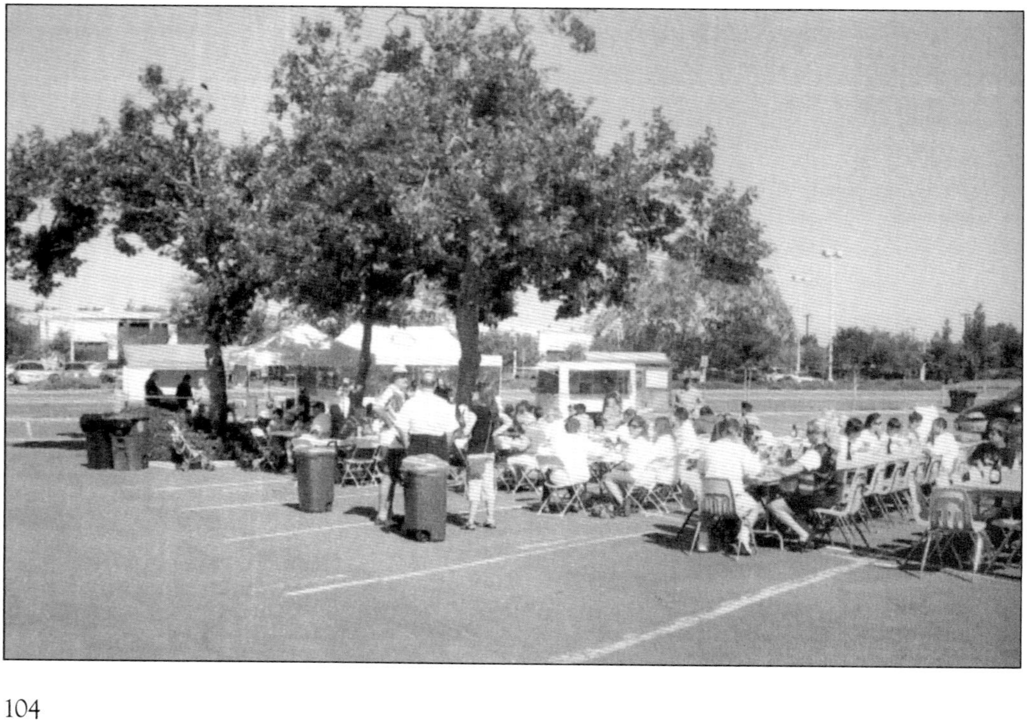

Nine

The Spirited People

Citrus Heights abounds with examples of spirited people striving to create a better community for all.

In the mid-19th century, early Citrus Heights settler Constantina Hirtzig Van Maren worked for her sister Emily Hirtzig Wilson Johnson and her husband, Levi Johnson, who owned the 12 Mile Roadhouse. When Constantine did not receive compensation for the work she provided, she filed suit against the Johnsons for 27 months of back wages. In the midst of the ongoing litigation, Constantina married Peter Van Maren. The case eventually went to the California Supreme Court, which ruled in favor of Constantina. The main question of the case was as to the liability of the community property. With this 1863 decision, the court ruled that both husband and wife were to be responsible for the acts of either partner.

The Sacramento County Board of Supervisors approved an access road from Auburn Road to the eastern part of the district in 1864. Known today as Greenback Lane, it cuts through a number of ranches from Auburn Road to Folsom. The ranchers were in dispute with the county over the treasury greenback bills that the county wanted to use in payment for the land. The ranchers argued that the currency was worthless. They wanted to be paid in cash. A 1990 California State Senate proclamation notes that officials from the county came back to Constantina, a leader among the other ranchers, and asked her what to call the road. She replied, "Why don't you call it Greenback Lane."

In 1928, community residents were highly charged over the lack of support from the county to provide funds to maintain the rural roads and keep them free of potholes. The Community Club sponsored an annual Road Day. The spirit of the residents was outstanding. About 50 members would show up to patch up holes, clean drainage ditches, and improve school and cemetery grounds.

The greatest community action occurred when residents challenged the Local Agency Formation Commission (LAFCO) and the Sacramento County Board of Supervisors over the incorporation of Citrus Heights. The issue of a new city in Sacramento County was placed on the ballot. The momentum and spirit of the citizens led to establishment of the city on January 1, 1997. Residents received assistance from the local chamber of commerce, Citizens for Citrus Heights Incorporation, and the Citrus Heights Community Council. This effort demonstrates the power of the electorate when the cause is meaningful.

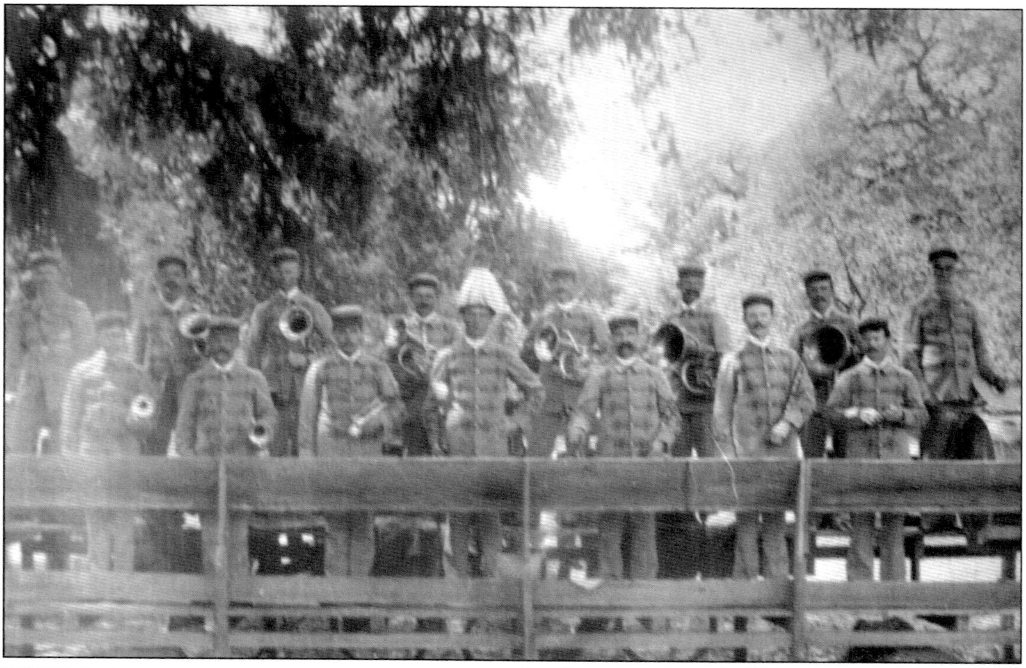

In this image is Schellhous Brothers Band at the Cobb's Service Station arbor at Sylvan Corners in 1906. (Courtesy Leonard M. Davis.)

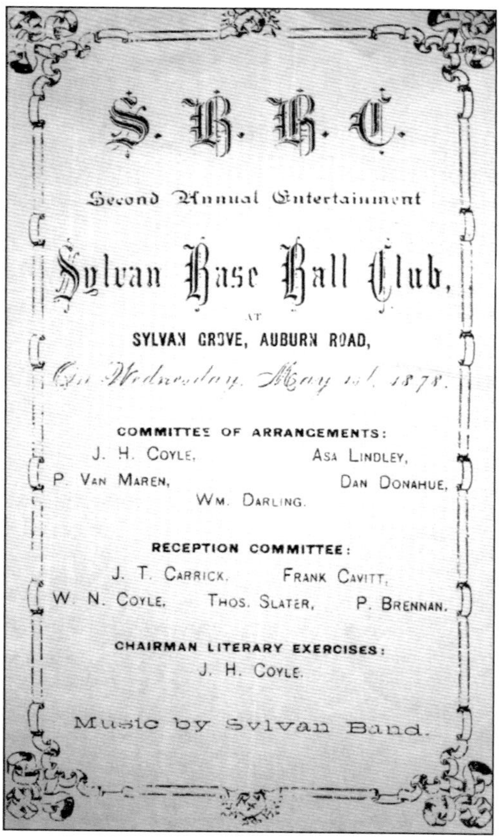

S. B. B. C.

Second Annual Entertainment

Sylvan Base Ball Club,

AT

SYLVAN GROVE, AUBURN ROAD,

On Wednesday, May 1st, 1878.

COMMITTEE OF ARRANGEMENTS:

J. H. COYLE, ASA LINDLEY,
P. VAN MAREN, DAN DONAHUE,
WM. DARLING.

RECEPTION COMMITTEE:

J. T. CARRICK. FRANK CAVITT.
W. N. COYLE. THOS. SLATER, P. BRENNAN.

CHAIRMAN LITERARY EXERCISES:

J. H. COYLE.

Music by Sylvan Band.

Members of the Sylvan Base Ball Club (S.B.B.C.) held a gala in 1878 at Sylvan Grove on Auburn Road (now Auburn Boulevard). (Courtesy Leonard M. Davis.)

Listed here are the 1878 members of the Sylvan Base Ball Club. (Courtesy Leonard M. Davis.)

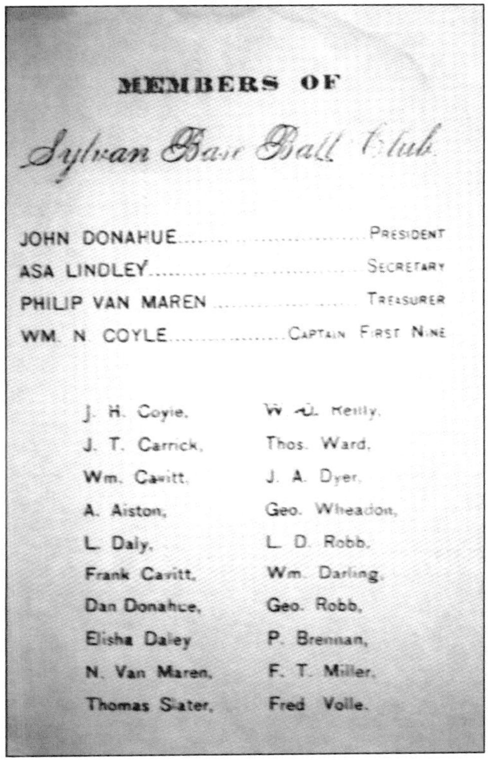

MEMBERS OF

Sylvan Base Ball Club

JOHN DONAHUE	PRESIDENT
ASA LINDLEY	SECRETARY
PHILIP VAN MAREN	TREASURER
WM. N. COYLE	CAPTAIN FIRST NINE

J. H. Coyle,	W. J. Kelly,
J. T. Carrick,	Thos. Ward,
Wm. Cavitt,	J. A. Dyer,
A. Aiston,	Geo. Wheadon,
L. Daly,	L. D. Robb,
Frank Cavitt,	Wm. Darling,
Dan Donahue,	Geo. Robb,
Elisha Daley	P. Brennan,
N. Van Maren,	F. T. Miller,
Thomas Slater,	Fred Volle.

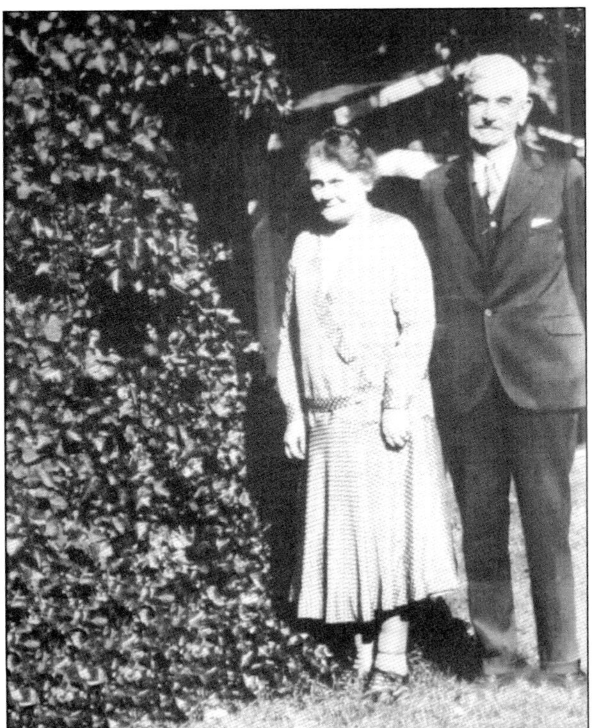

Adolph ("Pa") and Catherine ("Ma") Van Maren, owners of the Van Maren Ranch, are pictured here in 1937. Adolph was the son of Peter Van Maren, who settled in Citrus Heights in 1854. Catherine was well known for contributing food and clothing to the unfortunate in the 1930s. Adolph was very active in developing the grammar school and San Juan High School. (Courtesy Jim Van Maren.)

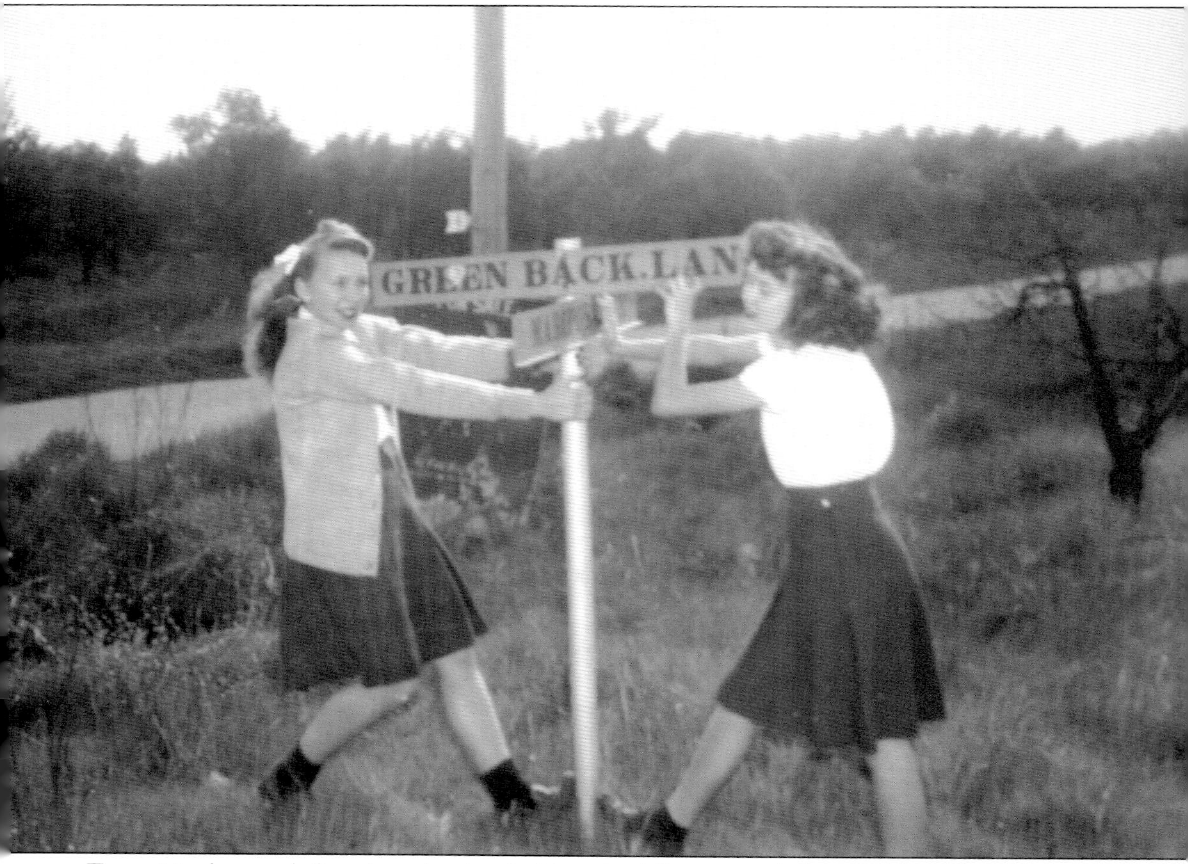

Two spirited young ladies place the sign for Greenback Lane near Auburn Boulevard in the 1940s. (Roseville Historical Society Photograph Collection, City of Citrus Heights.)

Pictured here are advertising fliers for the Florida Inn, a popular nightspot. (Courtesy Coldani family.)

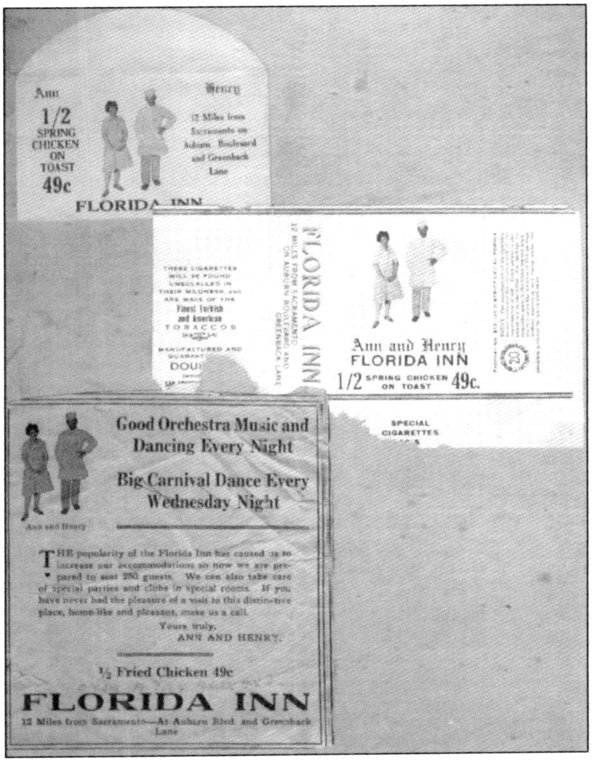

An evening of dining and dancing at the Florida Inn was captured in the 1920s. Note the curtained cubicles for private dining. (Courtesy Coldani family.)

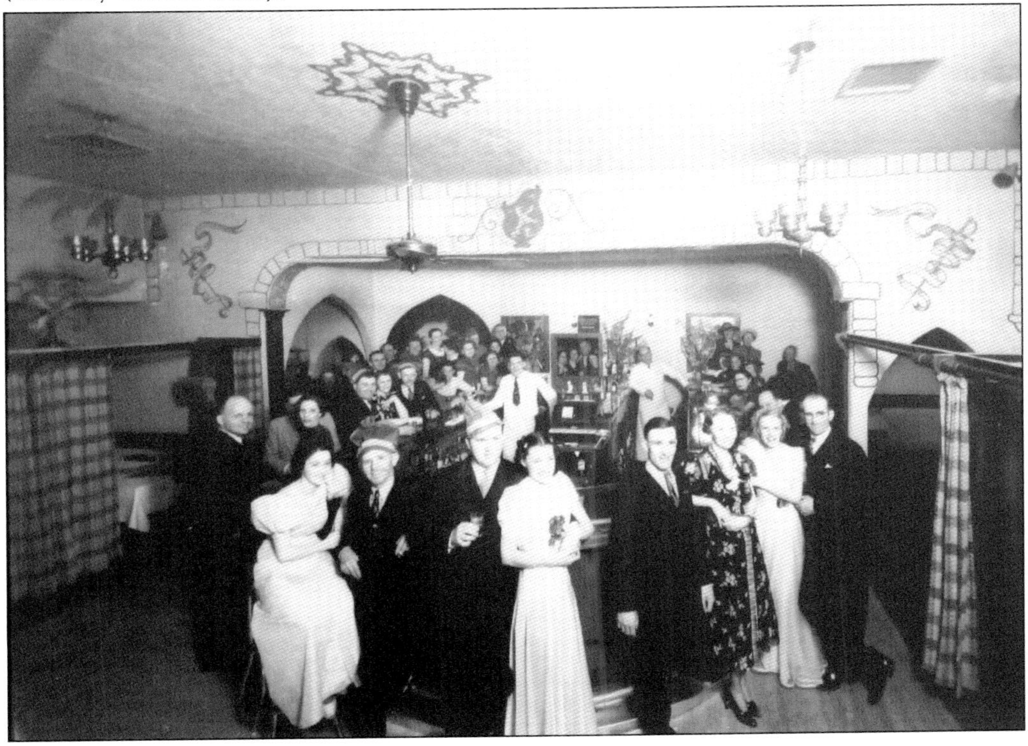

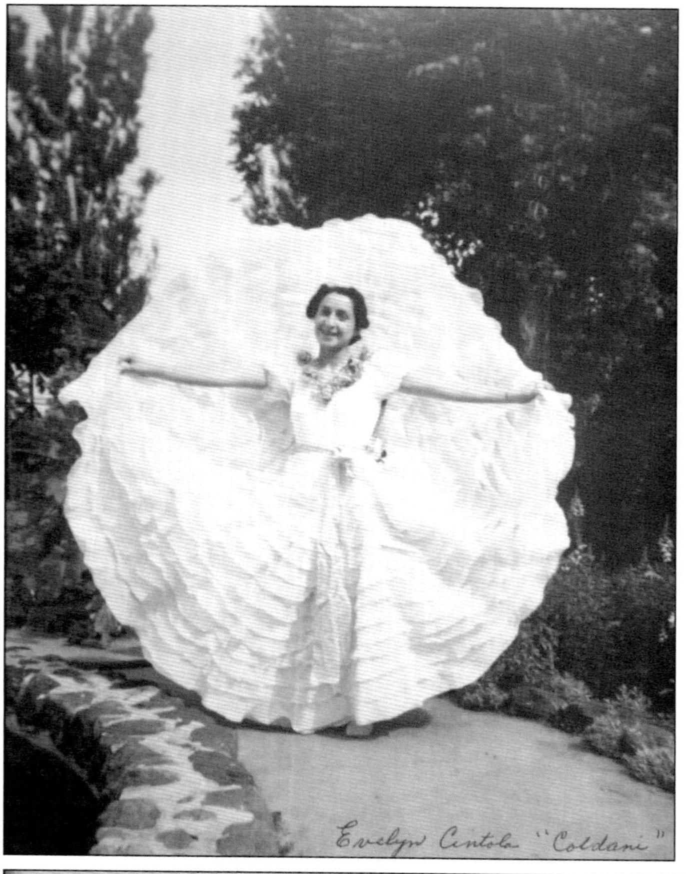

In this image taken at the Florida Inn, Evelyn Cintola shows off her Italian dress. (Courtesy Coldani family.)

Lena and Ann Coldani are seen playing musical instruments. (Courtesy Coldani family.)

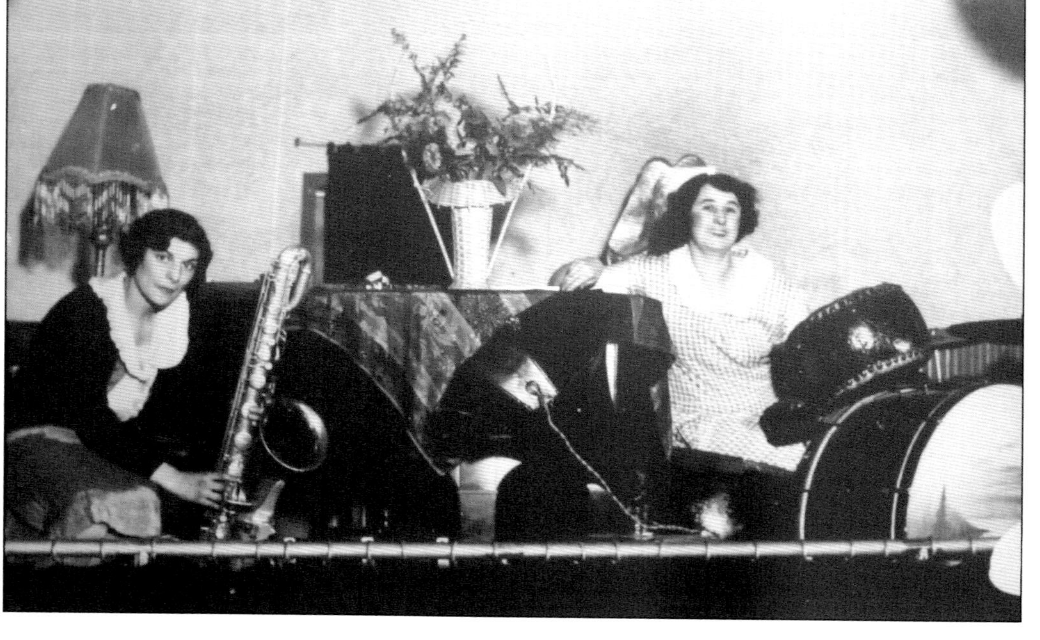

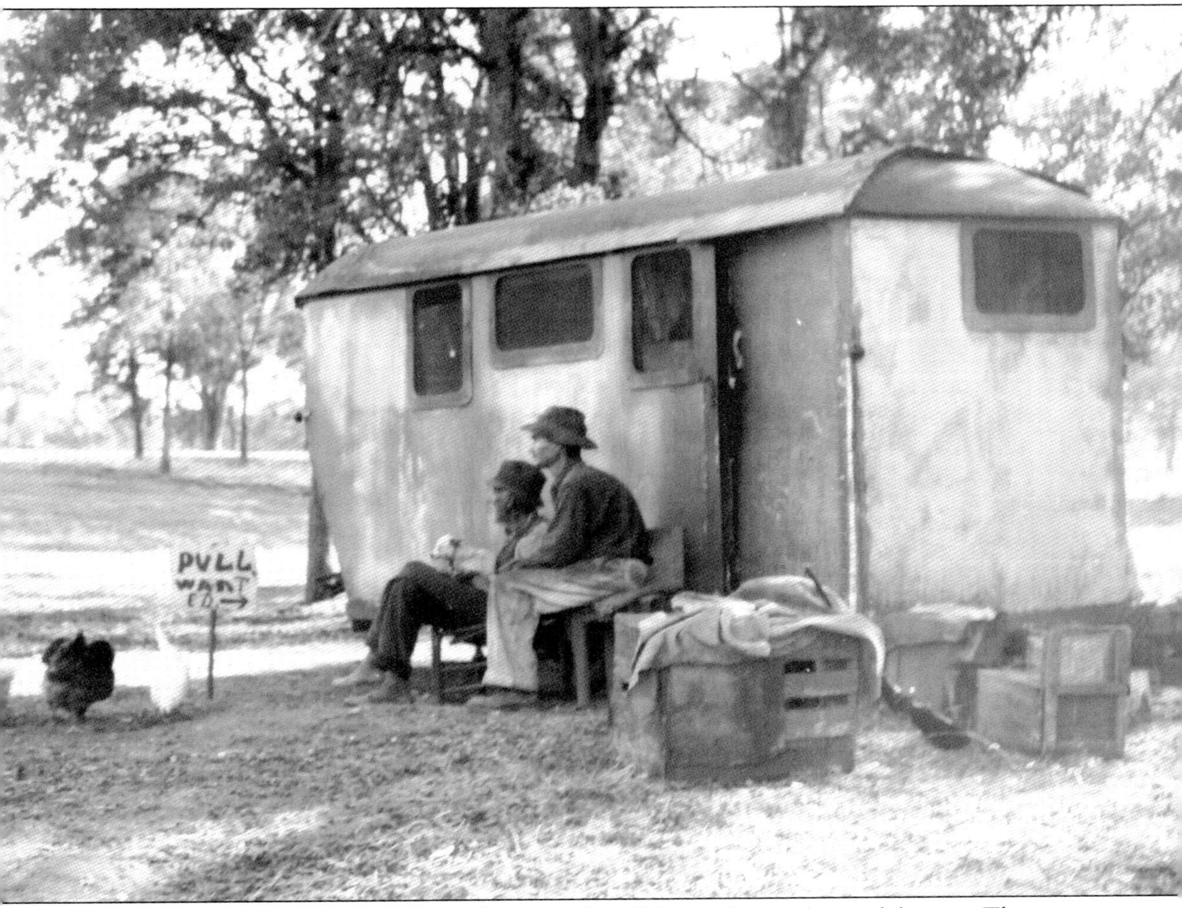

Pictured is an example of a sheltered home of the 1930s on the outskirts of the city. These men are hoping for help getting the trailer pulled to another location. (Roseville Historical Society Photograph Collection, City of Citrus Heights.)

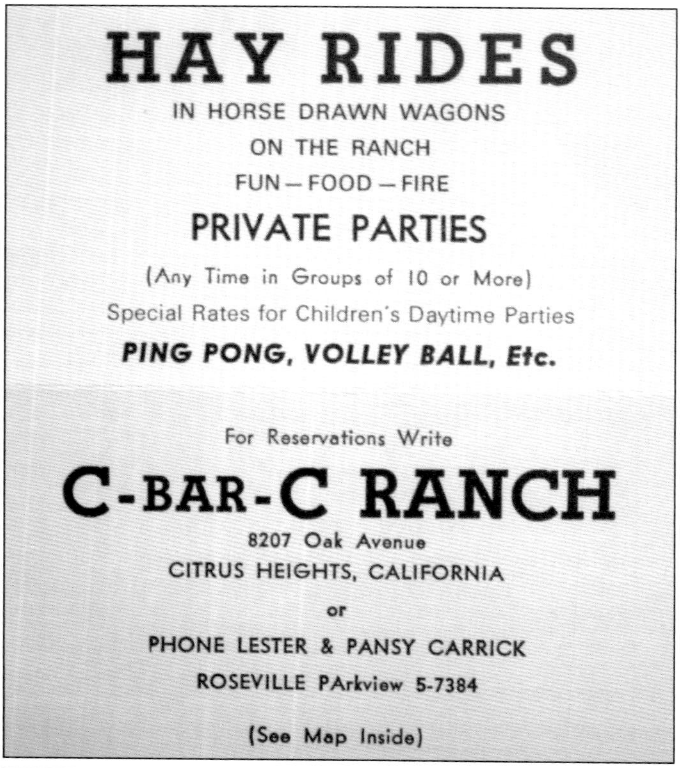

Hay rides in horse-drawn wagons were popular at the C-Bar-C Ranch on Oak Avenue. The hay wagon (below) is driven by Lester and Pansy Carrick. (Both, courtesy Roeley Giusti.)

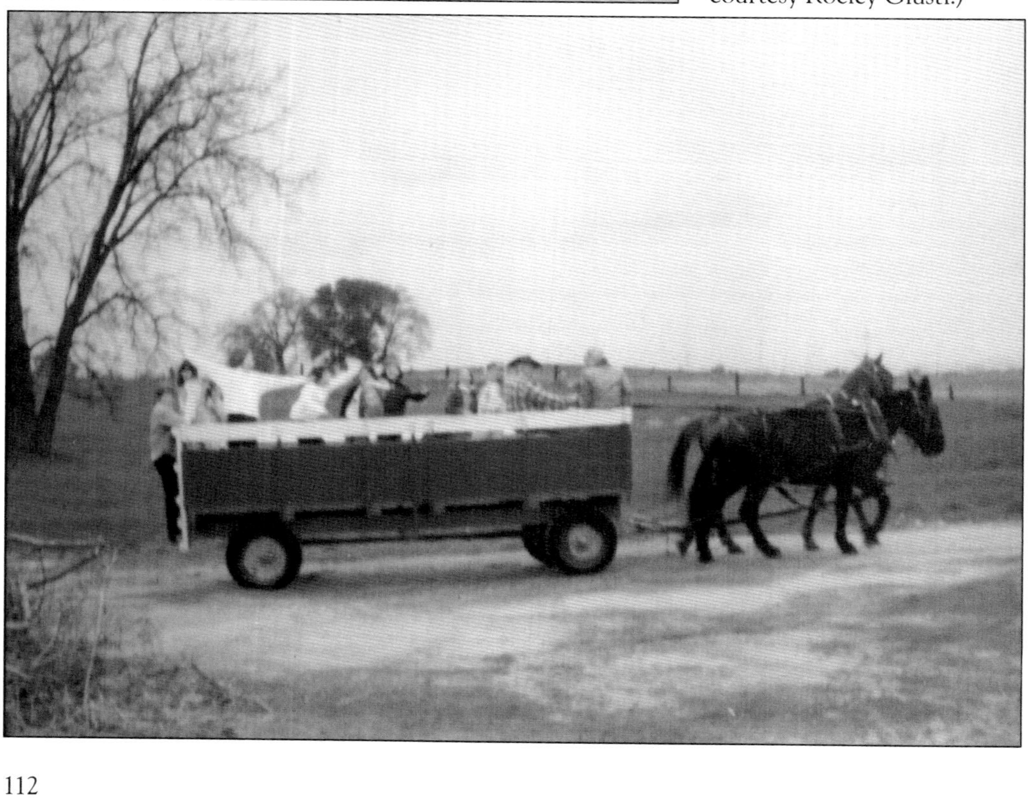

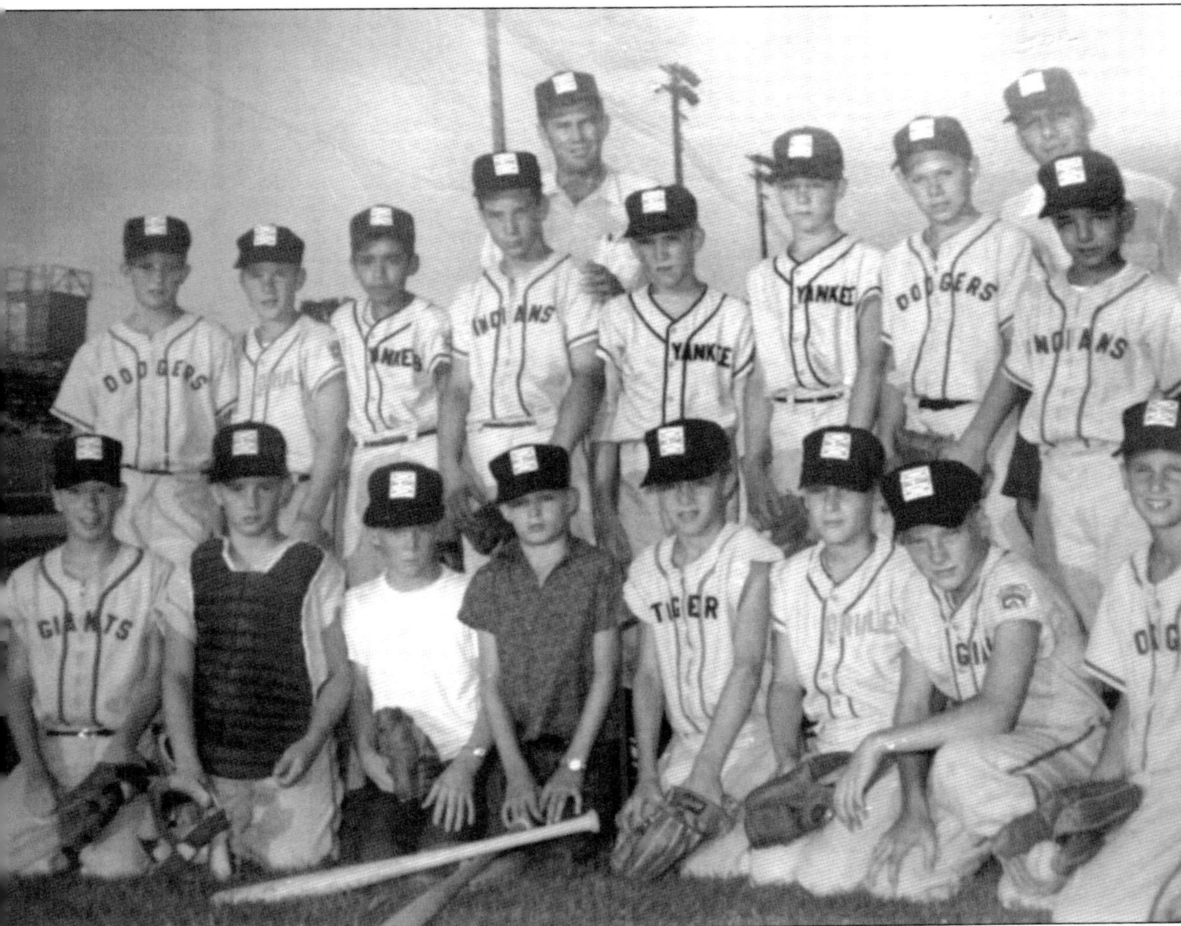

Pictured is the first official Little League all-star team in 1960. (Courtesy Roeley Giusti.)

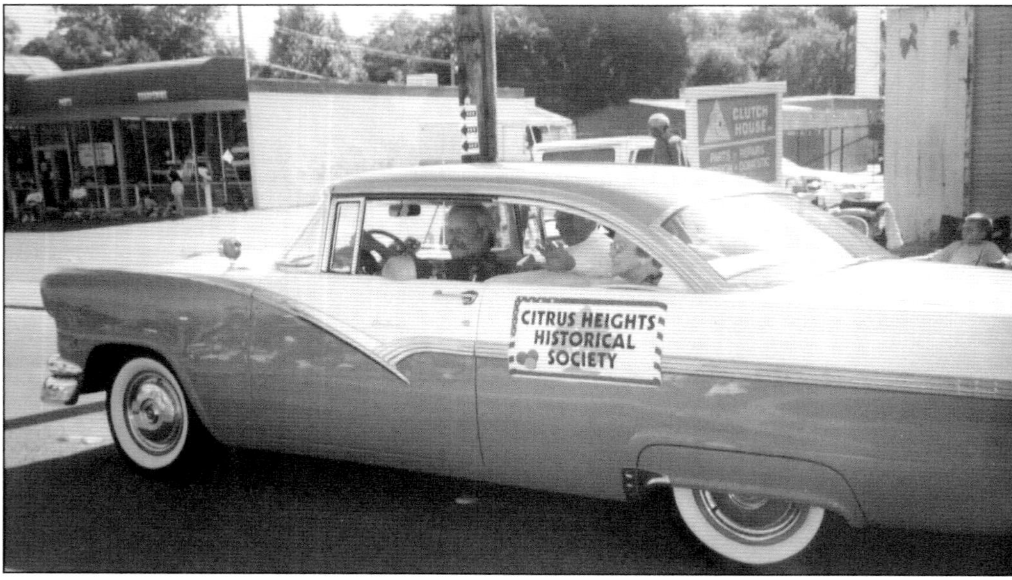

A 1955 Chevrolet in the 1982 Citrus Heights Parade showcases the Citrus Heights Historical Society. (Courtesy Jim Van Maren.)

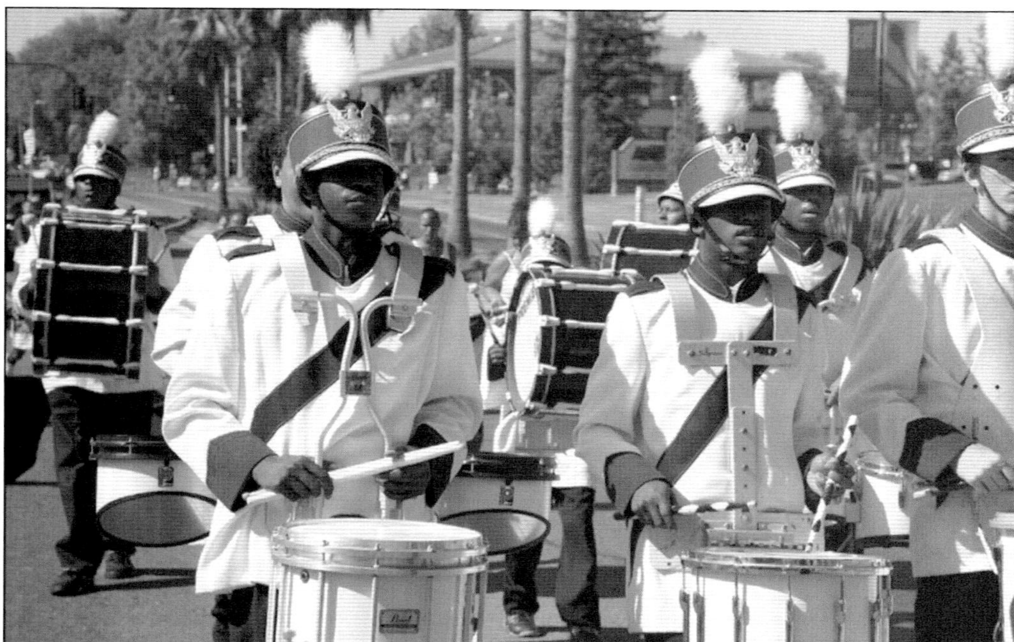

A drum corps unit marches in the city's Red, White, and Blue Parade. (Courtesy City of Citrus Heights.)

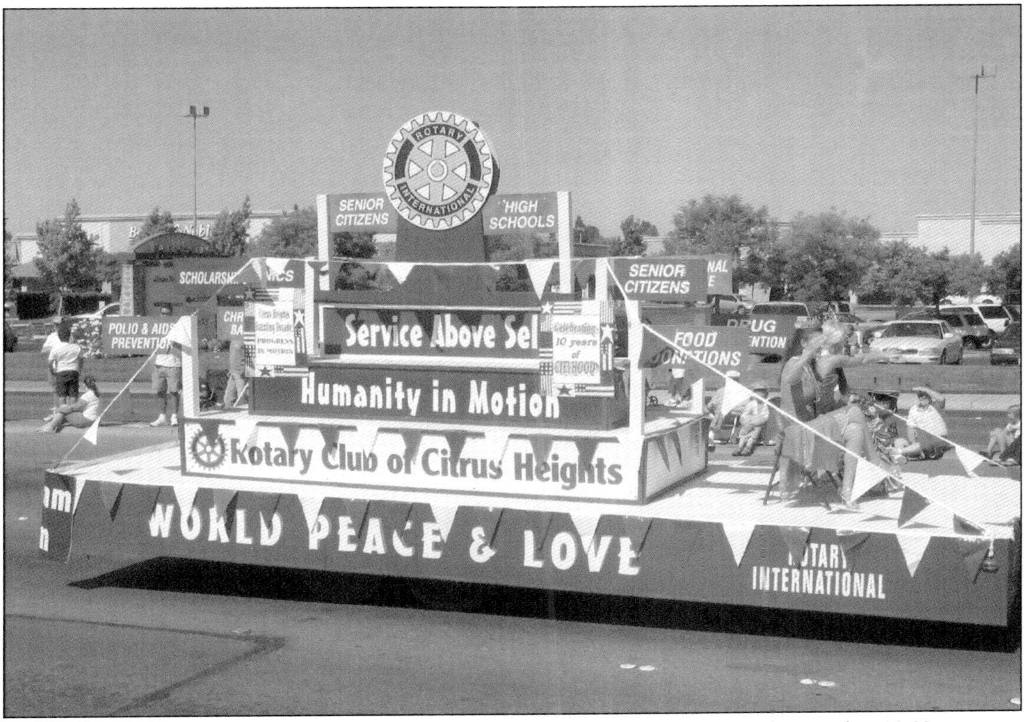

In June of each year, the city sponsors a Red, White, and Blue Parade. In the 1960s, it was originally called the Children's Parade in honor of two local children who died tragically. These photographs shows the 2009 entries of a float (above) and marching band. (Both, courtesy City of Citrus Heights.)

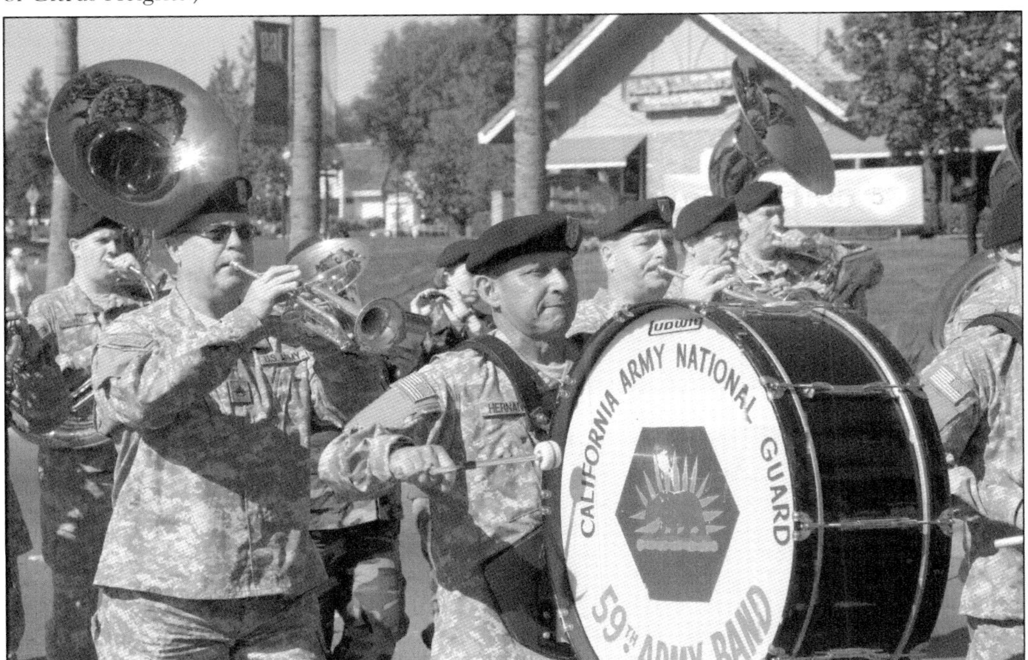

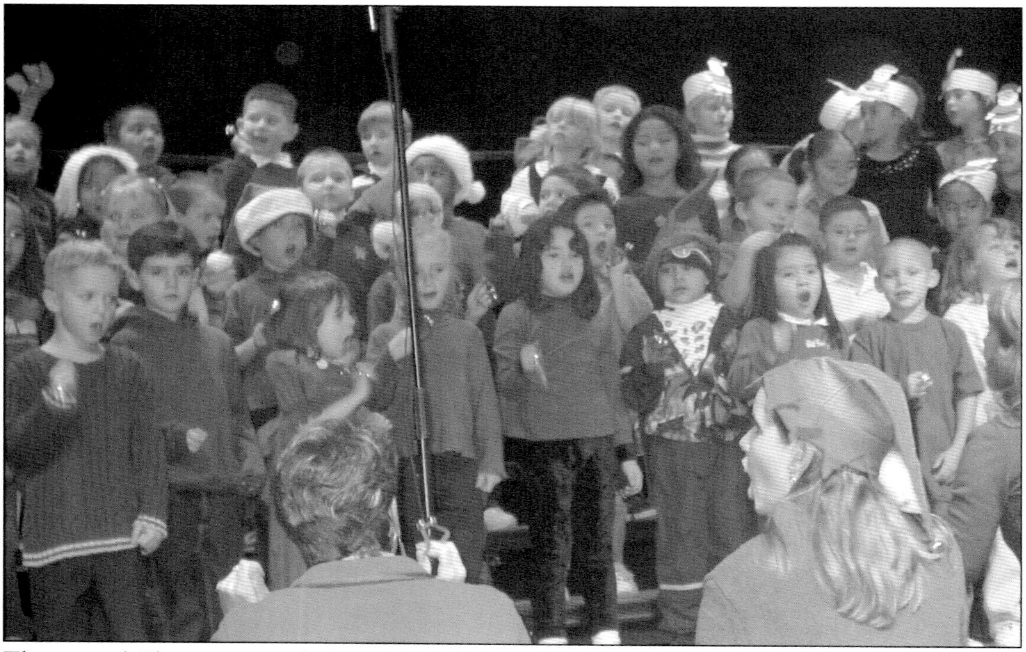

The annual Christmas tree lighting provides an opportunity for the youth of the community to sing carols at the ceremony. (Courtesy City of Citrus Heights.)

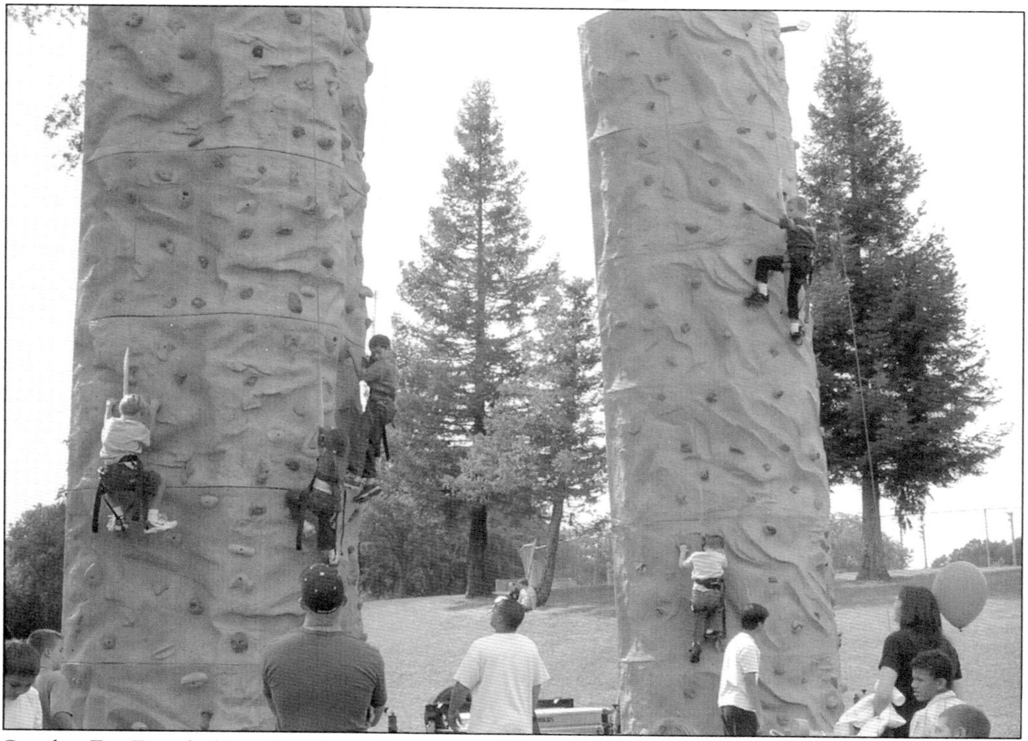

Sunday FunDay, held at Rusch Park, is an annual city event free for the community. It has an average of 10,000 locals attending. (Courtesy City of Citrus Heights.)

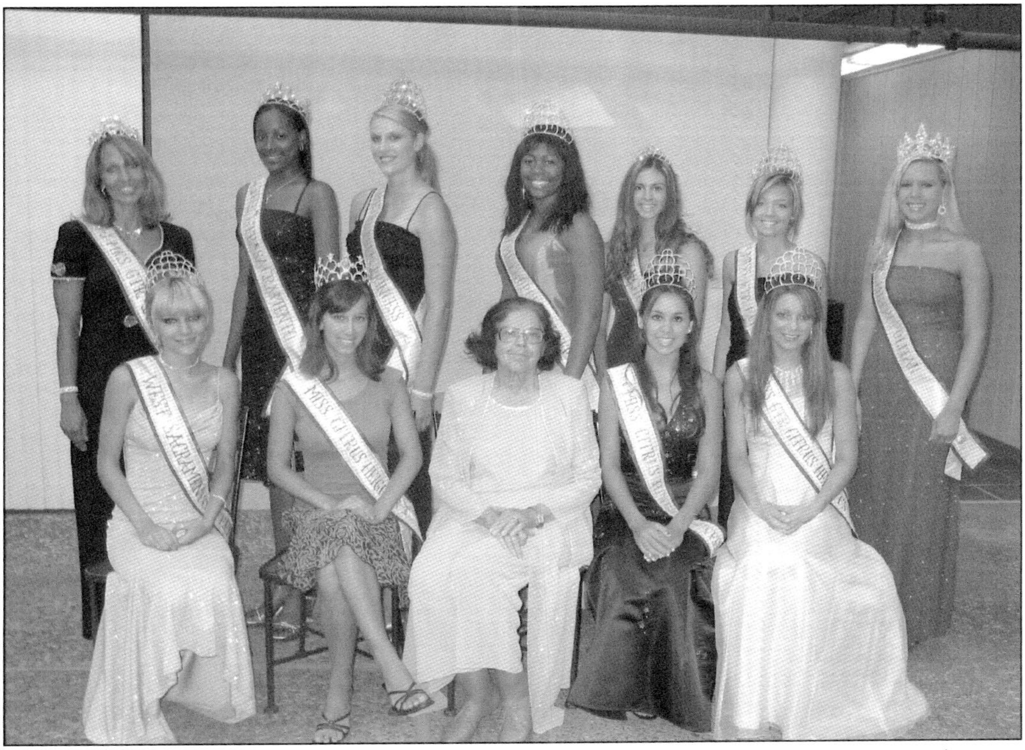

Mary Purvis (center, first row), director of Northern California Pageants, leads talented young ladies at a local pageant. (Courtesy City of Citrus Heights.)

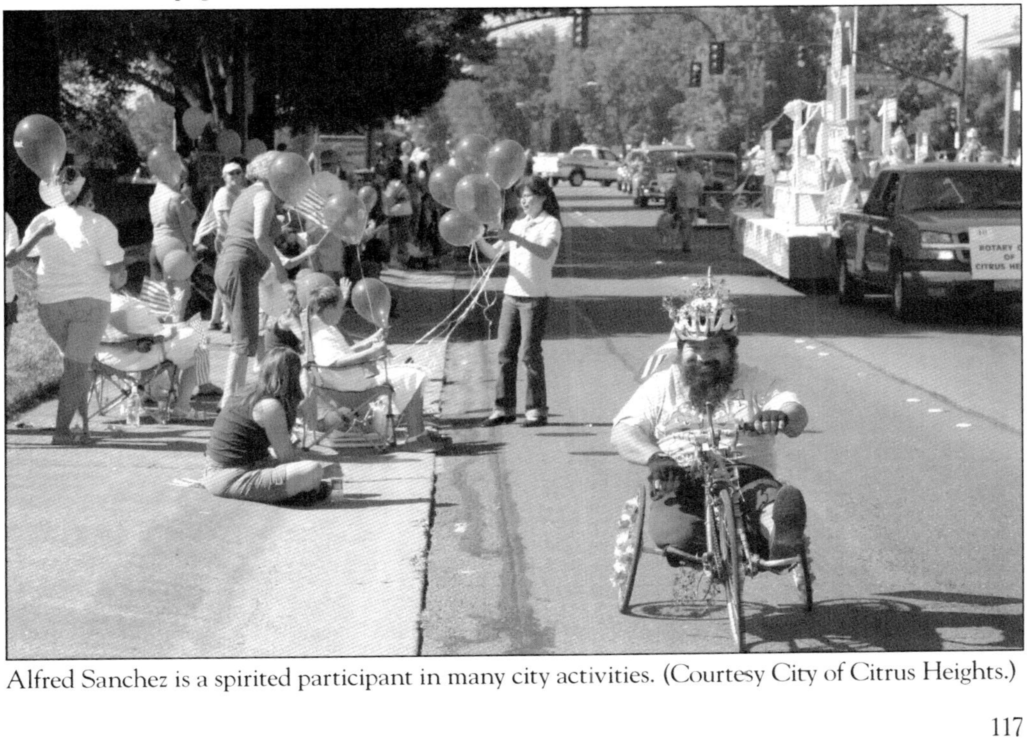

Alfred Sanchez is a spirited participant in many city activities. (Courtesy City of Citrus Heights.)

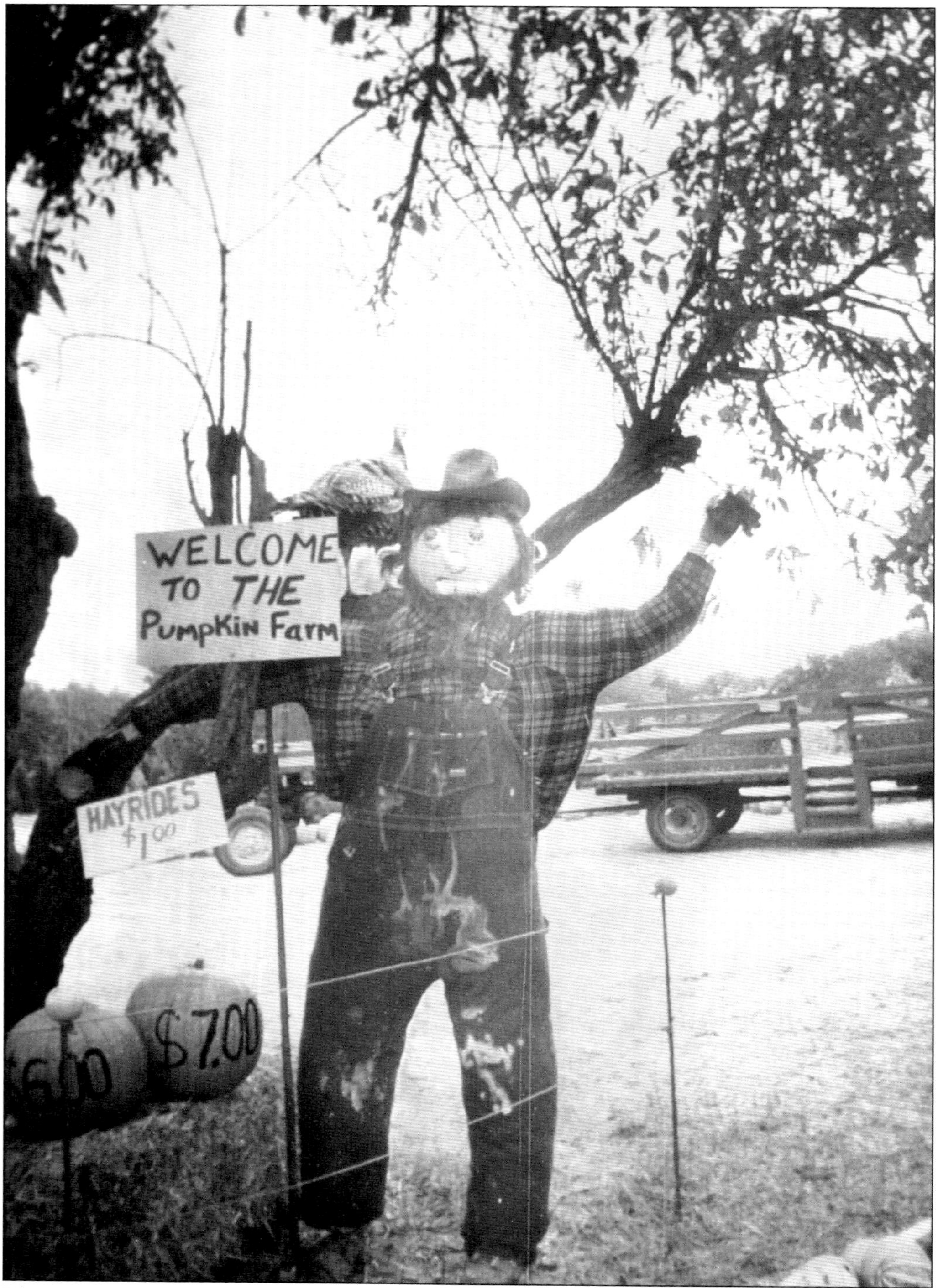

The Pumpkin Farm at Old Auburn Road and Mariposa Avenue is a local favorite and delights schoolchildren to this day. Note the wild turkey over the shoulder of the scarecrow (1990). (Courtesy City of Citrus Heights.)

Ten

The New City

Local control manifested itself in many ways after Citrus Heights became a city in 1997, with community involvement a cornerstone of municipal development. Residents have numerous ways in which to interact with civic leaders and city staff, including city council meetings, public workshops, and the city's 10 neighborhood associations (REACH). In order to oversee the city's development and land use, a planning commission was created. To preserve and promote the city's historical resources and to foster, develop, and enrich art programs, the History and Arts Commission was formed. Both of these groups consist of citizen volunteers. These municipal activities depend on the people and encourage their participation. The city is not a full-service municipality, so it actively participates in organizational partnerships in order to further economic development and other mutual goals. One example of this collaboration is working with the Sunrise MarketPlace. Traditional city services—such as firefighting, education, libraries, water, and parks and recreation—are provided by regional entities, including the Sacramento Local Conservation Corps, Citrus Heights Water District, and the Sacramento Metropolitan Fire Department. In order to provide heightened law-enforcement services, the city launched its own police department in 2006. To fulfill a pressing need, a community center was opened in 2010.

Since incorporation, the city has demonstrated that a locally controlled municipality can make a positive impact on the quality of life of its residents and enhance the business community, all while being fiscally responsible. The City of Citrus Heights believes in the core values of diversity, integrity, teamwork, innovation, respect, responsive customer service, and trust. This community exhibits economic vitality and an inherent vibrancy; it gets its strength from community involvement, the people and their neighborhoods, and innovative government.

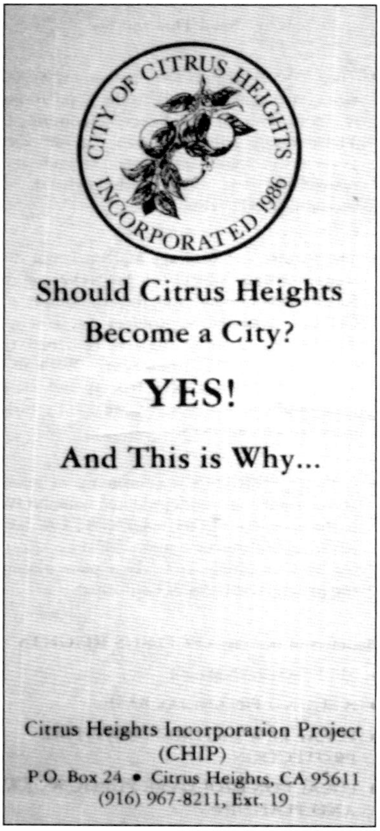
CITY OF CITRUS HEIGHTS
INCORPORATED 1986

Should Citrus Heights Become a City?

YES!

And This is Why...

Citrus Heights Incorporation Project
(CHIP)
P.O. Box 24 • Citrus Heights, CA 95611
(916) 967-8211, Ext. 19

The desire for incorporation in Citrus Heights began in the 1920s. By the 1980s, an organized grassroots committee called the Citrus Heights for Incorporation Project (CHIP) began the process that ultimately led to incorporation in 1997. (Courtesy City of Citrus Heights.)

Pictured below are civic leaders and community members essential to both the incorporation of the city of Citrus Heights and the success of the organization thereafter. (Courtesy City of Citrus Heights.)

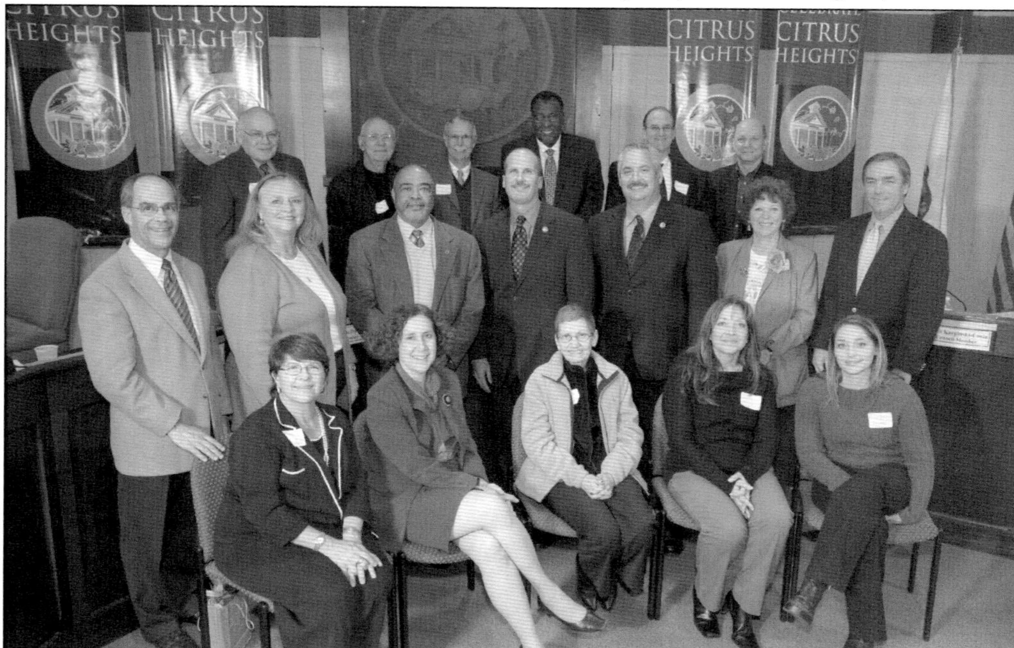

Community excitement ran high as news of the city's incorporation was broadcast after the 1996 elections. (Courtesy *Sacramento Bee*.)

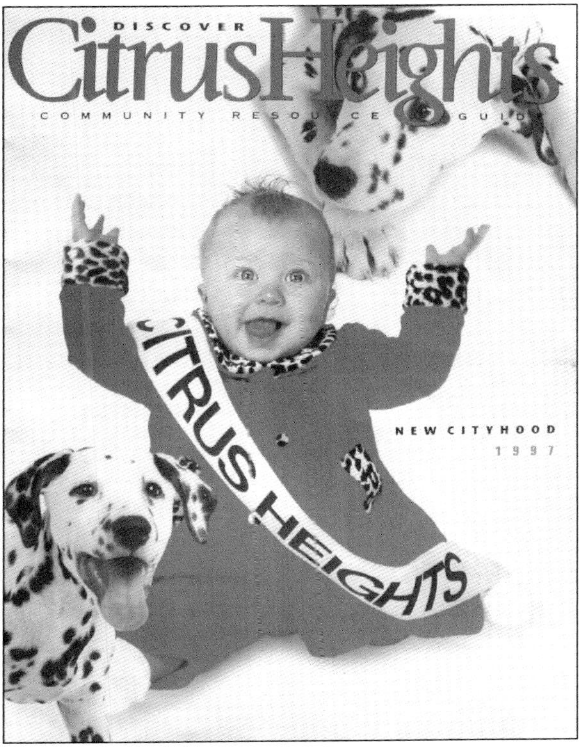

Here, members of the Veterans of Foreign Wars prepare to hold the opening flag ceremony at the beginning of a city council meeting. (Courtesy City of Citrus Heights.)

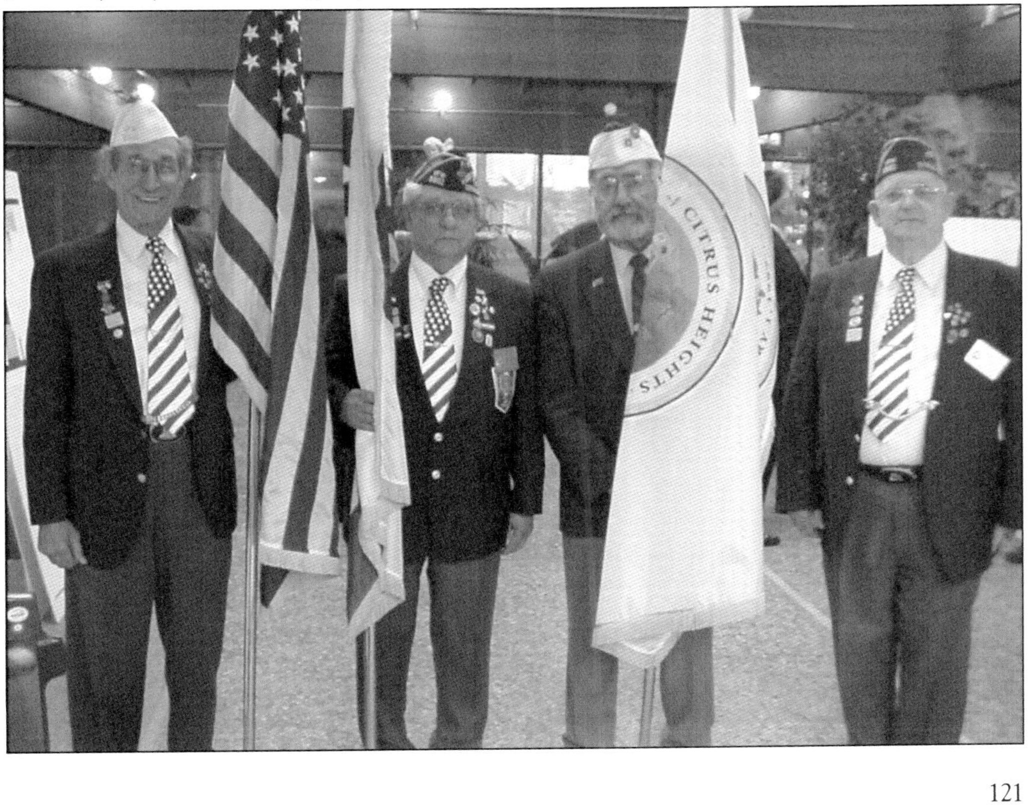

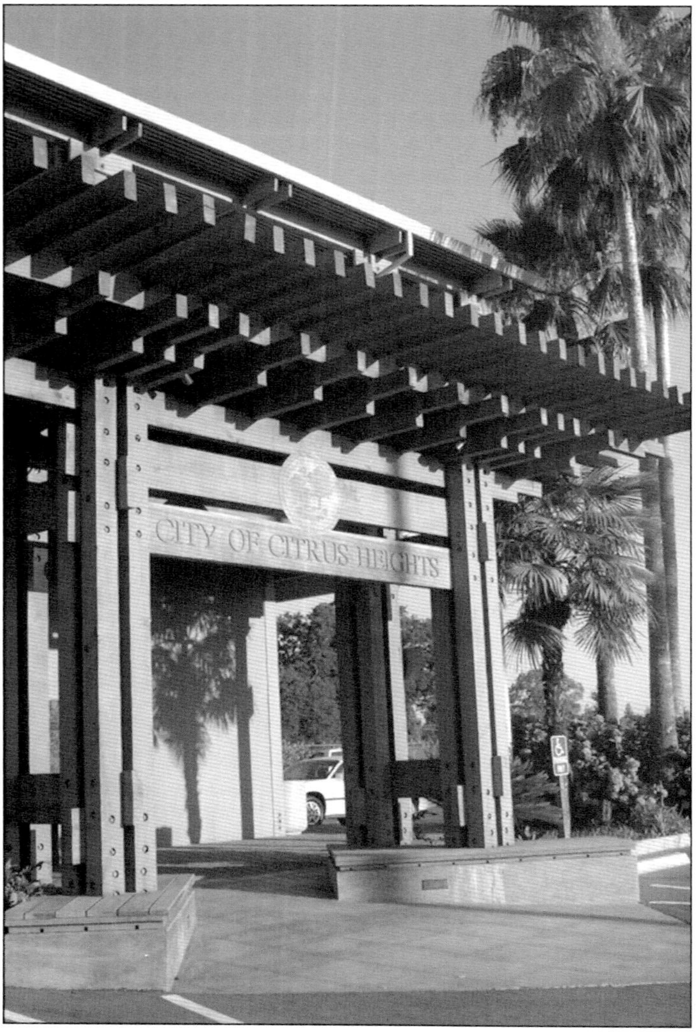

The front entrance to city hall is pictured in 2007. (Courtesy City of Citrus Heights.)

Behind this unique government complex lies an award-winning rose garden. (Courtesy City of Citrus Heights.)

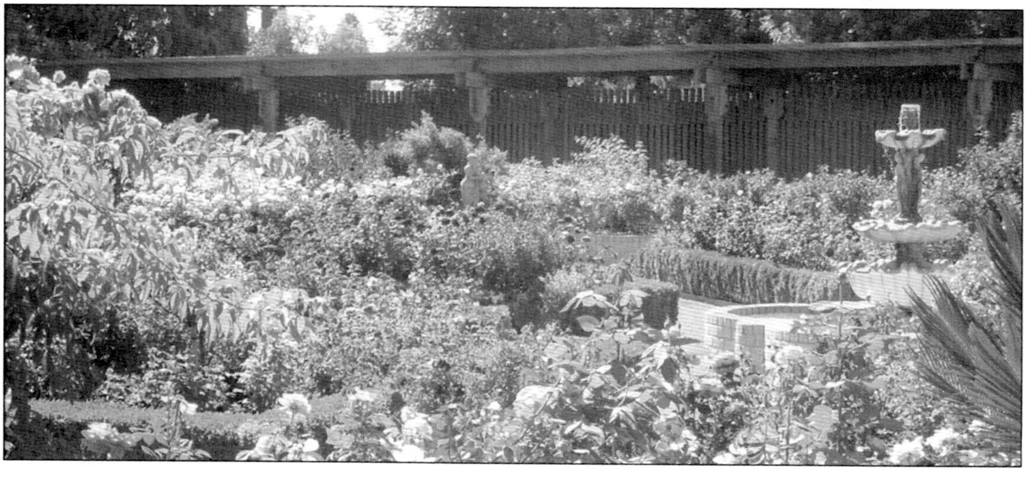

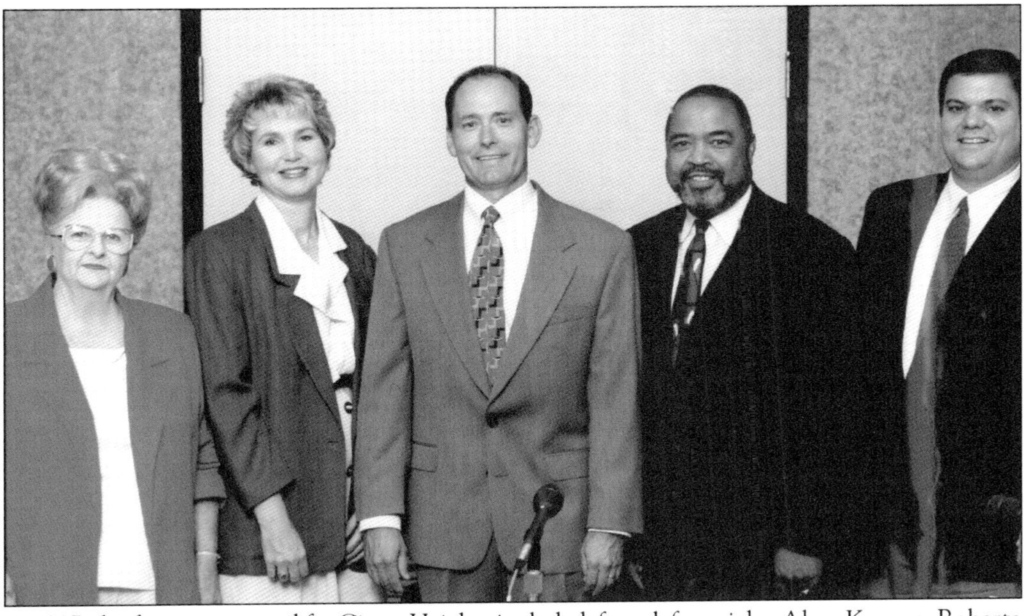

In 1997, the first city council for Citrus Heights included, from left to right, Alma Kenyon, Roberta MacGlashan (vice mayor), Bill Hughes (mayor), James Shelby, and Tim Raney. (Courtesy City of Citrus Heights.)

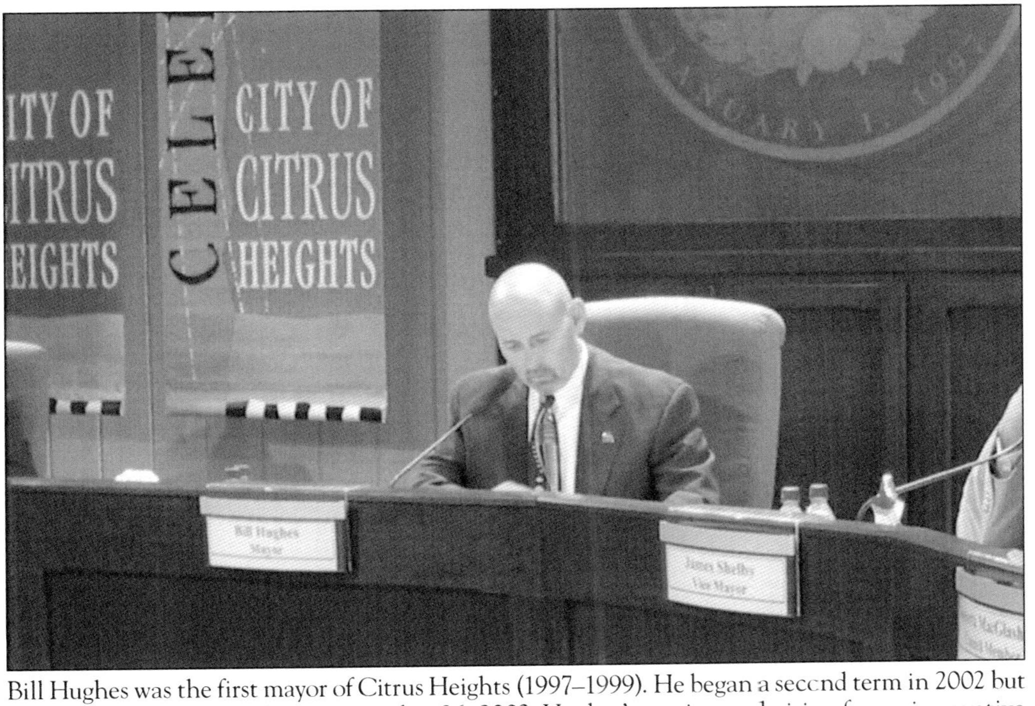

Bill Hughes was the first mayor of Citrus Heights (1997–1999). He began a second term in 2002 but passed away unexpectedly on November 26, 2003. Hughes's passion and vision for an innovative government set the city's high standards. (Courtesy City of Citrus Heights.)

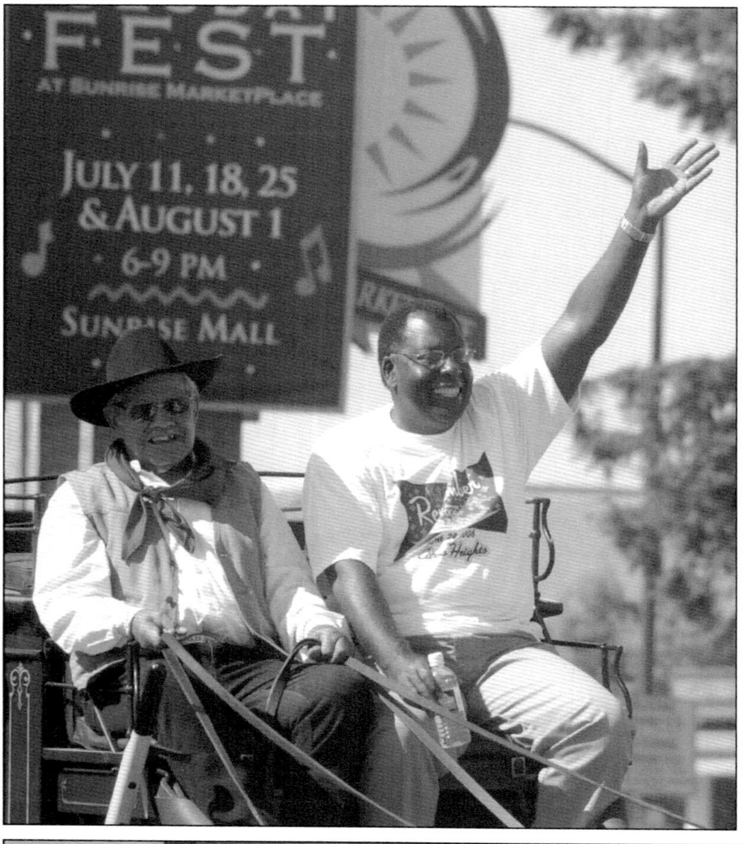

City Manager Henry Tingle (right) has led the city with focus, compassion, and integrity. Under Tingle's leadership, the city now has its own employee-based police department, a dramatically improved infrastructure, and a strong financial foundation. (Courtesy City of Citrus Heights.)

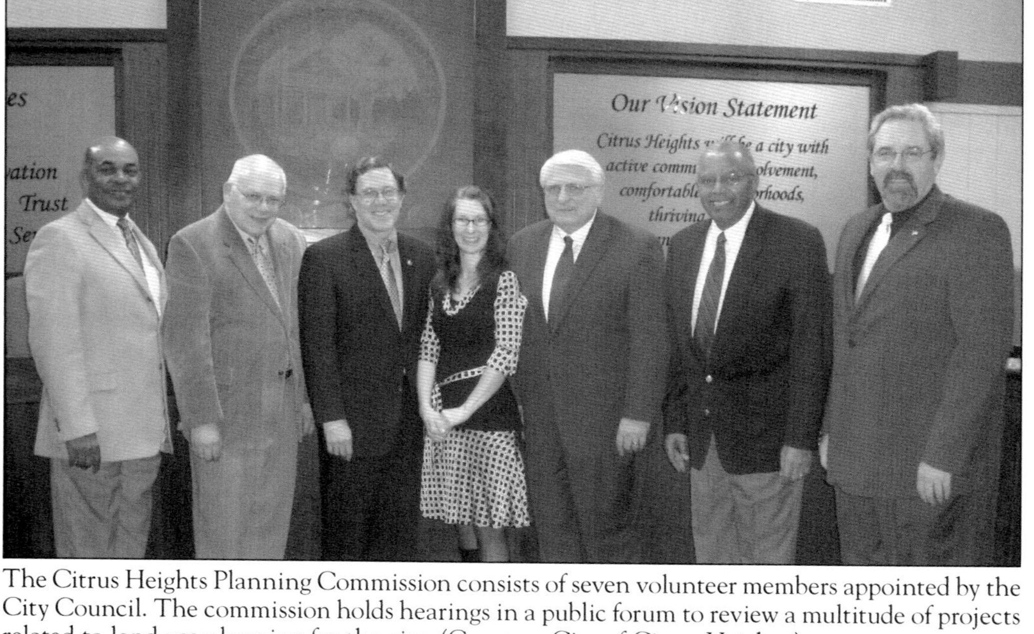

The Citrus Heights Planning Commission consists of seven volunteer members appointed by the City Council. The commission holds hearings in a public forum to review a multitude of projects related to land-use planning for the city. (Courtesy City of Citrus Heights.)

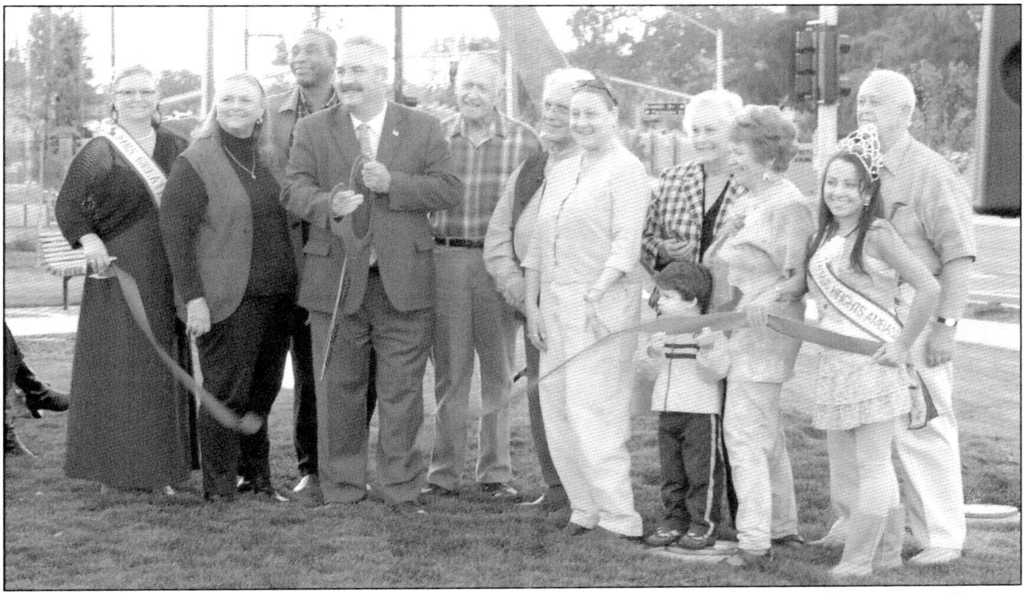

The History and Arts Commission preserves and promotes the city's historical resources; fosters, develops, and enriches art programs; and encourages citizen participation. It has identified local sites and buildings with historical significance and sponsors a revolving Art in City Hall program highlighting the artwork of local students and artists. Members of the History and Arts Commission, city council, and the Northern California Pageant are seen in November 2008 at the ground-breaking of the city's first piece of public art, *Up and Away*. (Courtesy City of Citrus Heights.)

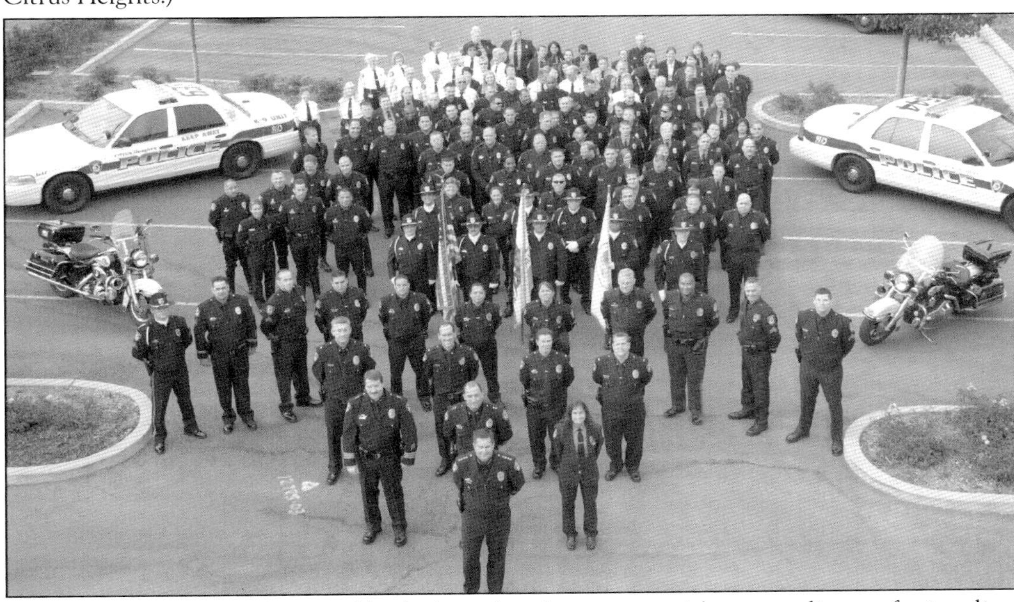

Chief of police Christopher Boyd leads the police department with outstanding professionalism. The department covers a population of almost 85,000 people. The officers have dramatically improved the safety and security of the area. The department also offers informative outreach presentations. (Courtesy City of Citrus Heights.)

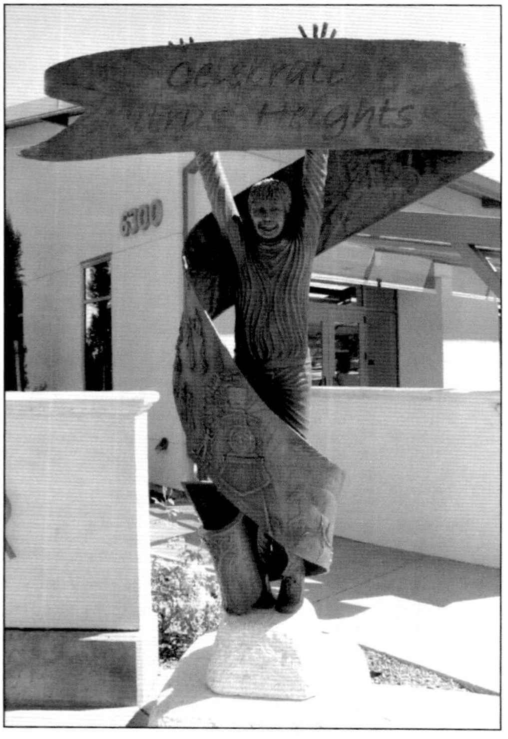

Created by Philip Sciortino, *Celebrate Citrus Heights* is a statue of a boy with a sash wrapped around him. Important historical events and sites within the city are depicted on the sash. The statue is located in front of the community center. (Courtesy City of Citrus Heights.)

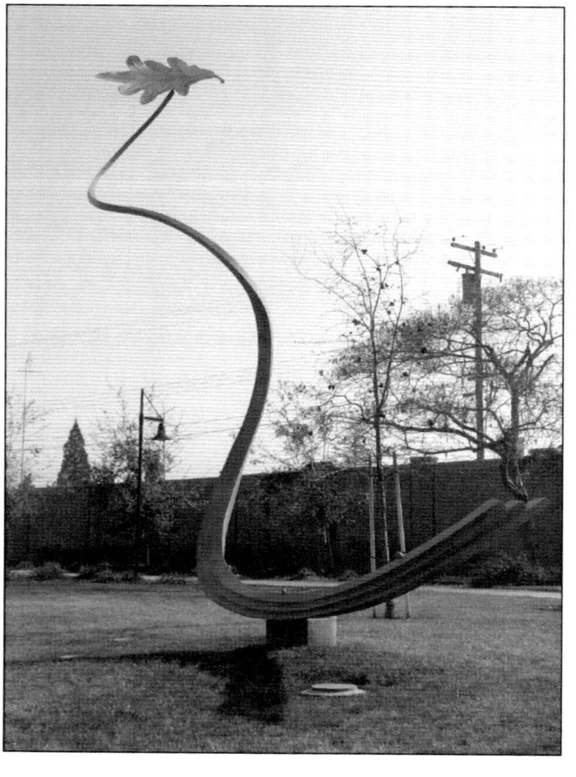

The History and Arts Commission requested that public art be displayed within the city. In 2008, the first piece of public art, *Up and Away* by Colin Lambert, was installed in the open-space area south of Greenback Lane. The spiral movement trail was constructed using bronze sheets built over a steel internal skeleton and now stands 18 feet high. At its tip, the piece holds aloft a 4.5-foot, gold gilded, carbon fiber oak leaf that rocks and sways in the wind. (Courtesy City of Citrus Heights.)

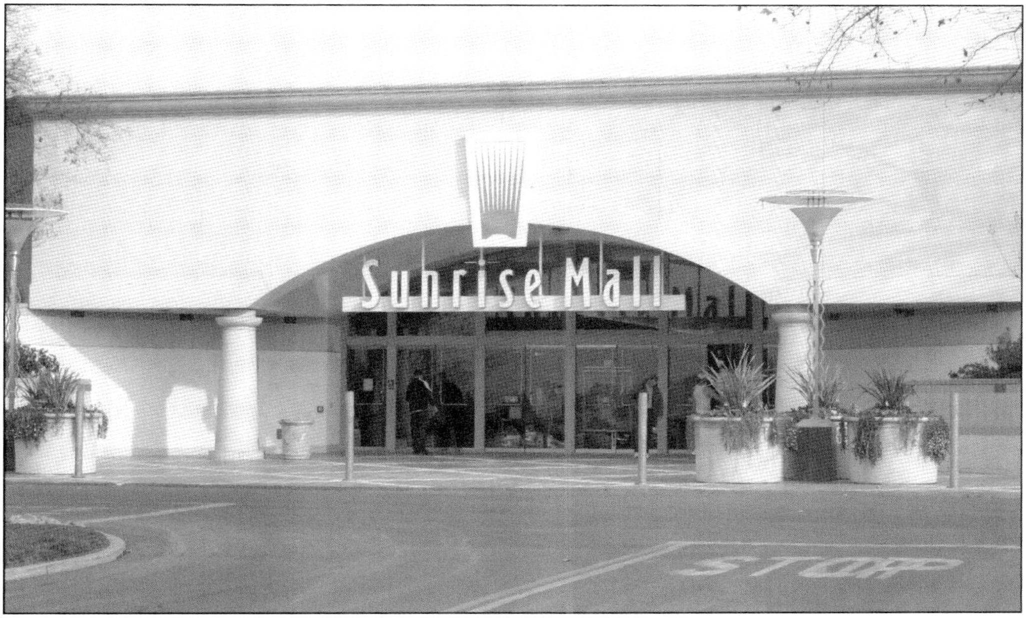

This is the main entrance to Sunrise Mall, which is located at the intersection of Sunrise Boulevard and Greenback Lane. When it opened in 1972, it was the first major retail mall in Citrus Heights. Today, it is the cornerstone of Sunrise MarketPlace. (Courtesy City of Citrus Heights.)

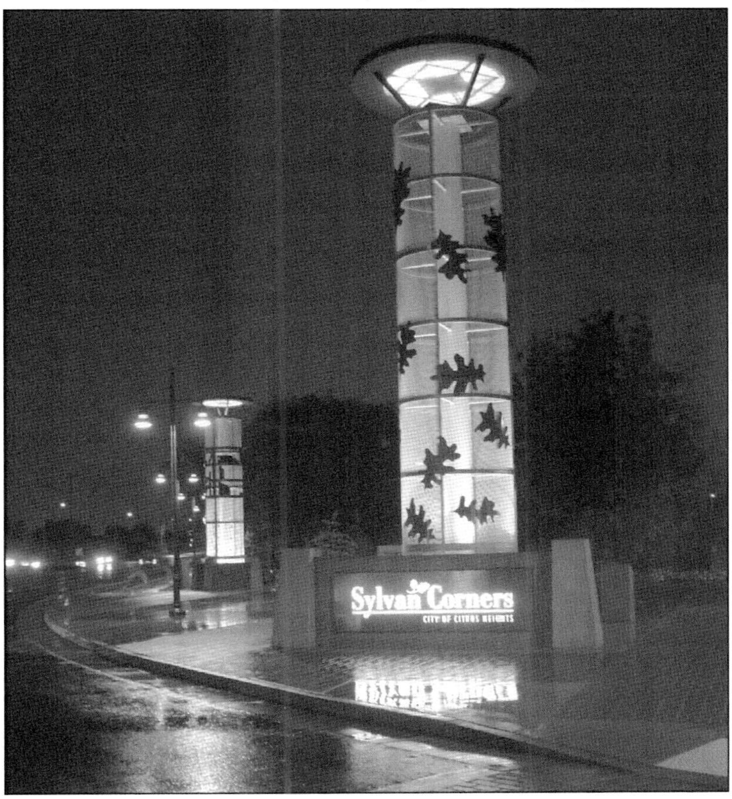

Sylvan Corners is at the intersection of Auburn Boulevard and Sylvan Road, a central area for Citrus Heights. Today, the intersection and its six columns represent a focal point for the historical and geographic center of the city, once part of the Lincoln Highway and Highway 40. (Courtesy City of Citrus Heights.)

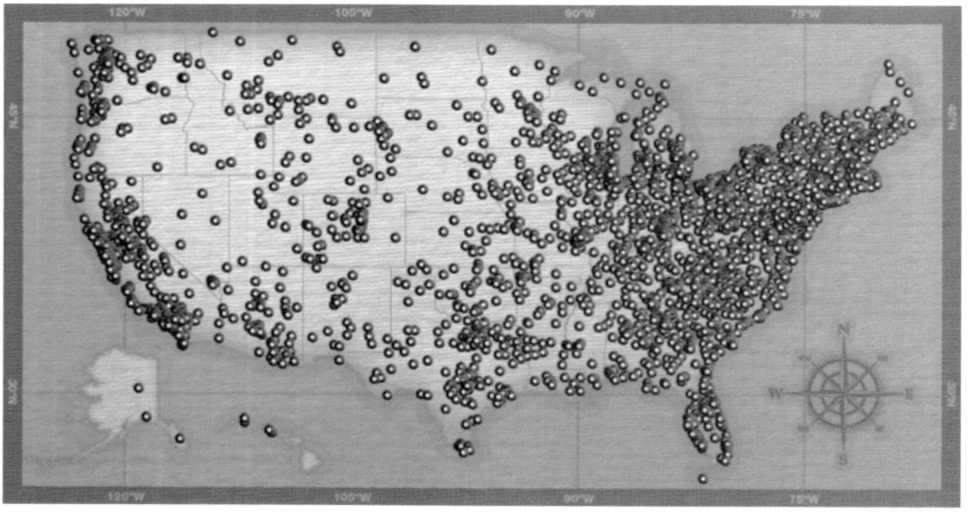